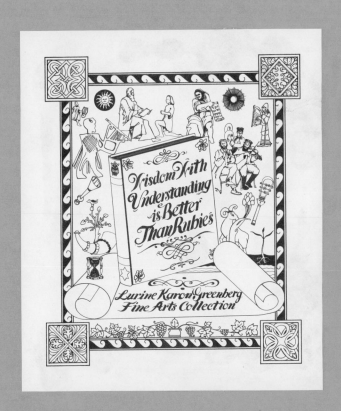

Wisdom With Understanding is Better Than Rubies

Lurine Karon Greenberg
Fine Arts Collection

Wiel Arets

Edited by Xavier Costa
Photographs by Hélène Binet

Wiel Arets

Princeton Architectural Press

Published in 2002 by
Princeton Architectural Press
37 East Seventh Street
New York, New York 10003

For a free catalog of books, call 1.800.722.6657.
Visit our web site at www.papress.com

Published simultaneously by Ediciones Poligrafa

Copyright © 2002 Ediciones Poligrafa
05 04 03 02 5 4 3 2 1 First edition
Images ©2002, Wiel Arets Architect & Associates, Maastricht
Photographs ©2002, Hélène Binet, Kim Zwarts
Texts and translations ©The authors

For Princeton Architectural Press:
Project coordinator: Mark Lamster
Projet editor: Nicola Bednarek
Specials thanks to: Nettie Aljian, Ann Alter, Amanda Atkins, Janet Behning, Megan Carey,
Penny Chu, Jan Cigliano, Clare Jacobson, Nancy Eklund Later, Linda Lee, Brooke Schneider,
Jane Sheinman, Lottchen Shivers, Jennifer Thompson, and Deb Wood of Princeton
Architectural Press–Kevin C. Lippert, publisher

Library of Congress Cataloging-in-Publication Data

Arets, W. M. J.
    Wiel Arets: works, projects, writings / edited by Xavier Costa;
    photographs by Hélène Binet.
        p. cm.
    ISBN 1-56898-335-2
    1. Arets, W. M. J. I. Costa, Xavier. II. Title.
NA1153.A74 A4 2002
720'.92—dc21
                                                2002000529

ISBN: 1-56898-335-2

Dep. Legal: B. 2.486 - 2002 (Printed in Spain)

Contents

Xavier Costa

Towards an architecture of mediation

The architecture of Wiel Arets has been characterized from its beginnings by bringing together a wide-ranging body of production with a constant interrogation of the ideas that underpin the design work and provide its impetus. This interrogation is intimately linked to Arets' continuous academic commitment, in the various architecture schools in which he has exercised a decisive influence. It is also related to the production of texts that are crucial to understanding the development of his architecture over the last fifteen years and to interpreting the inflections of his work.

In Arets there is a continuous investigation of concepts that synthesize in some tangible, visualizable way the flow of ideas of contemporary thought. Consequently, metaphors drawn from the physical world and on other occasions from biology or science constitute some of the main referents in his theoretical corpus. Virology, rhizome, translucency and prophylaxis are among the concepts that tend to be enunciated in terms of the reflections or questions that emerge from specific projects, but which make possible an effective dialectic between the design and the thought that feeds it.

In view of the continuity of these interrogations, which at times take a more developed form and at others are simply brief commentaries in the margins of a detailed description of a particular work of architecture, it clearly makes sense to read and interpret the main texts by Arets in tandem with the exercise of documenting his works. In this introduction I have sought to place the emphasis on four key essays, four texts that outline various stages in Arets' architecture. Casa come me is a text about Villa Malaparte in Capri; Grid and Rhizome sets out from a commentary on the project for the Academy of the Arts in Amsterdam and goes on to posit a surprising reconciliation between two concepts that simultaneously feed the project; An Alabaster Skin explains the importance of the surface and the relationship with the environment of the city; A Virological Architecture introduces a series of different biological, corporeal and even pharmaceutical metaphors.

The ideas put forward in Arets' writings frequently come across as highly synthetic, producing in the reader the impression of a thought packed up in a partial exposition that needs to be unfolded and allowed to develop to its full extent. It is this unfolding that I would like to outline in this introduction, by way of a detailed commentary on the concepts that have shaped the intellectual and creative evolution of Wiel Arets.

In undertaking this task, it is useful to incorporate a number of critical texts that expand on his ideas or relate them to other and broader fields. When it comes to interpreting Arets' writings, it proves especially productive to draw on the interpretations of Anthony Vidler, Bart Lootsma, Greg Lynn and Stan Allen, which here accompany the texts and architectural projects.

Malaparte

The writings of Wiel Arets present an implacable transition from a position that corresponds to the state of architectural thinking characteristic of the early 80s towards perspectives that redirected the course of his architecture and allowed it to evolve very considerably in a short period. The conceptual distance between Casa come me and A Virological Architecture is a reflection — one of the most revealing mirrors — of the intense debate that has taken place in architecture over the course of the last few years, and of the permeability between a variety of different areas of knowledge.

As Bart Lootsma has established, this trajectory of constant transition in Arets stems from his interest in certain examples of Italian, Japanese and Mexican architecture. This stage is perfectly exemplified by the essay on Villa Malaparte, Casa come me, written jointly by Arets and Wim van den Bergh and originally published in 1989.[1] The essay describes the authors' experience of visiting the house and explores the extent of Curzio Malaparte's personal intervention in the conception and realization of the work.

In the reading proposed by Arets and Van den Bergh in their essay — coinciding with others who have written about this architecture — the part played by Adalberto Libera was purely secondary in relation to that of the true architect and owner of the house, Curzio Malaparte. The Malaparte house is, in the words of the author of La pelle, Malaparte himself, "a temple dedicated to the principle of identity," "a metaphysical void"; in other words, a shrine to reflexivity, to the self-referential quality of architecture. According to Arets and van den Bergh, the fascinated — that is, literally spellbound, turned to stone, as in the fascinum of classical Latin — gaze of the writer Malaparte was turned on that construction come me, "like me"; in other words, the house is a reflexive extension of the subject who conceived and realized it.[2]

The Malaparte house is described as a solitary construction — a metaphor or simile, once again, for the solitarius Malaparte, who, in the period just before the house was built, had endured the isolation of five years' exile on Lipari. "Too much sky and too much sea for one man alone; but not enough land! . . . From the terrace of the castle I dominate the sea . . . I look down, toward the sea, and I feel I am contemplating a town square from the height of the tower."[3] The isolated individual is enclosed in a house-macchina, his fortress clinging to the rocky Capri cliff-top like some archaic construction, a kind of colossal stylobate, an inhabitable pedestal.

The basilica of Lipari is an evident source for the flight of steps of the Malaparte house, but in Lipari these steps lead up to the enormous mass of the church, while in the Malaparte house there is a clamorous void above the stylobate. This can be interpreted as a fragment or ruin, as a construction of echoes from a world of myth: Malaparte makes indirect references to himself as a latter-day Ulysses, even as Aeolus, the master of winds and storms. The house can be seen, perhaps, as a great but incomplete temple in honor of its creator.

The 1989 essay is evidently interested in a model of architecture that unites in exemplary fashion the formal restraint of its design with the symbolic density of the references and evocations. As in some of the work of Luis Barragán or of other architects of the period — Tadao Ando and Giorgio Grassi come to mind — there is an ambition to conjugate a series of spatial, tectonic and formal

Malaparte

....
[1] Wiel Arets and Wim van den Bergh, "Casa come me: A Sublime Alienation," **AA Files** 18 (1989), pp. 136–141.
[2] "fascinum is that which has the effect of arresting movement and, literally, of killing life. At the moment the subject stops, suspending his gesture, he is mortified. The anti-life, anti-movement function of this terminal point is the fascinum, and it is precisely one of the dimensions in which the power of the gaze is exercised directly," in Jacques Lacan, "What is a Picture?," in **The Four Fundamental Concepts of Psycho-Analysis.** Alan Sheridan, Eng. tr. New York, Norton, 1978.
[3] An extract from "On the Island of Lipari," by Curzio Malaparte, published in **AA Files** 18 (1989): p. 14. This text first appeared in English in 1936.

poetics with a rigorous design based on simple repetitive volumes. The text on Casa Malaparte describes to perfection the horizon of these architectures, which ask to be compared with some of Arets' own first projects and built works, such as the Academy for the Arts in Maastricht, and at the same time also invoke the more rigorous and austere exercises of his later architecture.

Historically, we can identify a wider context for this highly eloquent episode. The slow death-agony of modern architecture over the course of the 60s and 70s saw the production of a number of works that sought to maintain the geometrical, formal and constructive rigor of the most austere rationalism, while incorporating a set of significations that had little or nothing to do with the "Fordist" productive optimism of the avant-garde movements. In various centers of theoretical research — Italy in particular — efforts were being made to establish a phenomenological relationship with the history and the symbolic contents of architecture. The book L'architettura come mestiere, by Giorgio Grassi, was one of the most influential contributions to this endeavor. Those years, so rich in ideological development, pointed towards possible new lines of work, which will be explored in subsequent articles in this volume.

This first theoretical work by Wiel Arets marks one of the most eloquent — and at the same time least orthodox — trajectories in relation to the debate and the new approaches in architecture that were being forged during these years. As is customary for Arets, he decisively underpins and explains this direction in certain key texts from this period. The Malaparte essay is evidently one of these and a useful point of departure from which to pursue the evolution of Arets' architecture.

Academy for the Arts and Architecture, Maastricht

Grid versus Rhizome

A year later, Arets published Grid and Rhizome, a text that inaugurates a different line which proved decisive in the subsequent course of ideas in his work. Grid and Rhizome is posited as a pairing of apparently irreconcilable terms and concepts. By contrasting them, Arets seems to be deliberately seeking to provoke. How is this juxtaposition of two mutually exclusive orders to be justified?

The concept of the rhizome is put forward as a model of spatial and biological organization characterized by multiplicity and dispersion. The botanical example of the rhizome serves as the model for a conceptual organization that is introduced and articulated by the text Mille plateaux by Gilles Deleuze and Félix Guattari, published in 1980.[4] The rhizome is an organism with no beginning or end, with no recognizable center, visible only in a fragmented and apparently chaotic way. According to the text, the rhizomatic city par excellence is Amsterdam, a city labyrinthine in its physical organization, and a multiple and culturally diverse place.

The actual text of Mille plateaux itself is organized and presented in the semblance of a rhizome, its apparently unconnected chapters referring to diverse subjects and chronologies with no evident order. What seems to be an accumulation of arbitrarily grouped writings should be understood as a rhizomatic structure that "emerges" at distant points. Below the surface, however, there is a common body that explains the relationships between them. The Mille plateaux of Deleuze and Guattari thus provide a mode of discourse and knowledge, but also of spatial organization that in architecture has, on certain occasions, been translated literally into specific projects.

In spite of the frequency with which the rhizome concept appears in the writings on architecture produced in the 90s, the text by Arets represents a pioneering effort by introducing it into a direct reflection on his own work. In Grid and Rhizome, the two terms are used as a means to describe the complexity of the siting and the program of the project for the Academy of the Arts in Amsterdam.

In this context, he proposes a reconciliation between the two concepts. Amsterdam is described as rhizomatic city, and at the same time the presence of the orthogonal grid is noted in elements at various scales: from the details of buildings in the area of the project (the Portuguese synagogue, the Zuiderkerk, the old

Academy of the Arts, Amsterdam

....

[4] Gilles Deleuze and Félix Guattari, **Mille plateaux,** Paris, Editions de Minuit, 1980. Eng. trans. by Brian Massumi, **A Thoussand Plateaus**, Minneapolis, V. of Minnesota Press, 1987.

arsenal and others) through to a reference to the importance of the democratic and egalitarian spirit in the culture of the city, with its fusion of different religions. As Arets explains, "as democracy has developed in these societies of belief and commerce, it knows no hierarchy, but unfolds in the transparency of the light."

Grid and Rhizome represents an intermediate, transitional moment in which Arets' ideas and architecture were striving to maintain their link with a set of references specific to the 80s, while they were, at the same time being, redirected towards new issues and interests that would be developed more fully in his later writings.

Alabaster

In affirming that "architecture is . . . a skin of alabaster," Arets is giving his discourse an even more emphatic inflection. The metaphor of the translucency of architecture is a figure rich in implications: "a between, a membrane, an alabaster skin, at once opaque and transparent, real and unreal. . . ." On the one hand, the translucent skin speaks of the importance of light, a light that is omnipresent and diffuse, a light captured by continuous, superficial membranes. At the same time it speaks to us of the protagonism of this surface: the skin of alabaster effectively equates architecture with a surface — an unexpected equivalence that seems to ignore any spatial definition of architecture — by virtue of its luminosity. The most important aspect of the various implications of this skin of alabaster is the diminishing sense of architectural autonomy that is apparent here. The stony, self-referential and hermetic volume of Villa Malaparte dissolves away to leave a space infused with light and transparency. This is a space that relates to the exterior, to the environment of the city. For Wiel Arets the membrane is the architectural and strictly buildable response to the complexity of the debate on contemporary urbanism and the civic context of architecture.

The relationships that Arets' architecture establishes with its urban context have been written about on a number of occasions. At first sight, buildings such as the Academy for the Arts in Maastricht, the AZL Pension Fund offices or the Central Police Station in Heerlen seem to point to a relationship of contrast or resistance, even a certain isolation, with regard to the city around them — "bastions" for our disturbing cities, as Bart Lootsma has so aptly described them.[5] Nevertheless, as Anthony Vidler points out in his essay "Oneirism" on Arets, this is an architecture that produces careful responses to the continual change of the city. The reorganization of crystalline volumetries speaks eloquently to us of the impact of the flow of the city, the city that Julien Gracq defines as that which "like me, never ceases to change."[6]

In An Alabaster Skin, Arets refers to an architecture that "appears only in order to disappear," a notion that constitutes the point of departure in Greg Lynn's essay "Intensive disappearance," in which the skin of alabaster "represents disappearance through the partial, cunning reflection of contexts on a milky surface." The translucent skin points to the building's complex relationship with its context, a relationship in which violence is inevitably present: the violence, Arets would say, of refusing to be a victim of the environment, while at the same time being able to influence and dominate it.

The peculiar relationship that some of Arets' works establish with their urban setting is manifested in the treatment of the accesses to the buildings' interiors. This characteristic can be perceived, for example, in the creation of accesses on levels other than the street, and circulation routes that explicitly divert the possibility of direct continuity between the level of the public space and the interior. In works such as the Police Station in Vaals or the AZL Pension Fund building, this kind of elaboration is produced to eloquent effect.

Gianni Vattimo has described postmodern society as La Società Trasparente, the notion of transparency here alluding to the supposed permeability of communication and information in the

Academy for the Arts and Architecture, Maastricht

Headquaters AZL Pension fund

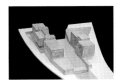

Police Station, Heerlen

Police Station, Vaals

....

[5] Bart Lootsma, "Creating Space for the Unpredictable," in **Wiel Arets,** Antwerp: De Singel, 1996, pp. 10–32.
[6] The quote from Julien Gracq appears in the essay by Vidler and is originally from Gracq's book **La forme d'une ville,** Paris, José Corti, 1985.

contemporary world though the essay in fact questions this transparency. The society of generalized communication and the mass media constitute for Vattimo the possibility (albeit unrealized) of such a transparent society. "These means of communication have been decisive in bringing about the dissolution of centralized perspectives, of what the French philosopher Jean-François Lyotard calls the 'grand narratives' ".[7]

The centralized perspectives to which Vattimo refers have been diluted in the power — literal and metaphorical — of the surface. The corporeal nature of the "skin" is extended by means of references to scarring and the ritual modification of the visible surface of the body. This anthropological reference is made concrete in Arets' text on virology in relation to the Masai people and the practices they use to alter their skin and, on certain occasions, the actual morphology of their bodies.

Arets' architecture is concerned not with the tautened depth of perspective (static, monocular, spatial or figurative) but with the two-dimensional splash of the transparent-translucent surface. The skin of alabaster is a corollary of the cinema screen, a surface on which the lights and shadows of the projection dance. The flat projection and the graphé on the surface are themes that contribute to the nuancing of an idea that is made visible, with its various shadings, in projects such as the library for the university campus in Utrecht.

University Library, Utrecht

Virology

Arets's text A Virological Architecture introduces a new stage in the trajectory we have followed thus far. The reference to virology continues in a more incisive form, an interest in models of knowledge derived from science — not for nothing did Arets study physics before becoming interested in architecture — and more particularly from the life sciences. The rhizome as an arboreal metaphor, the skin as a corporeal model for architectural surfaces, the processes of scarring and artificial modification of the body; such themes predate Arets' interest in a component of the most dematerialized corporeality.

The relationship between corporeality and architecture has been covered extensively in both classical and contemporary literature. Whereas the human body tends to be presented in classic texts (including Le Corbusier and his Modulor) as a "construction," both material and geometrical (the laws of proportion, the parts of the body as basis of systems of measurement, medicine as a form of knowledge comparable to architecture), the scientific understanding of the human body in modern times has tended to shift away from tectonic models towards models in which the body is understood not so much as a stable, erect construction with a certain permanence but as a permeable organism sensitive to forces of a fluid order that can affect it, make it sick and even destroy it.

The classical notion of the pharmakon or drug is an early reference to a substance that is both curative and poisonous, a minuscule body possessing the power to spread through and impregnate the whole of the body to which it is administered. The pharmakon could be applied to the body of an individual, but also to the social body, which may be similarly affected and modified by the "foreign" elements. The body around which drugs and other philters circulate is permanently exposed to the temporality of external influences, to contamination, and Arets asks to what extent the drug is different from the disease or whether, like a vaccine, it should be understood as a sickness that neutralizes the one that has already entered the body.[8]

Since the Enlightenment, modern science and medicine have taken a special interest in ethereal phenomena and their influence on our bodies: electricity, magnetism, gases, etc. The organicist model — as opposed to the mechanistic model so cogently described by historians of scientific thought and its strategies of visualization, such as Barbara Stafford and Georges Canguilhem — has presided over a shift in thinking away from constructive and

....

[7] See Gianni Vattimo, **La società trasparente,** Garzanti, 1989. (Gianni Vattimo, **The Transparent Society.** David Webb, Eng. tr. Baltimore, Johns Hopkins University Press, 1992.)
[8] On the pharmakon, see the reading of Plato proposed by Jacques Derrida in "La pharmacie de Plato," included in **La dissémination,** Paris, Seuil, 1972.

stable (mechanistic) models to procedural and unstable (organic) models.[9]

If the tectonic, constructive body is above all a visible body, the corporeality that virology is interested in is, in contrast, an **invisible** corporeality which seems to escape the patterns of perception and representation with which we are familiar. To the extent that architecture is dependent on its techniques of representation, virology raises complex questions about the current state of architectural knowledge. A virus is a parasitic organism; that is to say, it needs some other organism in or on which to live. But this relationship becomes more complex in so far as the virus infiltrates and imitates the genetic codes of its "host" in order to reproduce itself; in terms of genetic information, the virus will resemble the host to a high degree. The virus opens up the possibility of understanding matter not as a stable substance but as encoded information: its very existence is dependent on its capacity to transform itself continually on the basis of the host organism it occupies.

This permeability is also present in virology, which equates living organisms with electronic systems. Virology speaks to us of instability and uncertainty with regard to the processes of contamination, an instability and a temporality that can be extended to social systems through the logic of the Platonic **pharmakon**, on which Jean Baudrillard and Arthur Kroker, two of Arets' key references, have written.

This shift away from the interpretation of architecture as visualizable and static corporeality — be it anthropomorphic or prosthetic — towards a corporeality based on the logic of invisible fluids, toxins and other phenomena studied by virology emerges from the ideas of Kroker and Eric Bolle, together with the reading of Baudrillard's "La transparence du mal."

In Baudrillard's words, "Virulence takes hold of a body, a network or a system when it expels all of its negative elements and resolves itself as a combination of simple elements. This is due to the fact that the networks have been transformed into virtual beings, nonbodies in which viruses are released, and these 'immaterial' machines are far more vulnerable than traditional mechanisms. Virtual and viral go hand in hand. This is due to the fact that the body itself has become a non-body, a virtual machine taken over by non-viruses."[10]

Setting out from the notion of spatial "over-exposure" and a concern over the impact of the information technologies and the new forms of virtual relationship, Paul Virilio has written about the over-exposed city, an environment in which architecture's responsibility for configuring relations between interiority and exteriority is giving way in the face of other forms of control and spatial segregation. The over-exposed city seems to evoke the image of a body stripped of its usual defences and which is particularly vulnerable to the circulation of those flows (of information, communications, population and so on) that can no longer be controlled by architectural elements. Such over-exposure seems to be a product of the failure of traditional architecture to provide an effective response to the new phenomena of mobility that are increasingly reorganizing the space of the city.[11]

Arets proposes a simile between the virologist and the architect, in that the latter is also trained to recognize the various intangible mental, sociological, political and economic processes that take place in the city, and seeks to influence these by means of projects. There is an evident proximity between Arets' interest in virology and his interest in the techniques of cinematographic representation. The image in movement flows through the interior of the inhabited space and could be said to penetrate and alter it by its very production, thereby altering our perception and our understanding of such spaces. Arets' interest in both film — including its construction, its montage techniques and its iconic narratives — and virology reveals subliminal links that share a common grounding in those ideas that see architecture, too, as a virus that spreads

....

[9] Georges Canguilhem, "Machine and Organism," in Jonathan Crary and Sanford Kwinter, eds., **Incorporations** (Zone 6), Cambridge, Mass., The MIT Press, 1992. Barbara M. Stafford. **Voyage into Substance.** Cambridge, Mass., The MIT Press, 1987.
[10] See Jean Baudrillard, "Prophilaxie et virulence." In **La Transparence du Mal. Essai sur les phénomènes extrêmes,** Paris, Galilée, 1990.
[11] Paul Virilio, "The Overexposed City." Published in English in **The Lost Dimension,** New York: Semiotexte, 1991. Originally published in l'espace critique (Paris, Christian Bourgeois, 1984).

through the city, infecting and curing it at the same time. It is, in short, the concept of architecture as process that presides over the elaboration of this figure of virology.

In his writing on "liquid" architecture, Ignasi de Solà-Morales raises the possibility of an architecture that would be "materially **liquid,** attentive to and a configurer not of stability but of change, and thus at one with the fluid and shifting nature of all reality," and asks if it might be possible to have an architecture that would work with time more than with space, an architecture whose objective would be the ordering of movement and duration over and above the plane of dimensional or spatial extension.[12] Some notable gestures have been made in this direction in the visual arts, as in the case of the Fluxus group or, as Arets himself observes, in the work of the French artist Yves Klein.

Arets' interest in virological processes is accompanied by an ongoing attention to cinematic forms, and he has expressed a particular admiration for film-makers such as Jean-Luc Godard. Indeed, Arets proposes a comparison between cinematic montage and an urbanism based on a mode of perceiving and constructing the physical space that seems to depend on the use of techniques intrinsic to film montage: "The way we perceive a city has been structured beforehand by films."

In his celebrated essay on the reproducibility of the work of art, Walter Benjamin presented photography as an illustrative instance of the profound impact of mechanical reproduction on our perception. "The processes of reproduction can bring to the fore certain aspects of the original work that are inaccessible to the naked eye." In the same text, Benjamin also suggests a direct relationship between film and architecture, two visual products which, he claims, both call for a "distracted" perception. The writings of Gilles Deleuze, a major influence on Arets' ideas, provide a more immediate grounding for discussing the impact of the language of film on architecture and its relationship with the city. The cinematic referent serves to introduce the discussion of fluid space, mobility, velocity and architecture, with montage serving as the "constructive" model for both cinematographic and architectural production.

Contemporaneous with the invention of cinema, Henri Bergson distinguished three types of movement: perception, affection and action. These three movements speak to us of mediation, of that intermediate position that the "skin of alabaster" also speaks of.[13] This is the mediation called for by Deleuze when, after quoting Bergson, he invokes intermediate relationships between the domains of art, science and philosophy.

In the architecture and above all in the writings of Wiel Arets we can also discern these three Bergsonian movements; that is to say, the **perception** of concepts habitually external to a specifically architectural knowledge, an **affection** or incorporation into the work itself, and its simultaneous **mise en œuvre** — the **action.**

....

[12] Ignasi de Solà-Morales, "Liquid Architecture," in **Anyhow,** Cynthia Davidson, ed. Cambridge, Mass., The MIT Press, 1998.
[13] See Gilles Deleuze, "Mediators," in Jonathan Crary and Sanford Kwinter, eds., **Incorporations** (Zone 6), Cambridge, Mass., The MIT Press, 1992. Originally published in L'Autre journal 8 (1985).

13

Anthony Vidler

Oneirism

"I am an ephemeral and not too discontent citizen of a raw modern city."[1]

    The form of a city, Baudelaire noted with irony and some nostalgia in the face of Haussmann's reconstructive fury, changes more quickly than the heart of a mortal. But, as successive "modernisms" and "countermodernisms" have demonstrated, often the heart changes even more quickly than the city itself. Le Corbusier's impatience at the obstinate survival of old Paris — "Imagine all this junk, which till now has lain spread out over the soil like a dry crust, cleaned off and carted away"[2] — is only one extreme example of the radical shifts in sensibility toward the city in this century, shifts that have more often than not been resisted by the intractable nature of the existing urban fabric. More recently, debates over the fate of the "historical" city, whether couched in terms of Rossi's neorationalism or Krier's neoclassicism, have themselves foundered over the unwillingness of cities to be turned into historical museums of themselves. Maurice Halbwachs's observation that "the stones of the city . . . have a fixed place and are as attached to the ground as trees and rocks," that "Paris and Rome . . . seem to have crossed the centuries without interruption to the continuity of their life for a single minute," remarks written during the Second World War, seem to attest to this durability of the city, its incorrigible will to live its past in full modernity.[3]

    A contemporary philosopher of urban architecture is faced then, at the end of the twentieth century, not so much with the absolute dialectic of ancient and modern posed by the avant- and rear gardes of the last eighty years, as with the more subtle and difficult task of calculating the limits of intervention according to the resistance of the city to change. And, as writers from Rimbaud to Julien Gracq have perceived, this resistance is not only one of stone but also, and perhaps more importantly, of mentality. In Halbwach's words "spatial images play such a role in the collective memory." The place occupied by a group is not like a chalkboard on which one writes, and then erases, numbers and figures.[4] The black-

---

[1] Rimbaud, **Les illuminations.**
[2] Le Corbusier, **Urbanisme.** Paris, 1925, p. 280.
[3] Maurice Halbwachs, **La mémoire collective,** preface by Jean Duvignaud. Paris, Presses Universitaires de France, 1968, p. 134.
[4] Halbwachs, **La mémoire collective,** p. 133.

board, after all, remains profoundly indifferent to the figures inscribed on its surface, while a place receives the imprint of a group, and vice versa — a salutary caution to the urban architect in front of a seemingly passive plan of streets and houses.

In the development of such a sensibility to the limits of urban change, the projects of Wiel Arets stand as evocative experiments in the intersection of the mental and the physical. From the outset, in the urban block projects designed with Wim van den Bergh (1984–1985), the traditional modern dialectic between ideal type and real context has been avoided, or rather replaced, by a more complex intercalation of intellectual narrative and material proposition. Here the city, as existing, stands as the object and generator of so many possible futures, each calculated according to the nature of its opposition to those futures. The architectural project, while crystallizing one or more of these futures, is then presented to the city, so to speak, as a whole, not as a replacement or substitute, as in the utopian urbanism of Modernism, but as material to be submitted to the life and consuming power of the context. Apparently totalizing "types" will thereby inevitably be fragmented by the counterforce of the site. Thus the social "resistance" of Arets and Van den Bergh's Moscow tower housing, imagined for a dissident population at the heart of the old city, is doubled and reciprocated by the city itself, in such a way that architecture, defining its own limits, a bulwark against the world, is in turn limited and partially invaded by its surroundings. Here Arets and Van den Bergh have at the same time refused the image of a "modern" superimposed on a tabula rasa, or raised above it on pilotis, and also rejected any comforting simulacrum of a historical context. Their vocabulary belongs resolutely to a century of technological change, echoing while not imitating the already historicized language of the first avant-garde; but their strategy is built on a countermodern heritage, out of the **Illuminations** of Rimbaud, the **vases-communicantes** of Breton, the **flânerie** of Aragon and Benjamin, and, of course, the hallucinatory world of Roussel's **Locus solus**. Their contemporary "urban imaginary" is thus fabricated out of the dialectic between memory, as defined in the long post-Bergsonian tradition, and situation, as phenomenologically described by writers from Bachelard to Lefebvre.

This dialectic is perhaps most clearly evident in the later project by Arets and Joost Meuwissen for the "completion" of the Ca'Venier dei Leoni, the home of the Peggy Guggenheim collection in Venice. The historical foundations of this project, the "sea story" of an eighteenth-century palace, the very scale of which seemed already to have forbidden its completion, is here taken for the ground of a scheme intended to pay homage to two denizens of the collective memory of Venice, the musicians Franz Liszt and Richard Wagner. Physically ephemeral but mentally eternal, music becomes the preferred figure for this apparently absurd erection of (Otto) Wagnerian towers on a classical base; in one sense, both base and superstructure are mutually exclusive — if one exists, the other must be fiction — but on another level, their solid juxtaposition throws into relief the precise nature of Arets' art of memory, the forced reconciliation of present and past in an image that refuses any reduction to one or the other.

These almost archaeological superpositions, similar to those that Freud articulated in the realm of Roman memory, where two contents that **spatially** would find it impossible to locate in the same place find their reconciliation in the mind, are extended into images of territorial occupation in the OFI-sports center and the Columbusworld projects, again by Arets and Wim van den Bergh. In these designs, sited on apparently open ground, the land in fact plays the role we have ascribed to the city as both ground and formidable opponent, filled equally with memory — to collective memory, as it were, of the landscape, of Greek athletics on the island of Crete, and of Columbus and his discoveries in Portugal. In this latter project, which recalls Le Corbusier and Paul Otlet's vision of a Mundaneum, the attempt is to construct a form of contemporary memory theater, along the lines suggested by Giordano Bruno, that will allow the visitor to trace the multiple paths offered by the idea of Columbus, paths that echo a history and propose a future. Whether in city or country, these designs seem conscious of the special psychogeography of places — that complex mixture of memory, experience, and space intimated by the situationists in the late

OFI-sports center

Columbusworld

1950s and theorized by Henri Lefebvre — in contrast to the mechanical memory lifted from history by a postmodernism that relies more on quotation than on interior strategy.

And this consciousness, it must be said, is not allowed to remain in the domain of the pictorical but, in Arets's more recent projects, is itself forced into the physical domain with technical and formal mastery. Thus the remodeling of the House and Pharmacy of Brunssum, the Medical Centre and House at Hapert, the Keent-Moesel pharmacy at Weert Zuid, and, most importantly, the Medical Centre Weert, all display a drive toward a language of simplicity, realized with a deliberately reduced technological repertoire that allows for an elegant functional solution without impeding the play of memory and experience. In this sense, Arets' often-lauded "purity" approaches the "difficult simplicity" noted by Aldo Rossi in the geometrical reductions of Boullée, and evoked by Rossi himself in early projects for schools and houses. The deceptive absence of high architecture in these built designs serves to heighten the effect of what Le Corbusier unambiguously defined as the fundamental architectural elements — light and shade articulating masses and surfaces. Here the memory theater and the architectural object find their intersection in an unobtrusive typological imagination, one that, for example in the Pharmacy of Brunssum, underlines the virtues of the Corbusian Domino model by stressing the horizontal floors and by framing all interior divisions on translucent glass block, but without destroying the nature of the existing pitched roof. Typology is confronted with context as a means of measuring, once more, the necessary recalcitrance of the already built. Other projects exhibit a similar attitude toward the typical, most especially the design for the Fashion shop in Maastricht, where the space for cultural consumption is articulated by architectural elements that resist the decorative or the stylistic in favor of a simple contrast between the "loft" volume and the vertical stair. Other not yet realized designs for domestic settings, such as the Villa Romanoff, Miami, continue this precise calibration of the minimum number of architectural events necessary to shelter function and to liberate thought.

Perhaps the most advanced combination of architectural typology and urban discourse is demonstrated in the design for Rotterdam's North Urban Core, proposed in the context of nine schemes commissioned by Architectural International Rotterdam for the "Railway Tunnel Site". A strongly modulated but delicately inserted string of architecturally defined types, composed of diverse combinations of glass towers echoing the first urban block projects, is deployed in a city whose fabric is entirely respected yet profoundly transformed. The long thin line of glass towers leads from the center to the river's edge, marking a route and a thought at one and the same time. Yet for all the powerful visual character of this intervention, the surrounding city is left untouched, save, of course, for the mental reverberations of this "translucent" machine. The metropolis as an architectural container for individual and collective memory, "a void which is filled only with thoughts," in Arets' words, takes on, in this project, a catalytic rather than an instrumental role. In lieu of the modernist "social condenser," calculated with Benthamite fervor to transform the daily life of the citizen according to fixed ideals of bourgeois reform, Arets' envisions a shimmering and broken curtain of translucent walls that reverberate with the multiple "stimuli" observed by Georg Simmel as the leitmotivs of the "mental life" of the metropolis.

But this substitution, one that affirms the possibilities for urban architecture at a moment when, politically and aesthetically, the modern tradition seems in defeat and disarray, is, by the same token, more than a literal recombination and recalculation of modern architectural types. Its strategy emerges here as even more important than any (less than final) result. For the practice outlined by Arets equally privileges city **void** and city **thoughts**, a difficult dialogue to sustain but one based on a belief in the permeability of things to ideas and ideas to things. No longer are things either the result of thoughts or their simple signifiers; rather they are constituted in that ambiguous realm of memory that is at once experience and recollection of experience in such a way as to remain inseparable. Thus the early design for the Farsetti garden in the Veneto, founded on a narrative recalling both a description from the Tipaldo and the more recent "garden" imagined by

Pharmacy, Brunssum

Medical Center and House, Hapert

Keent-Moesel Pharmacy, Weert Zuid

Medical Center, Weert

Villa Romanoff, Miami

Architectural International Rotterdam

Roussel, transforms a literary conceit into a spatial situation so as to permit the experience and recreation of as many narratives as there are visitors. In the Columbusworld or the Translucent City projects, despite the almost anatomical attention to the delineation and program of each separate architectural event with its corresponding metaphorical referent, the resulting composition remains open to multiple interpretations. Architecture, creating situations or events, demands a fictional starting point; the city, an "accumulation of effects whose causes are reversed," refuses any such limitation on its freedom to reconstruct the imaginary.

In other terms we might understand this procedure, so self-consciously developed by Arets, as a deliberate merging of the **locus solus** invented by the architect and the **locus suspectus**, or haunted site, of the city, a recognition that architecture and lived experience share the same sources. In this conflation, the traditional opposition between an ideal project and its real application is overcome by the essential **complicity** of the architect's project and the collective memory from which it derives. In the **unheimlich** environment that is thereby created, we might imagine that Arets' buildings take their place easily enough amidst the cacophony of walls and spaces that suffice to indicate the memory of a city; that they, following on from and juxtaposed to the concrete evidence of prior imaginaries, will in turn stimulate their own; that walking in them, in the steps of Julien Gracq, we might for a moment find as much permanence in the city as in the heart: "and the town, with me, changes and remodels itself, carves out its limits, deepens its perspectives, and on this course — a form open to all the impulses of the future, the only way in which it can be within me and be truly itself — it does not cease changing."[5]

....

[5] Julien Gracq, **La Forme d'une ville.** Paris, José Corti, 1985, p. 213.

Greg Lynn

Criticism: Intensive disappearance

"We want our buildings to fit into the existing context, yet to remain flexible and open to change."[1]

In this statement, Wiel Arets identifies two central issues for contemporary architecture. The first concerns disappearance, the second concerns pliability. Arets suggests that blending can offer flexibility and openness. This type of incorporation — of a building into its context — requires both a logic of intensity and disappearance. There are two recurring figures in the work of Arets that exhibit intensive disappearance. The first is the series of models built to describe the internal circulation of the buildings, the second is an alabaster skin. The former represents the organization of local, free intensities through the exploitation of external pressures; the latter represents disappearance through the partial, cunning reflection of contexts on a milky surface. Like a chameleon, these projects diffract and reflect their context through the combination of these two tactics. These systems, of intensity and a translucent skin, suggest a liberating opportunity for the cunning expoitation of what has become a bankrupt theory of contextualism in architecture. Despite the resemblances to a recent theory of contextualism, Arets' sensibility could not be more dissimilar.

The models of the Boulevard Complex for Domburg of 1990, the Academy for the Arts and Architecture at Maastricht of 1990, the Amsterdam Academy of the Arts of 1990 and the folded and unfolded urban corridors of the Dance Theater at Delft of 1991 are intensive to the extent that they actively incorporate external influences in the definition of their internal order. Intensive relations between a building and its context typically result in the context influencing the building so that the building seems to become the context itself. This expansion through incorporation is an urban alternative to either the infinite extension of International Modernism, the uniform fabric of Contextualism or the arrested conflicts of Post-Modernism and Deconstructivism.

Like viscous fluids, which develop internal stability in proportion to the external forces exerted upon them, these systems are stabilized as they become affected by exigencies and contingencies. This two-fold deterritorialization sacrifices autonomous, internal

Boulevard Complex, Domburg

Academy for the Arts and Architecture, Maastricht

....

[1] Wiel Arets, **AA files** 21.

regulation for a more fluid participation in a larger contextual field. The incorporation of contextual forces within a system that is open to influence results in the discovery of new possibilities for the reorganization of that same context. Unlike the more familiar architecture of organic, whole organisms — to which nothing can be added or subtracted — intensive organizations continually invite external influences within their internal limits so that they might extend their influence through connectivity. Intensive contextualism is a tactic for fitting in yet remaining flexible.

Perhaps the Boulevard project is the best example of an intensive organization device in that it accumulates out of and is deformed by local forces and events. In this sense it is not only a broken spine but a flexible, continuous, connector composed of heterogeneous, local programs such as shops, swimming pools, galleries, restaurants, conference rooms, hotels, villas and golf courses. The organization that emerges from the pedestrian and vehicular movement around the Amsterdam Academy of the Arts — the oval — and the internal requirements of the academy — the bar — are placed into a dynamically hinged relationship in which neither is subservient to the other. The movement around the oval is visibly related to and does not contradict the more secluded interior of the Academy. Intense systems are forceful and effective because their pliability allows them to maintain a multiplicity of disparate, local, heterogeneous characteristics within a continuous mixture.

Intensive contextualism employs a "logic of curvilinearity" that can be characterized by the involvement of outside forces in the development of form. If internally motivated and homogeneous systems extend in straight lines, curvilinear developments result from the incorporation of external influences. Such a curvilinear sensibility is capable of smoothly deforming a complex and differentiated system in response to local programmatic, structural, economic, aesthetic, political and contextual influences. This is not to imply that intensive curvature is more politically correct than an uninvolved formal logic, but rather that the smooth incorporation of a context through tactical mutability is often more effective. Many of these cunning tactics are aggressive in nature. This is acknowledged in Arets' texts and projects.

Curvilinearity is a condition of being deformed in response to vicissitudes. In Arets' work this deformation takes the form of rectilinear deflections rather than bending. This insidious reconfiguration of the Academy for the Arts in Maastricht through a system of new connections is perhaps the most cunning example. Whether insidious or ameliorative, these kinds of tactical connections reveal new possibilities for organization. These affiliations are not predictable by any contextual orders but occur through vicissitude. Here, urban fabric has no value or meaning beyond the connections that are made within it. Distinct from earlier urban sensibilities that generalized broad formal codes, intensive contextualism develops local, fine-grain, complex systems of intrication.

Intensity can be engendered by a multiplicity of forms as long as they are forms of multiplicity. Multiplicity is a term used to describe the co-presence of the one and the many. It differs from mere multiples, as a multiplicity is a composite mixture of free elements. For example, the word "hair" refers to both the local elements (hairs) and to the overall organization (hair). Multiplicities are represented as simultaneously single and plural, for example the architecture(s) of Wiel Arets. In this regard, multiplicity is a sign of schizophrenia. A multiplicitous body is always less than one organism, whilst also being an affiliation of many organs. The paradigm of the pack, swarm or crowd, as proposed by Elias Canetti, may be one such model for engaging a less than whole building with a context that is not a continuous fabric but an assemblage of disparate morphologies. The distinctions between part and whole, autonomous individual and collective are not necessary when describing the behavior of a pack, swarm, or crowd. To become intensively involved with such an organization, an individual must enter into the affiliations of a pack. In a pack, each individual defers its internal structure in order to benefit, by alliance, from the fluid movements of the pack.

As the proper limits of individual elements (multiplicity of wolves) are blurred, the pack begins to behave as if it were itself an organism (multiplicity of the pack). The pack itself is not regulated by or reducible to any single structure, as it is continually, dynami-

Academy of the Arts, Amsterdam

Dance Theater, Delft

cally and fluidly transforming itself in response to its intensive involvement with both the external forces of its context and the internal forces of its members. It is at once less than a single organism and a collection of multiple organs. Multiplicity describes the assembly of a provisional group formed from disparate elements. Multiplicitous bodies are always multiplicating and entering into relations and connections of alliance through multiplication rather than mere addition. These are systems of connectivity, making heterogeneous free intensities continuous in an unpredicted manner, often as a result of vicissitude. As Canetti illustrates, the sole meaning of a pack is in its desire to grow and proliferate.

The most familiar model of multiplicity and intensity in architecture has recently become the "rhizome", used by Gilles Deleuze and Félix Guattari as an introduction to A Thousand Plateaus. In discussing the work(s) of Arets, the theorists and architects Stanley Allen and Edward Mitchell have both separately been baited by the title of Arets' text Grid and Rhizome concerning the Amsterdam Academy of Arts. In this regard they have been willing victims for the trap set by Arets. Allen and Mitchell have primarily concerned themselves with delineating the meaning of the grid and rhizome — as forms in Arets' work. In order to evaluate Arets' work from within the dialectic of grid and rhizome, in which he sets it, a separation of two terms that are often elided is necessary; the rhizomatous and the rhizomorphous. The first term describes the affects of a rhizome, the second its form. In the former, the rhizome is curvilinear because it is deformed by external forces; in the latter, it is merely a curved figure.

Affects are different from effects primarily in one respect. An affect is a virtual response in meaning; for instance, the color red gives the effect of warmth. An affect is an influence or alteration in behavior, not meaning; for instance, paralysis affects the movement of the extremities. Affects do not involve mimicry or imitation but transformation. When a parrot imitates language, it is assumed that the parrot does not undergo an internal transformation; is not affected by language but merely effects the use of language. The four model studies are rhizomatous to the extent that they are intensively deformed. The rhizomatous and rhizomorphous are neither in direct proportion to one another nor mutually exclusive, but are always related in mixture. The operative term in discriminating between the merely rhizomorphic and the behavior of a rhizome is the aforementioned logic of curvilinearity. Rather than signifying the rhizome with vermiforms (worm forms), a logic of curvilinearity identifies the rhizomatous with deformation. Specific deformations are contingent upon manipulation by external forces. The formal consequences of deformations may be bent, folded, creased, angled, twisted, blended and/or mixed. The rectilinear deformation characteristic of Arets' work is one such example. A straight path is not so much deformed as a localized system of connections resulting from a shared deformation across elements. Deformation is a system of organization itself.

Arets' work then is concerned with the incorporation of his projects into a context within which the possibility for movement remains open. Arets describes a seemingly familiar alien presence in a contextual field within which it disappears. In several popular Hollywood films this theme of an alien blending into a context is exploited due to its ability to evoke horror. There are two types of disappearance of an alien into a context. The first involves either an alien taking over a human body from the inside, as in "The Hidden", or replicating a human body, as in "The Invasion of the Body Snatchers." Familiarity allows these aliens a certain mobility as the nature of their alien interior is hidden. This type of disappearance is effective by inviting recognition as something or someone familiar. These aliens disappear by deceitful detection. Similarly, Robert Venturi's Molecular Biology Center at Princeton University houses an advanced genetic research facility that is sheathed with decorative skin approximating the Gothic structures surrounding it. With a single visit to Euro-Disney, Postmodernism in architecture could be broadly characterized by this shared strategy of inviting deceitful detection. A second type of disappearance is alluded to in the title of Arets' book An Alabaster Skin. The surface of the building's skin is used by Arets as a cloaking device.

Mark Wigley has already argued that the color white itself was used by the Modernists as a kind of decorative sign that signified the absence of decoration. The Arets' projects, however, differ from this modern sensibility in their translucency. Arets' alabaster, milky whiteness acts as a cloaking device, disappearing by remaining translucent and reflecting a diffracted image of its context. This alabaster translucency can be seen most pointedly in the perspectives which are so influential on the development of the projects.

Translucency allows for a simultaneity of readings that are precluded by either transparency or opacity. The alabaster skin that encloses the internal volumes in Arets's AZL-Beheer Headquarters and the Delft Theater perspectives allows the spaces to be seen as discrete elements that are blended with one another. The free intensities of these volumetric elements are imbedded within each other in such a way that a multiplicity of spaces seem to be co-present at all times in the drawing. A precedent for this alabaster urbanism is Skidmore Owings and Merrill's Law Library at Yale University that utilizes an alabaster curtain wall that breaks down the boundary between the interior and exterior without transparency. Light is admitted from the outside during the day and the interior emanates a glowing light at night. The polished surface of the blank curtain wall reflects the adjacent buildings while allowing permeability. Likewise, in Arets' work there is the stealth of a chameleon or even an alligator operating.

"Architecture is therefore a between, a membrane, an alabaster skin, at once opaque and transparent, meaningful and meaningless, real and unreal. To become itself, architecture must lose its innocence; it must accept a violent transgression. It can only become part of the world by entering into marriage with its surroundings. Therefore architecture is not only untainted but violent, and its violence once again has two sides. On one side architecture is violent because it resists having to be the victim of its surroundings; on the other it can distort those surroundings. This relationship lends it cunning." (Arets, An Alabaster Skin.)

The familiar example of the resemblance between an alligator and a log might be useful here. An alligator resembles and behaves like a floating log not because it desires to embody "logness" but because by disappearing within its context the alligator is given a floating mobility and cunning. The alligator is affected by the log it becomes only to the extent that it behaves and resembles a log; it means nothing more. Unlike the log, it will devour a duck, for example, when it becomes expedient for it to begin to behave like an alligator again. There is no contradiction here. It should be relatively clear that whether or not Arets' circulation elements are rhizomorphous, they are certainly more a log than a duck. As the work of Arets is influenced by and incorporates its context, it should be observed that these connections are meaningless outside of the possible lines of disappearance and escape that they provide. A rhizome, such as a potato, looks the way it does because of the way it grows; it develops intensively by incorporating the adjacent materials and forces present in its context. A potato is a **pomme de terre,** or apple of the earth, because it is as much like its subterranean context as it is a discrete fruit. The degree to which Arets' work is contextually deformed can be suggested by the degree to which it looks like a potato, or a rhizome, yet the true test is in its ability to intensively disappear by becoming fluid, becoming mobile, becoming its context.

Headquarters AZL Pension Fund

Stan Allen

Leveraging theory

"Just because Napoleon was nothing, he could signify everything except himself." With this unambiguous statement Marx signals the potential emptiness of the signifier and he underlines a corresponding instability in the meanings which might attach to the name. How often do place names, for example, fix and memorialize accident, mis-identity and error? Something similar — but more extreme — occurs in architecture under the mediated conditions of late modern capitalism. It has become impossible to separate out the "object" of criticism from the web of representations and affiliations within which it appears.

This insight is intended to point to the paradox under which the work of Wiel Arets is presented. A young architect with significant built works to his credit, Arets has gained a reputation as a careful constructor well within established modernist paradigms. His work is precisely detailed, and he favors the trabeated frame as a means of expression. Working within the parameters of an apparently reductive modernist language, and with clear antecedents in Dutch modernity, he is also able to allow the particularities of context to lightly inflect these rigorously formal compositions. Projects like the Academy for the Arts and Architecture in Maastricht (1990) map local conditions with great precision and on the basis of thorough local knowledge.

Educated at Eindhoven, living and working in the small city of Maastricht, Arets' affinities would appear at first to be primarily local. Confirmation of this could be found in the first work of Arets to appear after his graduation: not a built work, but a monograph on the work of F. P. J. Peutz, an unorthodox, unclassifiable and slightly provincial modernist architect active in Maastricht. Like the work of Peutz or of the better known Dudok, Arets' production appears to be an architecture more connected to stable traditions of place and history than to the global drift of present-day international architectural culture.

But just as Maastricht has recently entered the lexicon of international economics, so Arets has a paradoxical postmodern presence as well. Teaching at the Architectural Association since 1988, and more recently at Columbia University (two privileged locations for international intellectual exchange), the architect himself lives out a nomadic existence between London, Amsterdam, Maastricht and New York, traveling to teach, build and lecture. Thus in a 1989 text on Arets' urban projects, critic Tony Vidler refers to Rimbaud, Lefebvre and the situationists. And since winning the Rotterdam-Maaskant prize for Young Architects in that same year, Arets' projects have been accompanied by a carefully choreographed strategy of publications. Images of his work circulate globally, further complicating the "regionalist" model.

Academy for the Arts and Architecture, Maastricht

This double articulation is made explicit in a recent **AA Files** publication of Arets' work. Here, the project for the Academy of Arts in Amsterdam is presented under a text headed Grid and Rhizome, linking in this way the emblematic geometrical configurations of the modern and the postmodern.

This paradoxical conjunction of "grid and rhizome" can of course be interpreted as simply opportunistic, deferring to the predominant critical models in an effort to establish legitimacy. In this regard, Norman Bryson has suggested the following connection between theoretical and economic paradigms: ". . . the cult of drifting, the interest in signs for their indeterminacy, the postmodern fascination with signs in collision, in fragmentation, in moving ruin, might be just what you would expect in a state of capitalism that had turned from producing goods to producing and manipulating a realm of commodity signs. The theoretical recognition that the world is composed of decontextualized, clashing, colliding fragments might not, in fact, be a description of how 'meaning' works, but of how meaning works in the stage of the market economy now opening before us." (The Erotics of Doubt, 1990.) In the contradictory grid/rhizome pair, therefore, are conjoined the verifiability of modern instrumental means and the seduction of random postmodern drift. The project for the Academy of Arts embodies this professional compromise. "We want our building to fit into the existing context, yet to remain flexible and open to change," write the architects in their description. At the same time they refer to the Deleuzian idea of Amsterdam as a place of labyrinthine horizontal interchange ("don't go for the root, go for the canal" as Patti Smith says). Yet far from engaging the challenge to architecture's conventions contained within the multiple texts of Deleuze and Guattari, this project reiterates traditional hierarchies of architectural form-making. The visible portion takes the form of rectilinear towers, asserting their vertical dominance over the rootlike circulation at and below the level of the street. Grid and rhizome, but uncontaminated, held apart by the separatrix of the ground-plane, which maintains each in its expected place — the towers in open air and the roots the site of exchange below the surface of the city.

This mismatch of theory and practice, the incommeasurability of the project and its theoretical description, suggests another reading. It suggests a non-literal reading, one that bypasses the logic of appearance and the strictures of classical mimesis. This by contrast might be a reading which preserves more of the fluidity of Deleuze and Guattari's language itself, and at the same time unravels the (vertical) authority of language over form, of theory over architecture. Deleuze and Guattari instead solicit a form of reading based not on morphological correspondence, but on material and semiotic textures, based on unexpected jumps of scale or perception. The rhizome does not have to **look like** a worm or a fungus. ("Comparing a sock to a vagina is OK, its done all the time, but you'd have to be really insane, to compare a pure aggregate of stitches to a field of vaginas: this is what Freud says." — A Thousand Plateaus, p. 27.) In the case of Arets, the rectilinear frame may function not so much as a stable regulator of meaning but as an empty slot awaiting the unpredictable event. Which reading is proper: the literal one which would read the rhizome as an incitement to substitute a supple geometry of fluid vectors for architecture's traditional preference for the rectilinear and the vertical; or one which would take Deleuze and Guattari at their word and read the rhizome according to a logic of association and multiplicity? This work provokes us to ask further, by what mechanism of meaning could we verify the association of stable forms with stable meanings? Isn't the symmetry of this logic precisely what Deleuze and Guattari set out to unpack: "An assemblage, in its multiplicity, necessarily acts on semiotic flows, material flows, and social flows simultaneously (independently of any recapitulation that may be made of it in a scientific or theoretical corpus)" (A Thousand Plateaus, p. 23). The **indifference** of Arets' grid might be noted in this context: continuously rendered as surface and equal in the vertical and horizontal dimensions, rather than as distinct tectonic elements assembled according to a logic of load and support. And what exactly are all those little bumps and holes all over Arets' buildings? Arets, then, despite the apparent strong form affiliation, might be seen to embody a "yes, but" logic of undecidability, but only when the work is seen in conjunction with the (mediated) frame of theory, project and publicity.

Another chain of references and affiliations suggests yet another reading, which in turn supplements and contradicts the first. I am referring here to Arets' attraction to the works of Antonin Artaud, Samuel Beckett, Adalberto Libera and Adolf Loos. Here, in place of a spreading network of affiliations, these figures, despite their evident dissimilarities, are linked by the common use of strategies of negation, by silence, alienation, renunciation, and **disaffiliation.** They have put into practice Karl Kraus' dictum: "Whoever has anything to say should step forward and remain silent." Here I note not only the research and documentation of Libera's Casa Malaparte carried out by Arets and his students, and the references to Artaud and Beckett in the texts, but statements like the following: "However, the theater of the absurd, in particular the plays of Samuel Beckett, suggests that culture might be something entirely different, something that involves futility and the loss of meaning, the void — in short the depletion of the very essence of humanity." ("Casa come me: A Sublime Alienation." Wiel Arets and Wim van der Bergh, **AA Files** 18.) It would be pointless to underline the degree to which this contradicts the Deleuzian line taken earlier. The project of Deleuze and Guattari is born precisely out of the effort to think a way out of and around these "blockages" of modern thought conceived entirely as negation. For example: "It is false to see novels such as Beckett's as the end of the novel in general, invoking black holes, the character's line of deterritorialization, the schizophrenic promenades of Molloy or The Unnameable, their loss of names, memory or purpose. [. . .] Molloy is the beginning of the genre of the novel." (A Thousand Plateaus, pp. 173–4.) As noted before, we should not necessarily look for consistency, propriety and correctness in the play of references, although a certain degree of opportunism should not be altogether ruled out.

It is within these multiple shadows that the project presented here, the Dance Theater in Delft (1991), should be seen. As before, the co-presence of the grid and rhizome can be detected, but a significant change should be noted: no longer held apart in their distinct realms, the grid inhabits the rhizome and the rhizome inhabits the grid. The separatrix has begun to be twisted. In the aerial photograph, the figure of the theater appears as a misplaced solid. Its internal structure is heterogeneous; the grid begins to stammer. The analytical model suggests why: the superposition of two lines of movement — the pedestrian who arrives through the labyrinth of the streets, and the automobile, the relic of the machine world, introduced into the volume of the theater from below, infecting the stable geometries with another modality. That this coincides with the "affirmative" gestures and professional imperatives of careful analysis of circulation, the preservation of the adjacent square from automobile traffic and the separation of functions necessary for the function of the theater is not a contradiction, but evidence of the suppleness of the design logic. We are presented not with a collusive assemblage of fragments (the holdovers of cubist compositional strategies, surrealist juxtaposition or dadaist negation) but with a rectilinear frame — essentially symmetrical on the axis of the theater — contaminated from within, structured by its voids, and inflected by foreign geometries. The symmetry is not so much broken as melted. It should not be surprising that these themes are continued in such details as the lozenge-shaped columns in the foyer, the bar which penetrates the cube of the theater or the screen of black synthetic rubber which drapes the upper story of the project, or that the competition project was presented with fully developed construction sections. The intention here is not to oppose construction to critique, but to attempt to build according to the contradictory logics of critique.

This position both resists closure and anticipates a complex clarification in completion. As such, it would be futile to attempt to predict or to sum up; I would conclude by continuing to read this work against the grain of the affiliations it privileges. Francesco Dal Co has written that "In Loos, the limit is never a point of contact or of passage; nor can his forms be conceived of as masks, since his design makes subtle differences manifest, plans for differences and separations, reflects upon the modern poverty of language by laying bare its fleshless reality, and points out that every reassuring possibility of reconciliation is past. . . . " ("The Phenomenology of the Limit," **Oppositions,** 1981.) By citing Loos — a "premodern" source, (and a critical text long "out of date") — I don't mean to suggest that Arets is nostalgic or retrograde; rather, that an examination of his work collapses those very distinctions that would allow us to read architecture by means of exhausted teleological histories.

Dance Theater, Delft

Bart Lootsma

Personality, craft and tradition
The architectural roots of Wiel Arets

The architecture of Wiel Arets resists labelling. On the surface it resembles minimalist architecture, but it betrays too much attention to aspects of the program and of meaning to be truly minimalist. It is a distinguished architecture, but also an architecture which has a beguiling fascination with subversive processes — with decay, even with violence and with alternative forms of use — which at first sight it seems to deny with its compelling severity. It is an architecture that continually evades qualifications, if only for the reason that the buildings themselves change over the course of time. Yet it is also a very recognizable architecture. It is recognizable in the same way as someone's handwriting, in which the same letters are repeatedly constructed in the same way. The same materials and the same solutions appear from project to project, and innovations are carefully imbedded, without conceding to the vogue of the day. Arets' architecture is also recognizable due to its strict sense of composition and by the uncompromising way the buildings are planted in the cityscape. In short, it is an architecture with a personality and with unmistakable self-esteem. Having come so far, however, I must hasten to correct myself, for Arets' architecture is not a purely personal architecture, neither in the sense of some kind of expressionism nor in the sense of embodying a highly personal universe. It has too many points of contact with the history of architecture, with the history, structure and meaning of the city, and with the function and program of the brief, for that to be true. The combination of personality and tradition produces an architecture of craftsmanship, and we can trace the roots of this craftsmanship in Arets' architecture both to the region in which he grew up and to his studies and first lecturing appointments at the Eindhoven University of Technology in the period from 1977 to 1983.

What does that mean, to be precise, a craftsmanlike architecture in which tradition and personality merge? It certainly does not mean that Wiel Arets builds a traditional architecture — on the contrary. Arets' position on the threshold between the twentieth and twenty-first centuries may perhaps best be compared to that of Adolf Loos a hundred years before. Tradition, specifically in the sense of craftsmanship, was important to Loos too. But Loos understood that tradition is subject to evolution, and he was moreover faced with the implacability with which modernism manifested itself as a rising force of urban culture — even in the countryside. Loos was one of the first architects to realize that he had to look to the international scene for his references, and not only America, but

Nice and Paris. To the outside world Arets is known simply as a Dutch architect, but we must seek his true formative roots in the Dutch province of Limburg. It was here that he grew up and it is here that he lives and works to this day. Limburg is a region unlike the rest of the Netherlands, a region where a field of tension between tradition and modernity, between provincialism and cosmopolitanism, has been patent and tangible since time immemorial. On the one hand, the province cherishes unique traditions such as its own language, a high esteem for the pleasures of life (in particular its cuisine and its exuberant Carnival) and the appearance of its villages, towns and landscape. On the other hand, poised as it is between Belgium, Luxemburg and Germany, it cannot avoid taking an international outlook. Cologne, Paris and Brussels are not far away and the Limburgers eagerly speak the languages of these places, if only because the local language is itself a heady blend of Dutch, German and French. The situation is not unlike that of Basel, located at the meeting point of Germany, France and Switzerland, where the national borders have a relatively minor importance in day-to-day affairs but are culturally and economically highly important.

Limburg is also the Dutch province where modernity has had its heaviest impact in the form of large-scale industry: lime quarries and coal mines, and the chemicals industry that settled there on their account. Modern industrial structures and industrial monuments of the past appear with harsh abruptness in the otherwise charming, hilly countryside. Industry, especially the coal mines, has inevitably also left its mark on social life — in the social cohesion necessitated by dangerous and unhealthy work underground, and in new social institutions such as insurance banks and sports clubs. When the mines closed, the wide consensus was that effort would have to go into the development of new technologies and knowledge industries to ensure survival. Wiel Arets' personality, character and work seem to have been broadly determined by these aspects of his Limburg background. If any one of his buildings is symbolic of this, it is his headquarters for the AZL Pension Fund in the city of Heerlen. The AZL originated as a pension fund founded for the mineworkers and was formerly housed in a solid, surly, traditionalist brick building in Heerlen with a squat tower that commanded respect. Arets retained large parts of the old building in his new design, including the symbolically important tower, but at the same time he hollowed it out like a lime quarry, replacing the resulting cavity with an office block engineered with the latest building technologies and equipped with a highly flexible office infrastructure. The new building is cut as though by a surgeon's knife into the old tissue and is angled somewhat in relation to the old building, as though intending to affirm the tension between tradition and modernity — although its volume alone would be enough to dominate the old building. Inside, everything is at the service of the new organization. The new main entrance is a severe mask, reminiscent of the installations of John Hejduk, alongside the old tower.

Arets is all too aware of his personal background. One of his earliest texts is a colloquium paper he presented (in a series of valedictory lectures for Professor Apon) shortly before his graduation from the Eindhoven University of Technology in 1982 while a research assistant to Professor Slebos. In the paper, Arets quotes extensively from the first diary extract in Cesare Pavese's *Il mestiere di vivere* and comments as follows. "Pavese saw his mission in life as being to use his skills to master and shape the material that was given to him in his childhood; in the way that one carves a sculpture out of a block of marble, or extracts a story from a series of happenings to which one wishes to give meaning. *Il mestiere di vivere* is a logbook in which he continually calls himself to order, criticizes himself, eggs himself on and tries to correct himself, and in which he expresses rising despair of ever mastering this business, life. (...) The 'craft of life' was for Pavese a way of trying to turn his life around; of mending his ways and thwarting his destiny. It was a program, a scenario for his life, a life on which he worked with the same precision as that with which he crafted his stories. It was a life that he was not willing to let slip away, but which he wanted to build up and round off; life as a work of art."[1]

....

[1] Wiel Arets, **Fragmenten en hun relatie,** lecture at Eindhoven University of Technology, 20 April 1982, unpublished manuscript.

The text does not make it clear whether Arets was himself reminded of his childhood when he took the passage from Pavese as an extended motto for his lecture. He did not state so explicitly. His lecture is primarily an exploration of a series of standpoints taken with respect to architecture during the twentieth century, standpoints with which he feels some theoretical affinity: those of Berlage, Loos, Kahn, Eisenman, Rossi and Grassi. "It is the fragments of life, of the history of this life and of the history of architecture, which will unite the Work of Art of the architectural discipline into a whole," Arets writes. "It is a matter of fragments and their relationships, of the recognition of the mental and material relationships, which are the point of departure for architecture, while the architectural means must be treated with craftsmanship." [2]

There is another respect in which there is a very personal side to this appreciation of Pavese. Those who are at all acquainted with Arets will know how fastidiously he dresses (Yamamoto, Comme des Garçons), the neat way he arranges his papers, his pen, his organizer and his telephone on the desk with everything aligned square. He is probably also one of the few architects who lives in a house of his own design, a house which is fused with his office.

In a broader sense, however, this approach to life and work is consistent with the climate that prevailed in the Architecture Faculty of Eindhoven University of Technology in the period that Arets studied there. The university had been established as a more technocratically inclined counterpart of the Technical University of Delft. In the area of architectural design, moreover, it laid a strong emphasis on the design methodologies such as those developed under John Habraken within SAR (the Foundation for Architectural Research). There was much interest in urban renewal, specifically in the form of "building for the neighborhood," in which the architect abandoned his cultural leadership. A strong counter-movement arose among the students during the 1970s, however. Its main representatives were Jo Coenen, Sjoerd Soeters and Rudy Uytenhaak, who, supported by similar initiatives abroad, aimed at the rediscovery of architecture. The appointment of Geert Bekaert as the Professor of Architectural History and Theory in 1974 effectively institutionalized this tendency. Bekaert organized a series of impressive congresses and symposia, in which practically all the important art architects, theorists and historians who were to set the course of architecture during the 1980s took part. The Technical University of Eindhoven developed into a hotbed of Postmodernism, not only in the Netherlands but internationally. People there are still in the habit of reminding you with quiet pride that it was at Eindhoven, during a lecture in 1978, that Charles Jencks first used the term Postmodernism.

Bekaert's ambitions reached further than Charles Jencks' architectural interpretation of Postmodernism, however. The program of the architectural history and theory department developed increasingly in the direction of a history of tractates and individual standpoints, which were handled in monographic fashion. Fine art became an important point of reference for architecture, a development which was above all stimulated by the flourishing artistic climate then prevailing in the city, where Rudi Fuchs was the director of the Van Abbemuseum and which was then astonishing the art-loving public with one brilliant exhibition after another and with a program primarily aimed at the in-depth exploration of European painting and sculpture. Students of the Architecture Faculty were thus encouraged to develop a personal standpoint, while placing this in the context of the European architectural tradition and history, as Arets himself so decidedly did.

Energetic though it may have been, the Eindhoven interpretation of this postmodernist program had a highly pessimistic and gloomy side to it. Perhaps this was due to Bekaert's belief that culture was in decline and had to be rescued from the technocrats and social scientists (a standpoint naturally resisted by the rest of the faculty); or perhaps it was the NO FUTURE outlook propagated by Punk, which was a runaway success among the students at the time. Perhaps it came through the economic recession, or perhaps it was due to Bekaert's fundamental despair of civilization. Whatever the case, it is certain that the writings of Manfredo

[2] Wiel Arets, **Fragmenten en hun relatie,** lecture at Eindhoven University of Technology, 20 April 1982, unpublished manuscript.

Tafuri had considerable influence in Eindhoven, especially his 1997 *Progetto e Utopia* in which he analyzed how every architectural avant-garde was ultimately and inexorably absorbed by the capitalist system.[3] In an article titled "L'Architecture dans le Boudoir" which appeared in **Oppositions** in 1974, Tafuri described postmodern architecture as an architecture reconsidering its own language in anticipation of better times.[4] Reading Tafuri gave the feeling that architecture, although it had something very important to say, was wasting its breath in a society that refused to listen. Perhaps it was therefore better for architecture to either keep its lips sealed, as did the architecture of Giuseppe Terragni during the 1920s and 1930s according to Tafuri's interpretation.

A group of Eindhoven students centered around Gert Jan Willemse and Johan Kappetein began turning out designs inspired by the architecture of Peter Eisenman and Terragni. To the great alarm of the lecturers, they were recalcitrant designs which made no secret of the fact that they would scar the city. Willemse and Kappetein had adopted a lifestyle that was not only based on strict discipline and hard work, but which also expressed itself in their clothing: Willemse wore long leather coats and slouch hats, while Kappetein demonstratively sported the overalls he wore on his parents' farm at weekends, alternating with leather motorcycle outfits when on his self-modified chopped Triumph. They would eat lunch together with ostentatiously exposed stilettos on the table.

Although Willemse and Kappetein's designs were exhaustively detailed and brilliantly drawn, their belief in them and their possible realization grew more and more tenuous. The perfection of the drawings and models mattered increasingly for its own sake, and many days or weeks of meticulous handiwork went into them. If for this reason only, life and work merged for the two makers. Their designs were generally presented to the accompaniment of performances, installations and films, although without verbal explanations. After completing their studies, Willemse and Kappetein continued drawing designs in self-imposed isolation for several years. These designs were more and more like "projects for a world without people" (Entwurf für eine Welt ohne Menschen) to quote the title of a book by the Austrian author Peter Rosei who, together with Thomas Bernhard, became an increasingly potent source of inspiration. Then Kappetein withdrew to the confines of his parental farm and, shortly afterwards, Willemse took his own life in a painstakingly planned ritual. A posthumous survey of his work was exhibited in the Netherlands Architecture Institute a few years ago.

The early work of Wiel Arets and Wim van den Bergh — from whom he seemed practically inseparable during his studies and for several years afterwards — clearly owes a great deal to Willemse and Kappetein. In retrospect it seems far from coincidental that Pavese's *Il mestiere di vivere,* from which Arets so extensively quoted, finishes on the day before the author's suicide; it is consistent with the atmosphere in which architecture was experienced in Eindhoven. It is evident that the more socially oriented lecturers in the faculty were concerned about this from the report of the jury for the annual show of student designs when awarding the 1984 prize for the best design to Wim van den Bergh for his beautifully drawn Villa for the Carnival Prince with its literary and philosophical inspiration. They hoped that by according the student the prize they would deny him "the chance to sideline himself."[5] The previous year, Helga Fassbinder, the Professor of Urban Renewal at Eindhoven, had already detected in the student designs a divergence between the world of public housing and that of free design, and had compared the latter to an escape from the everyday world into an illusory one. This prompted Bekaert in 1984 to defend free design research against an educational approach which in his view risked suffocating amidst dry statistics and constrictive programs, in an impassioned plea under the title of "The consolation of architecture."[6] Free design research was in Bekaert's view one of the last embodiments of the humanistic ideal of independent thought.

....

[3] Manfredo Tafuri, **Progetto e Utopia,** Rome, 1973.
[4] Manfredo Tafuri, "L'Architecture dans le Boudoir," **Oppositions**, 1974.
[5] Jury report on student designs 1984, as quoted by Hans van Dijk in **Wonen TA/BK** 4 (1984).
[6] Gert Bekaert, "De Troost van de Architectuur," **Wonen TA/BK** 5 (1984).

Despite the animation of his plea, however, an unmistakable melancholy also shows through. It was all too simple, he argued, to now conclude that "when things go badly with the architect and with architecture, when he has become superfluous to society and is no longer occupied with the reality of the times, when he has fallen into disfavor, he seeks his sanctuary and diversion in the private world of the imagination."[7] The consolation of architecture does not mean that it must close its eyes to reality, he argues, but that it invents new realities and projects them into a world which is otherwise a hostile wilderness. A few years later Bekaert resigned from the Architecture Faculty, alluding to a Dantean hell when recalling his period there.[8]

A number of competition entries and study projects which Arets and Van den Bergh made in the early days of their collaboration are clearly suffused with the spirit of Bekaert's position. Literary in their inspiration, they stand uncompromisingly amid their city surroundings. Most of them were published in Wiederhall, the brilliant magazine that Arets and Van den Bergh founded together with Joost Meeuwissen. But there is something strange about this series of projects by Arets and Van den Bergh in the magazine. Although ostensibly underlain by an attitude of fundamental pessimism towards the future of culture, somehow or other these designs have a visual impact that recalls the utopianism of Russian Constructivism. It gives them something **Unheimliches,** as was immediately recognized by Anthony Vidler in the article "Oneirism" about Arets and Van den Bergh in his book The Architectural Uncanny.[9] The reference to Russian Constructivism is not fortuitous, for Arets and Van den Bergh had learned much about the movement on a study trip organized by the Faculty of Architecture in 1980. The utopian aspirations of the Constructivsts, their belief in the emancipatory efficacy of architecture, must have been obvious to the student architects during their preparation for the trip, which included an inspiring introduction by the lecturer Hans Tupker, but their first-hand acquaintance with the actual buildings — or whatever remained of them — in a country that had already taken its leave of them and was itself already in a serious state of decline, left an equally deep impression on them. The contrast between the optimism of the drawings and the reality of the situation they encountered in 1980 could not have been greater.

In their series of projects in Wiederhall, Arets and Van den Bergh impressively succeeded in transforming that paradoxical experience. Their powerful graphic staging is coupled to a deeply melancholic, indeed grimly pessimistic, undertone. A certain influence of Constructivism, as an architecture which instigates processes of change, remains implicit in Arets' work to this day, but without the unambiguous ideological message. Arets' architecture is darker in character and does not speculate on some future outcome. Rem Koolhaas' interpretation of Constructivism and the way he incorporated it into his designs was possibly also influential.

All the same, it soon became clear that Arets' position was not that of a pure social pessimist. He still believed there was a place for a truly craftsmanly and cultural approach towards the architecture of everyday practice. While still a student, he began undertaking small alteration and building commissions, which he often designed together with Bert ter Haar. Several of these plans were carried out. These occasional jobs grew step by step into an architectural practice, which soon attracted attention. Arets won the Maaskant Prize for Young Architects with this early work. The publication accompanying the award revealed a small and idiosyncratic but coherent oeuvre, which was perfectly staged in splendidly crafted perspective drawings and in the intriguing, sullen photography of Kim Zwarts.[10]

It is not only this meticulous staging that indicates Arets' faith in the possibility of architectural practice. In the preceding years, he had carefully constructed his own theoretical framework for a practice within which the cultural value of architecture could be secured. The colloquium paper quoted above was just a prelude to this. In another lecture from the same series, "Realism and

....

[7] Gert Bekaert, "De Troost van de Architectuur", **Wonen TA/BK** 5 (1984).
[8] Ibidem.
[9] Anthony Vidler, "Oneirism," in Anthony Vidler, **The Architectural Uncanny, Essays in the Modern Unhomely,** MIT Press, Cambridge (Mass.) & London 1992.
[10] **Wiel Arets Architect,** 010 Publishers, Rotterdam 1989.

Rationalism", November 1982, he developed his ideas further.[11] It was a summary of and introduction to the theories of Tendenza, in particular Aldo Rossi and Giorgio Grassi, which had been launched in the Netherlands not long beforehand. The two Italians were introduced by a group of architects and theorists which included Joost Meuwissen, Umberto Barbieri and Cees Boekraad, who deployed their designs and ideas as ammunition in a conflict that was raging at the Technical University of Delft between Aldo van Eyck and Carel Weeber, a conflict in which the latter was regarded as a Dutch counterpart of the Italians. The battle was being fought at all levels and in all media, and made a considerable impression on the current generation of students. In his introduction, however, Arets gave an interpretation to Rossi and Grassi's work which in several respects was less likely to have been given in Delft for strategic and polemic reasons. This interpretation concerned firstly the relation between architecture and art, which was taboo at Delft because Van Eyck gave the artistic aspect of the profession a specific interpretation of his own. Secondly, more or less by extension, it concerned the subjective and autobiographical aspects of architecture, which were also taboo at Delft because Weeber insisted on maintaining objective criteria for architecture and planning. Arets' interpretation was thus not only much freer than the Delft one, but he was, able to develop a depth that was not possible there. It is true that Rossi and to a lesser extent Grassi have themselves built many designs in the Netherlands, but beyond this their theories have never successfully been transplanted into the national situation, as they have in Switzerland, for example, in the work of Herzog & de Meuron or Diener & Diener. Although there is no direct connection between them, it is therefore no coincidence that Arets' work is often compared with that of architects such as Herzog & de Meuron, even though Arets' work reveals greater concern for the program than for the built product.

The defining characteristic of architectural rationalism is, according to Arets, that it treats architecture as an autonomous discipline that becomes a field of scholarly research in its own right. "This research focuses on primary concepts, rational kernels, such as ideas and rules," Arets writes. "It is hereby assumed that architecture cannot be satisfactorily explained in terms of sensory perception, the imitation of an empirical reality and the sensed interior reality." But, he hastens to add, "when we speak of 'rationalism,' we make a distinction when defining the term between rational and subjective moments."[12] Arets sees a difference between the process of developing an architectural language and the use of that language. For that development, he draws on Giogio Grassi. He sees Grassi's attempts to expose the internal logic of architecture and to purify it as "the best answer to the empty professionalism of the architecture of an alienating capitalism."[13] Grassi eventually became an important beacon for Arets, and Arets even translated Grassi's texts on his own initiative into Dutch. But Arets' sympathy in his own writings seems to be mainly with Aldo Rossi, for Rossi succeeds in introducing the subjective element into an autonomous architecture, and in two ways. Rossi treats architecture as a science but he has an insatiable appetite for personal interpretations. He speaks the language of architecture but uses metaphors and analogies; he thus speaks it artistically. To clarify his concept of the analogue city, he refers to the capriccios of the painter Canaletto which convincingly establish a link between reality and expression by juxtaposing meaningful fragments. This opened the way for Arets himself to quote from sources outside architecture and to give these references the same status as those to Mies van der Rohe and Le Corbusier. Besides these two he could now also lay claim, in his monograph on Maaskant, to Robert Mapplethorpe, Paul Valéry, Jean-Luc Godard, Plato, Marcel Duchamp and Leonardo da Vinci as significant conceptual points of reference.[14]

But perhaps it is even more relevant to Arets that Rossi succeeds in incorporating subjective aspects of his native region, Lombardy, into the development of his architectural language, colouring it as

....

[11] **Wiel Arets, Realisme en Rationalisme,** lecture at Eindhoven University of Technology, 1 November 1982, unpublished manuscript.
[12] Ibidem.
[13] Ibidem.
[14] Anthony Vidler, "Oneirism."

it were, speaking a dialect. Here the autobiographical aspect, to which Arets alludes in his first text by quoting Pavese, takes on clearer contours. The realism in the title of his 1982 lecture thus refers to the postwar Italian neo-realism that had such a formative influence on the work of Aldo Rossi. "They are mostly themes he takes from his native region and with which he incorporates every-day objects such as coffee pots in the composition. The forms are general ones that have a close bearing on reality," Arets wrote. He went on to stress that everyone has to discover what forms have such a partly objective, partly autobiographical meaning for him or herself.[15] In this lecture Arets thus marked off a domain within which he could operate effectively as an architect while creating for himself a conceptual freedom with which to develop his own work.

Besides this, however, Arets also implicitly defined an area of architectural research in this lecture within which an exceptionally interesting topic soon presented itself. F. P. J. Peutz (1916–1966) was a remarkably original architect from Arets' own region of Limburg who had somehow been almost completely ignored in the official history of Dutch architecture. This neglect was wholly unjustified, as Wiel Arets, Wim van den Bergh and the lecturer William Graatsma demonstrated when they held a major exhibition of his work at the Eindhoven Technical University in 1981, publishing a weighty monograph on him at the same time.[16] Their efforts rescued Peutz from oblivion and even won him a certain posthumous fame. As an architect, Peutz could not be pigeonholed stylistically. He designed in a variety of styles, even mixing them in the same building. Yet he often succeeded in achieving a high degree of stylistic coherence in the result, for example his phenomenal modernist "Glass Palace" in Heerlen (currently being restored by Arets). In other cases he brilliantly played the various styles off against one another, as in the Town Hall in Heerlen. He used both modern materials like glass or concrete, and the traditional Limburg building stone, a soft yel-lowish chalk known as mergel. In his text in the monograph, Arets explores Peutz's theoretical development in depth, but he also identifies him as a predecessor of Rossi and Grassi on account of the way his work in Heerlen attempted to instigate new relations on the basis of the historic structure. It would also seem that Peutz occupied a similar position for Arets to that of Oud for Grassi in the latter's book La construzione logica dell'architectura: an architect who initially flirted with Modernism, but later reverted to contem-plating the historical experience and the "unchanging laws" of architecture. Peutz's Heerlen Town Hall is to Arets what Oud's Shell Building is to Grassi, a scandal to the Modernists, but in this day demanding reassessment as a courageous manifesto of what Grassi calls "the long ignored contradiction between experience and program".[17]

It is precisely these aspects that Arets has subsequently devel-oped in his own professional career: the building as a collage of fragments which changes the city by establishing new morphologi-cal and conceptual relations; an architecture with a strong autono-my that nonetheless offers a great deal of programmatic freedom and above all sets the scene for special experiences. Arets is still developing and refining that program, but he remains faithful to his basic principles. The same principles provide more or less the theoretical framework he uses when discussing the work of other architects, e.g. when introducing a number of Japanese architects to the Netherlands (as one of the first to do so, between 1980 and 1983), among them Tadao Ando, Kazuo Shinohara, Fuhimiko Maki and Itsuko Hasegawa. He organized the first exhibitions of Ando's work in Europe. The conflict between modernity and tradition that Arets is familias with from his Limburg background is even more sharply pronounced in the work of these Japanese architects, and each of them has problematized it in a distinct way.[18] Arets recog-nized this, and it must have given him the courage to address that conflict with increasing incisiveness in his own work.

....

[15] **Wiel Arets Architect,** 010 Publishers, Rotterdam, 1989.
[16] Wiel Arets, Wim van den Bergh, W.P.A.R.S Graatsma, **F.P.J. Peutz 1916-1966,** Eindhoven, 1981.
[17] Giorgio Grassi, **La construzione logica dell'architectura,** Marsilio Editori, Padua, 1967.
[18] See Wiel Arets, "De destructie van de eenvoud," **De Architect** 13 (1982) 20; Wiel Arets, "Shinohara's machine," **De Architect** 15 (1984) 2; Wiel Arets, "Tadao Ando's architectuur van contradicties," **De Architect** 15 (1984) 3; Wiel Arets, "Maki en het resultaat van transformaties," **De Architect** 15 (1984) 6; Wiel Arets, "Itsuko Hasegawa's Verhaal," **De Architect** 15 (1984) 7–8.

Unbuilt Work

Cathedral (068)
Cape Coast, Ghana 1997/2004

The Cathedral for Cape Coast is a project that responds simultaneously to the physical conditions of the surrounding landscape, a gently sloping hill overlooking the Fosu lagoon, as well as to new ideas on contemporary worship and liturgy. The main concept lies in assembling worshippers closely around the altar, aided by a folded floor inclined towards the sanctuary that reinforces a sense of sharing the same space.

The sanctuary is especially lit by a double wall that allows natural light to reach the altar, tabernacle and throne.

The building is designed as a suspended oval-shaped structure with a protruding Eucharistic chapel and a cone-like roof. It can accomodate up to 1,220 people. The box-shaped Eucharistic chapel can accommodate 80 people. Worshippers will have before them the Blessed Sacrament with a background view of the sea — through a large transparent glass window — stretching wide to meet the horizon. Parallel to the stairs leading into the cathedral, there is a gently sloping ramp that leads into the Weekday Chapel situated under the suspended part. The Weekday Chapel is designed to occupy a cut across the hill and to lie in between the sacristy and the vestry. The ramp leading into the Weekday Chapel is also designed to serve as a platform for open-air celebrations.

The building is to be constructed in in-situ colored concrete in bamboo moulding. As a new construction technique that seeks to take advantage of local resources and to minimize costs, bamboo is to be used together with steel as concrete reinforcement.

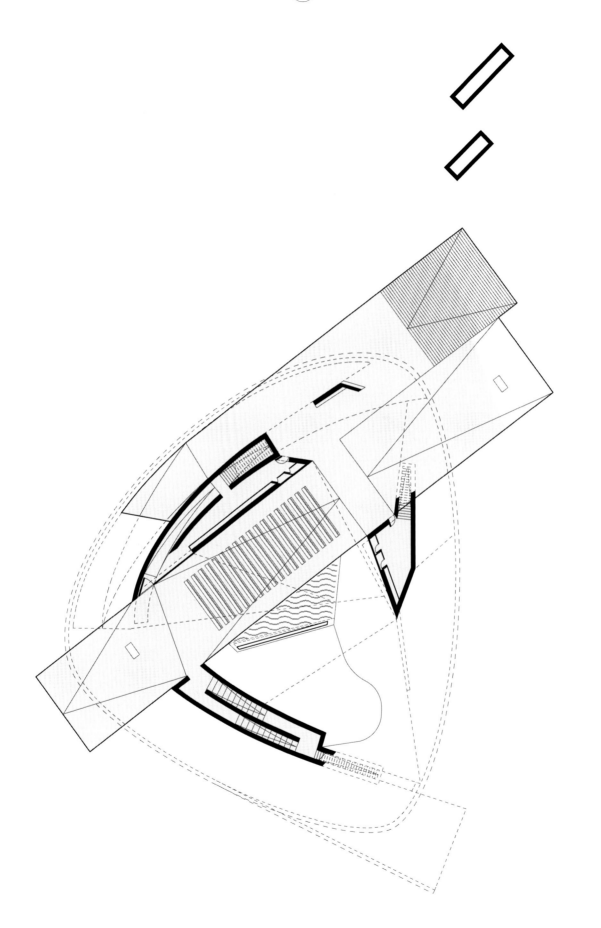

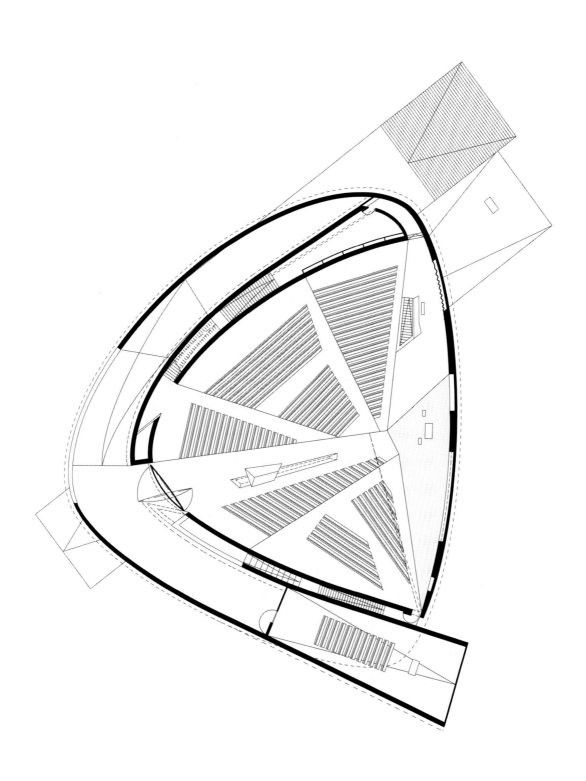

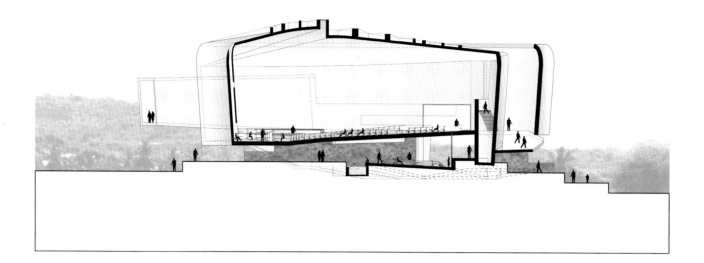

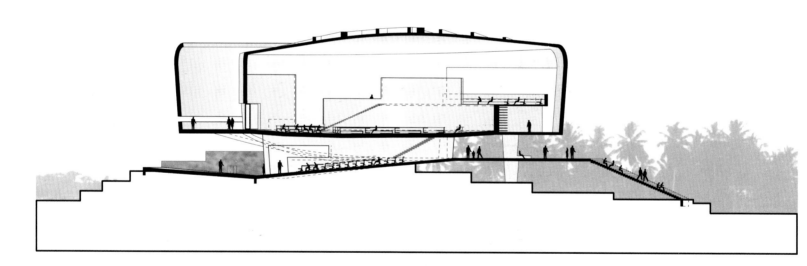

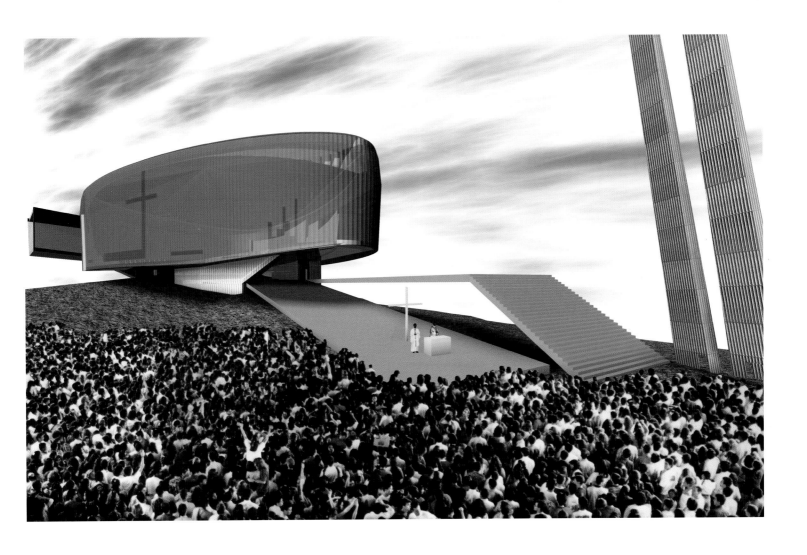

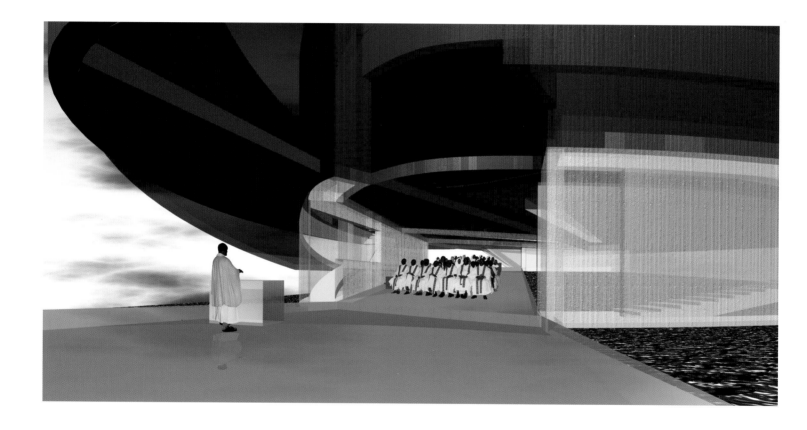

University Library (074)
Utrecht, 1997/2004

The University Library is an addition to the new university complex in the city of Utrecht. In any library, the storage of books and other light-sensitive items requires closed spaces, while the study space for students and researchers requires openness. This design seeks to reconcile such a paradoxical requirement of a university library in an ingenious manner. The closed volumes of the depots are suspended like opaque clouds in the air, yet the open structure gives visitors an experience of spaciousness and freedom. Patterns of leaves are printed onto the glazed facades to create the sense of a building in the woods and to reduce sunlight penetration. The new building is nine levels high, with a plan measuring 100 x 36 meters. There is one depot for pre-20th century documents — in the southern part of the building — and one depot for later materials — in the northern section.

From the main entrance, a wide staircase leads to the auditorium and exhibition space, and then continues further to the actual library area on the first level. Beyond the entrance gateways is the large lending area with the central desk. The void here rises to the very top of the building. Next to the void are the main staircases and elevators. These give access to all the reading rooms above and below. Next to the library, along the full length of the eastern side, a patio separates the library from the parking facilities and provides daylight on all sides. Located on the patio is the terrace of the reading cafe on the ground level. The parking facilities include a five-level garage and a separate bicycle shed.

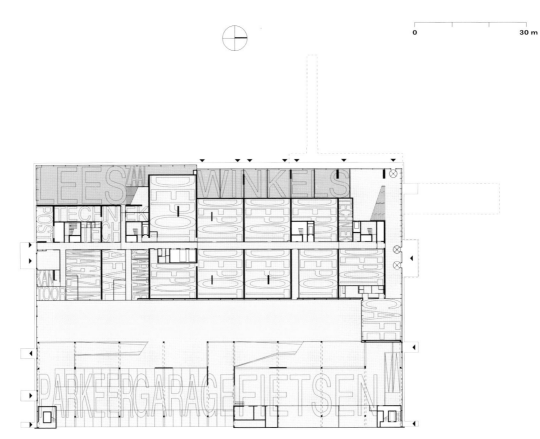

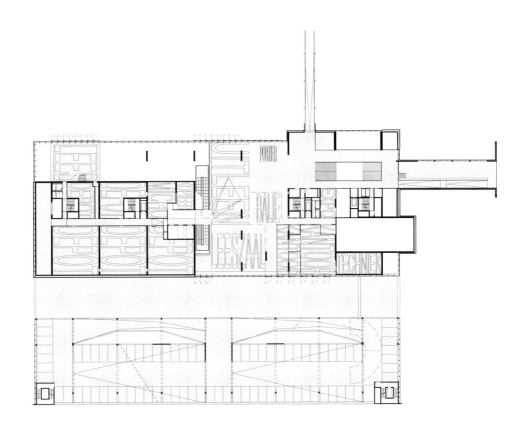

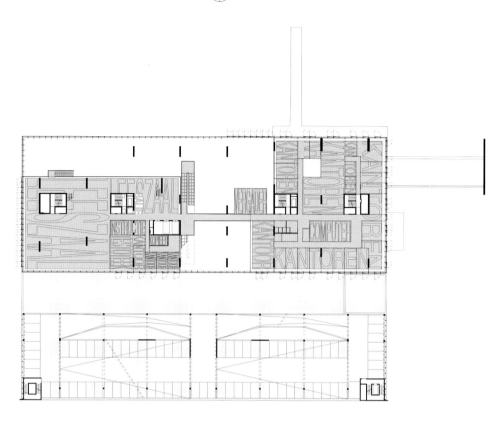

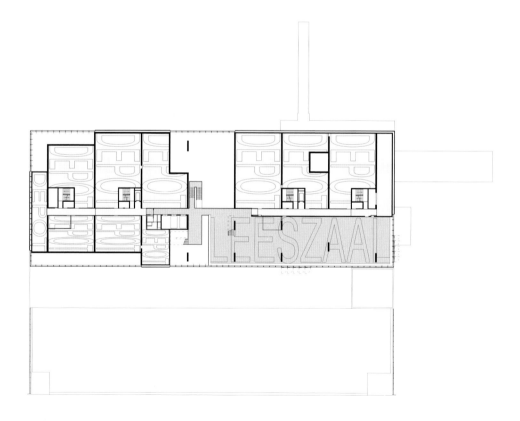

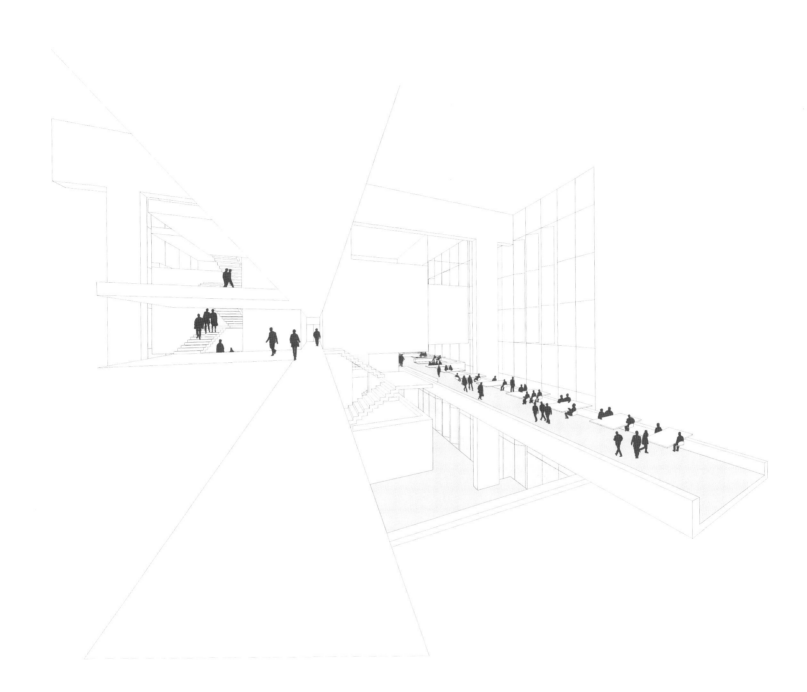

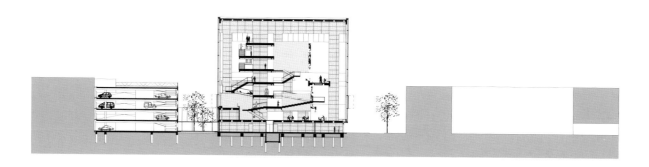

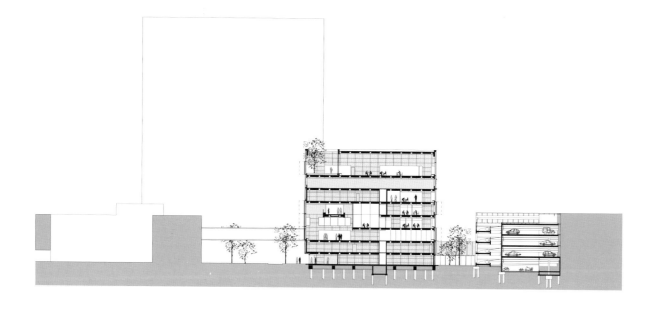

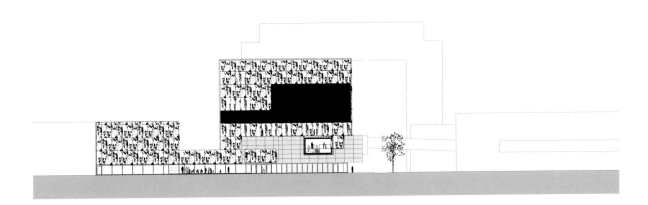

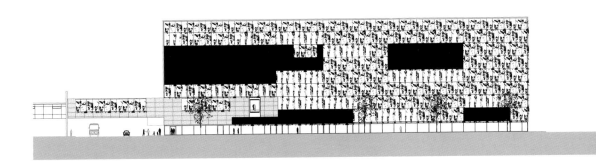

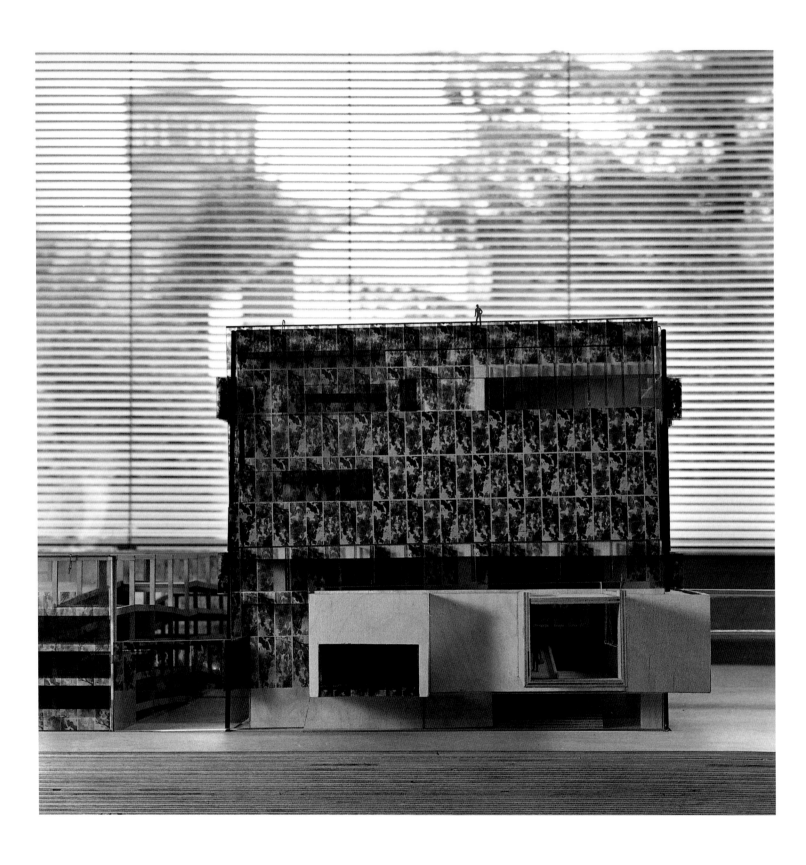

Hedge House [079]
Wijlre, 1998/2001

This gallery is conceived for a private art collection, and is intended to house a cafeteria, two greenhouses, tools and a few chickens. The gallery is located within the pleasure garden belonging to the Wijlre Castle. A linear exhibition space folds into one of its hedged fields, offering maximum wall surface, and defining exterior spaces between the hedge and the building. The itinerary of the exhibition becomes part of the overall routing in the park by way of two entrances-exits from the private and the public site.

The height of the hedges together with the stacked organization of the program creates an introverted exhibition space in the basement. The layered cafeteria, flowers, tools and chicken coops above, which are orientated to the outside, shape the ceiling of the exhibition area in different heights and define the sources of daylight. Top, side, indirect, and zenith light for the collection penetrates the building at the thresholds between the exhibition and the rest of the program. The materials inside and outside the gallery are limited to glass and exposed concrete, in addition to the plastered exhibition walls.

0   30 m

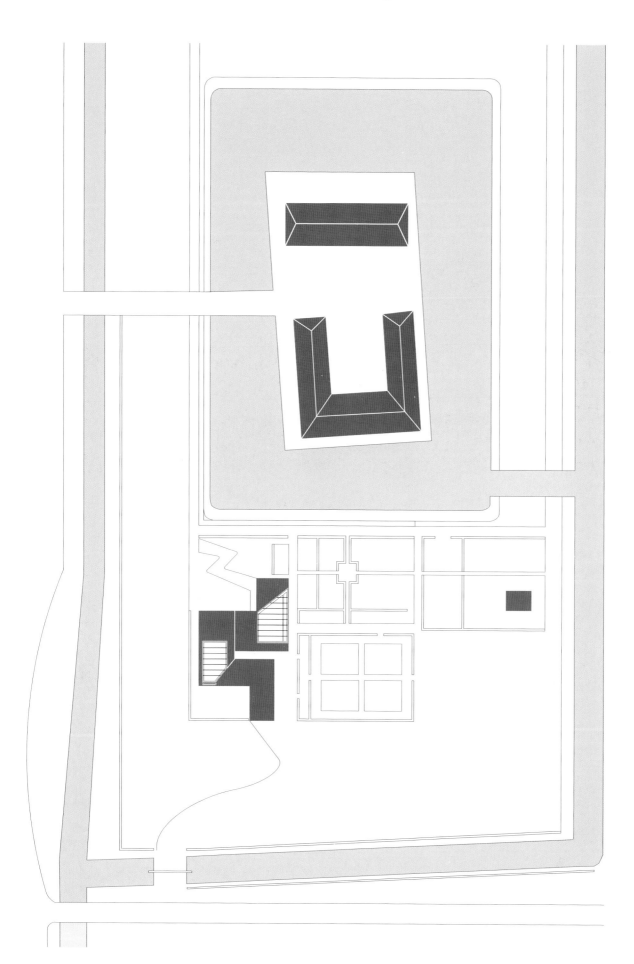

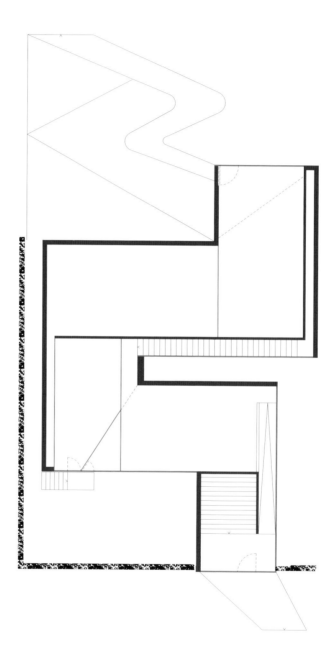

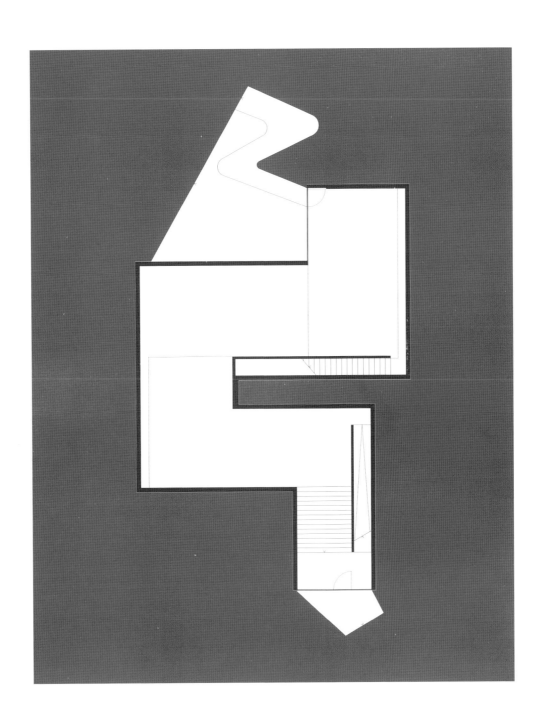

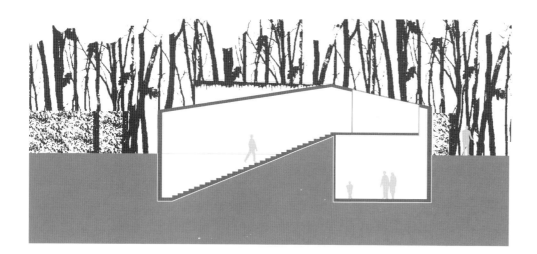

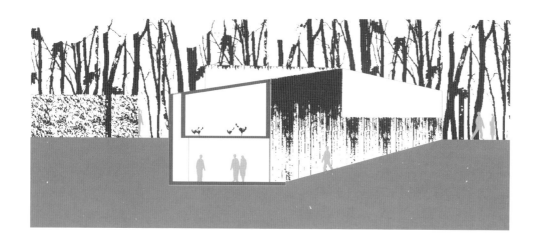

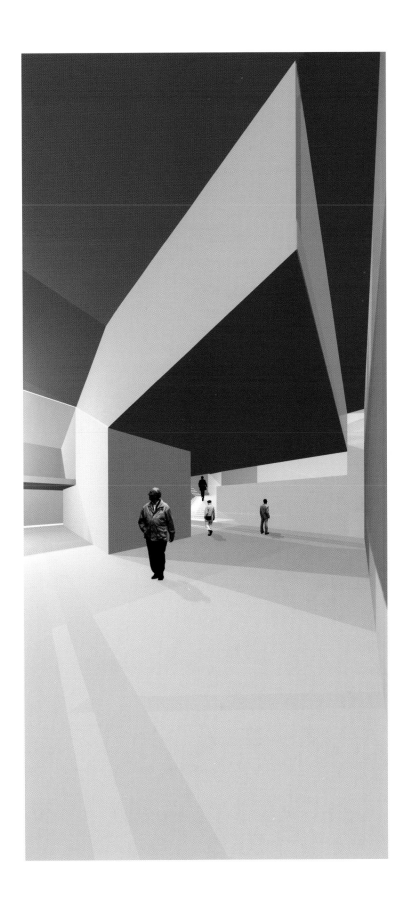

Theater Competition (080)
Almere, 1998

The theater is located on the waterfront of the city of Almere. The concept underlying the design seeks to incorporate the program of a contemporary cultural center, as well as the topographical condition of the waterfront. Both situations determine the design of a vertically oriented urban theater. Therefore, the architectural strategy embraces the notion of "highness" to organize the hybrid program of a cultural center in a vertical direction at the topographically privileged waterfront of Almere.

The program distributes one use on top of another, overlapping the large and small auditorium of the theater and the great hall of the art/music school as the main volumes within the hybrid structure. The vertical theater has protruding structures that stretch out, soaring onto the water. Accessibility is given a priority in the design of the city center. The cultural complex therefore establishes a compact entrance, together with a net of links with the projected flows of cars and people. In the entrance tube, both flows are brought together on different levels. The ground floor is constructed as an artificial ground, acting as a public foyer for the theater.

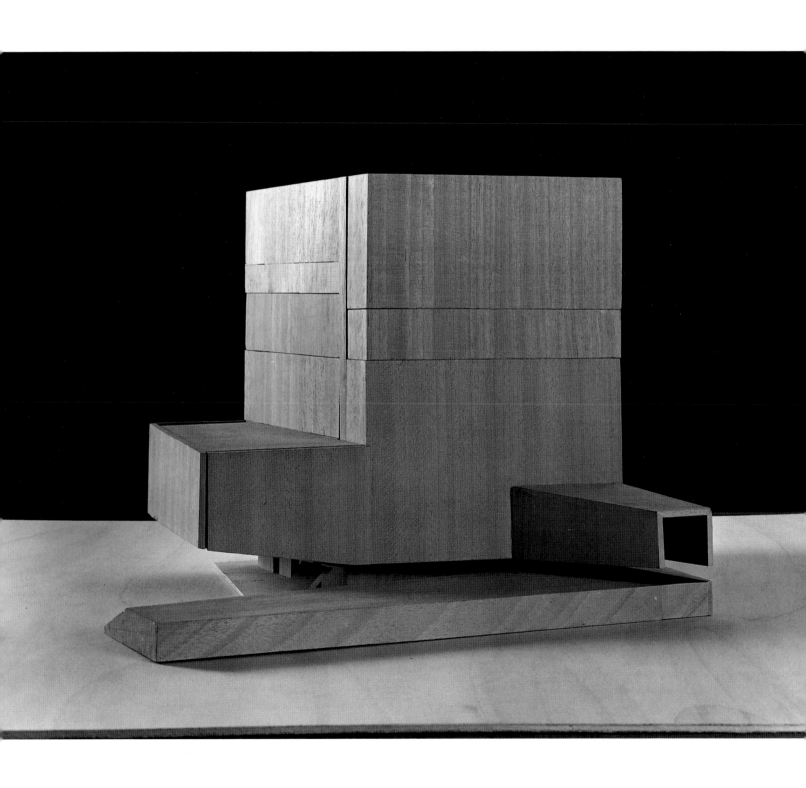

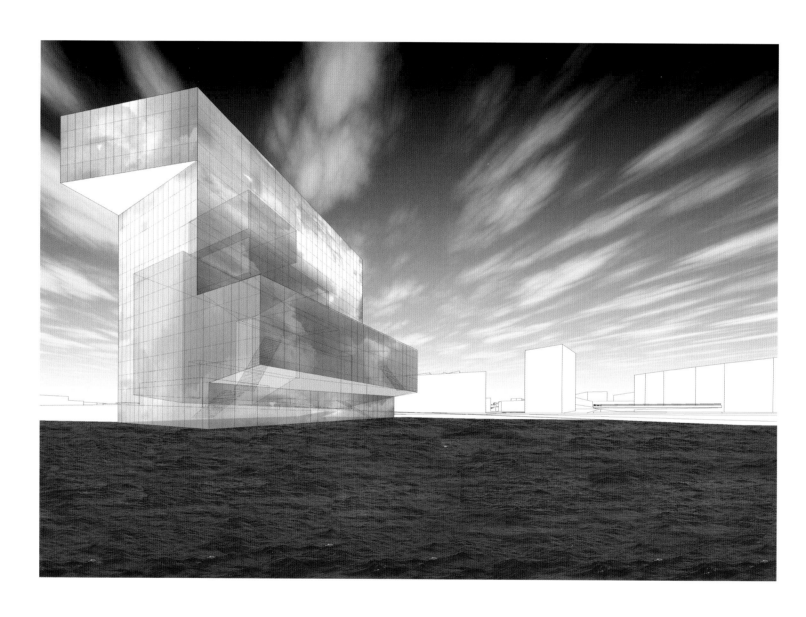

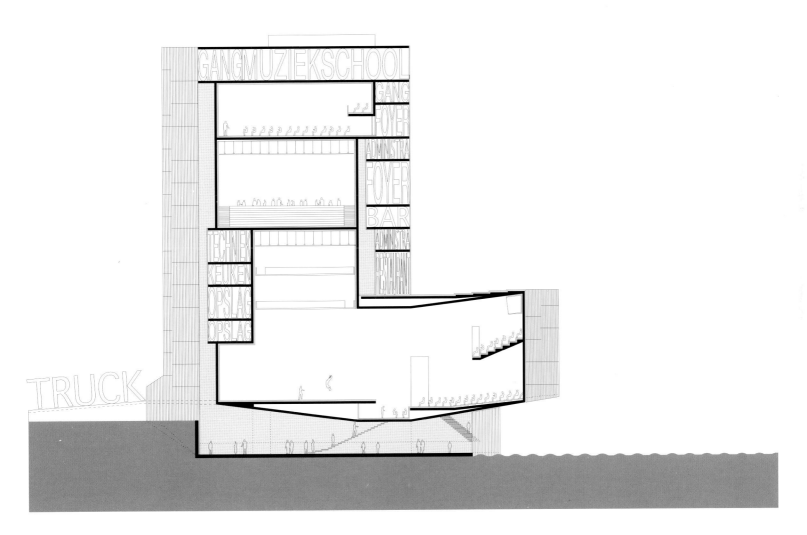

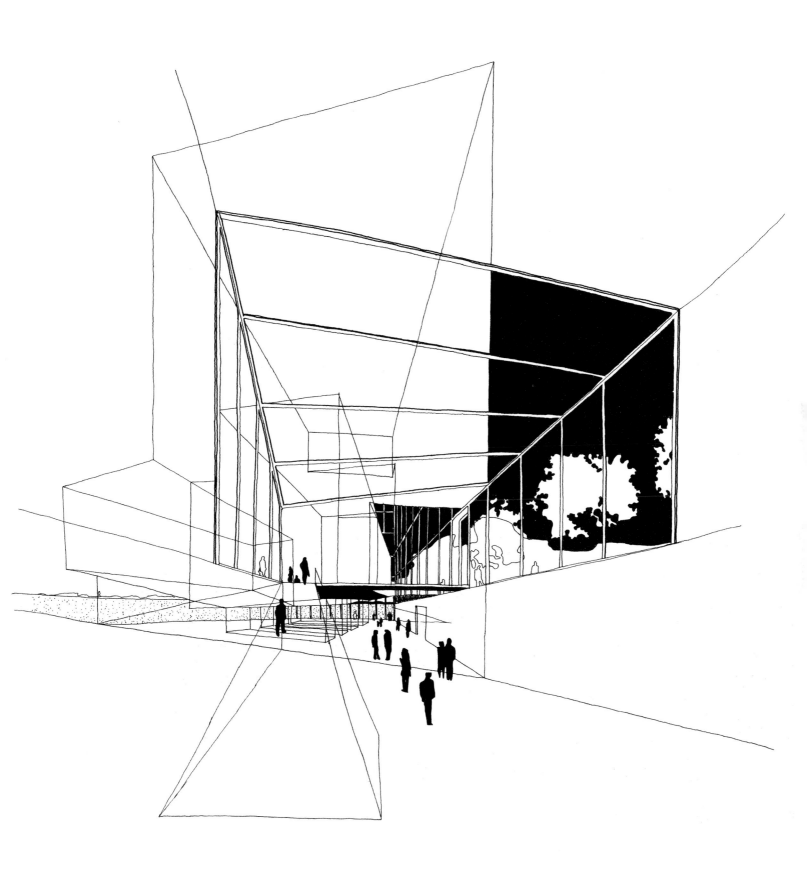

Europapark / Euroborg Stadium (081-082)
Groningen, 1998/2006

Groningen is a city centrally located in the northern part of the Netherlands. The current rivalry among cities is reflected in the tendency to organize an increasing number of urban events. Such an inclination towards the "festivalization" of cities aims at reaching a wider presence in the public domain. Groningen also finds itself taking part in this global competition for leisure programs. At its southern edge, at the center of an emerging neighborhood, a post-industrial terrain will be transformed into a new living and working environment. There is now no industrial production in this area, and it is therefore suitable for the new Groningen football stadium complex, as well as the Europapark railway station. The general program also includes mixed housing and office parks.

The new program benefits from its proximity to the cultural center and its attachment to the urban network. It occupies a key position in the link between the city center and the periphery. The hybrid stadium complex combines a manifold program — entertainment theaters, sport facilities, shops, offices, hotel and apartments. In contrast to a facility which is used only thirty days a year for sport events, this stadium is defined as an architectural void for 20,000 spectators, with a fluctuating contour around its perimeter. Lucca's amphitheater served as an urban model for this development. Over the years, it was transformed into a double-ringed plaza. The sports field, one meter below ground, can be lifted up to the roof level when not in use. This movement allows the space underneath to be used as a multi-purpose hall for other public events, and to access the field as a green space.

0   10 m

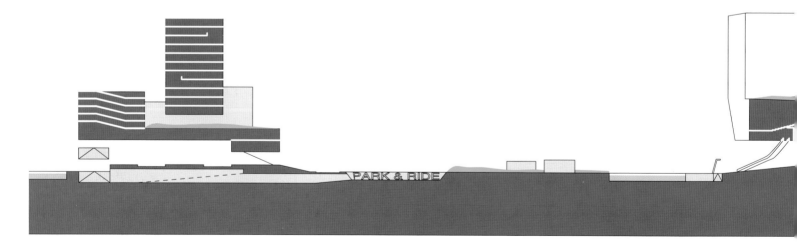

PARK & RIDE

STATION   PARK

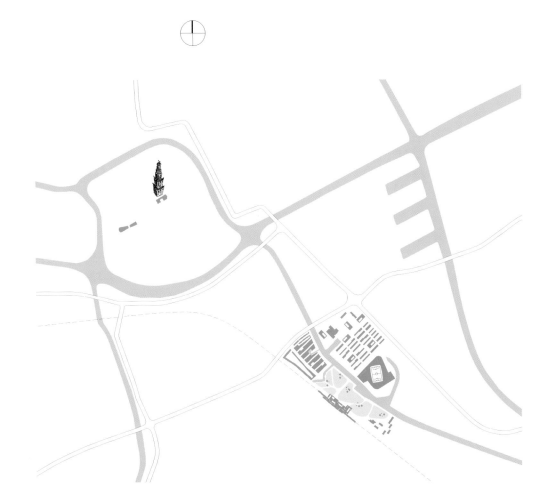

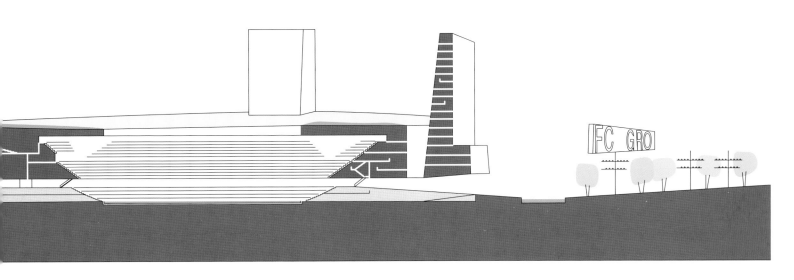

STADIUM

0   30 m

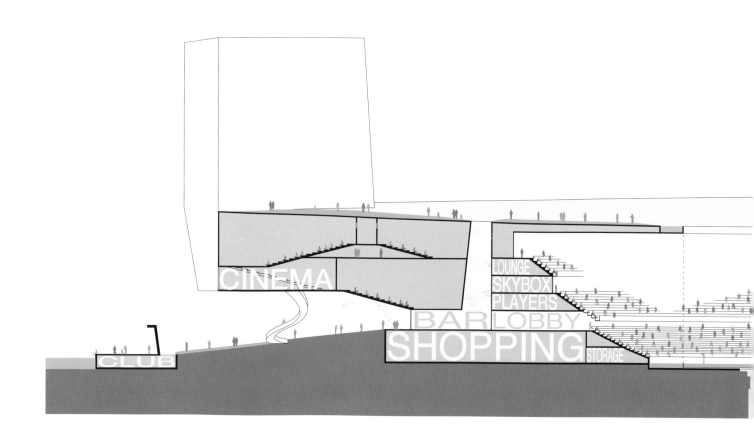

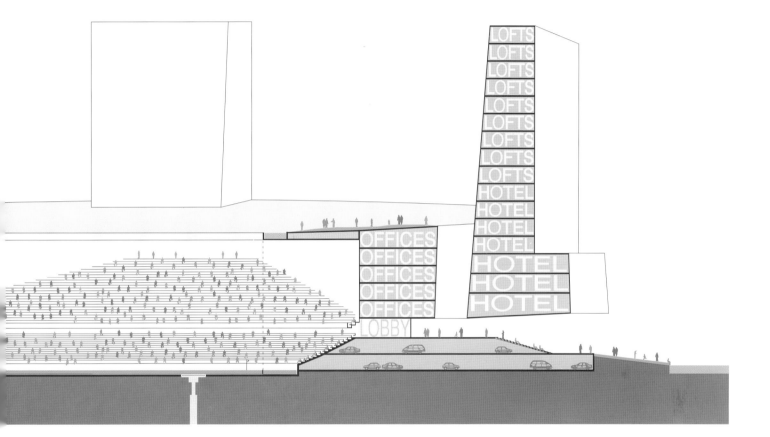

Jelly-Fish House ⁽⁰⁸⁴⁾
Marbella (Malaga), Spain, 1999/2002

The vacation retreat for the Wielheesen family is located on a slim lot
close to the beach. A long building in
front of the site blocks its view to the
sea on the ground. Therefore, the
swimming pool is programmed as an
extension of the roof terrace, which
enables a long-distance view. The
house is organized according to three
different routes. In addition to the
main entrance, the path from the
beach provides access to the ground
floor and to the roof garden, without
having to enter the house itself. A
third route provides an entrance for
guests.

Public and private programs overlap
taking full advantage of indoor-out-
door living throughout the house. The
public eating and living spaces face
their respective outside conditions at
opposing ends of the house, connected
via public circulation. A separate circulation path connects the family's private zones. Both circulation systems
intertwine and confront each other.
Each level of the house has a distinc-
tive orientation to the outside, as the
movement increasingly becomes freer
from lower to upper floors.

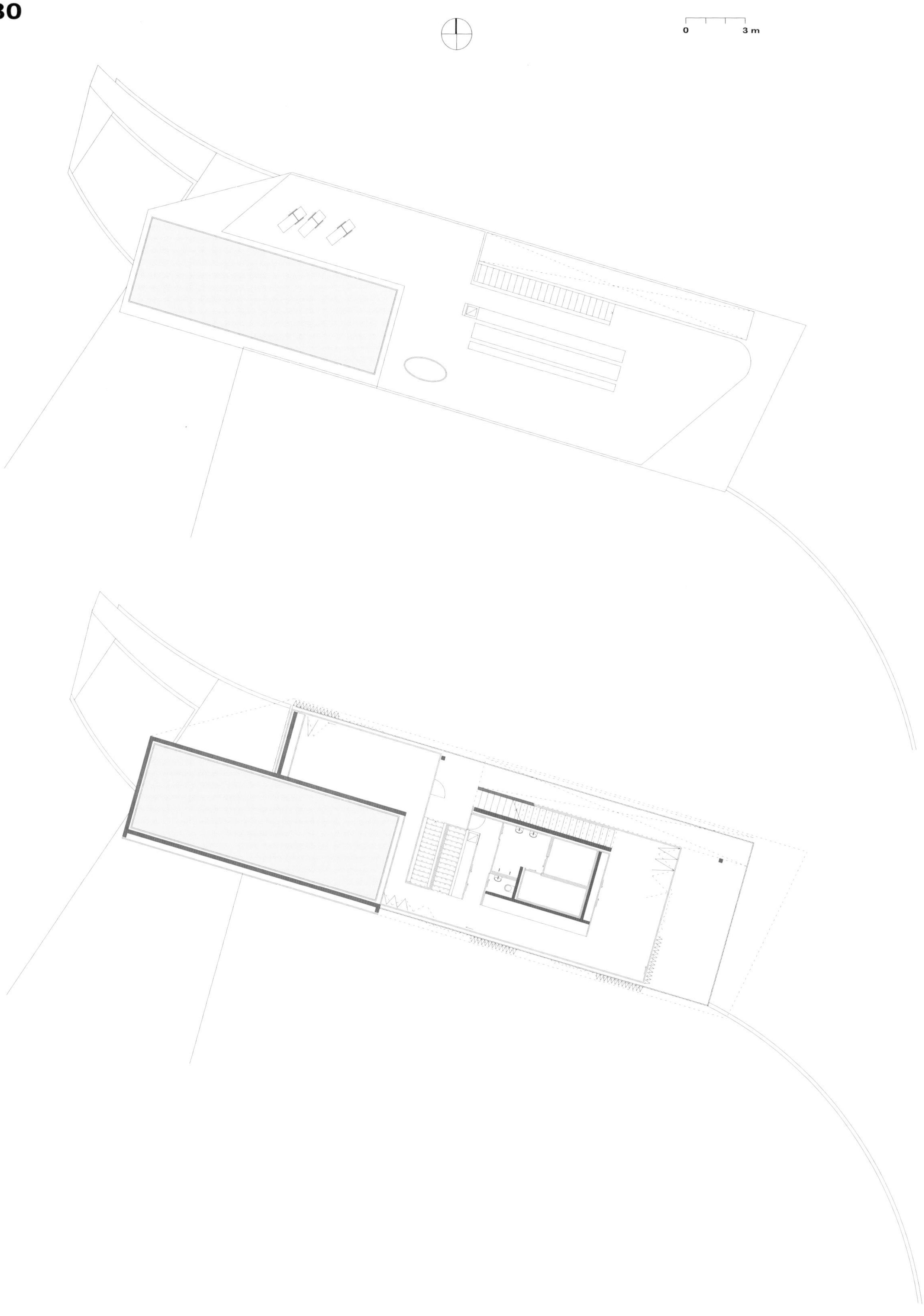
0
3 m

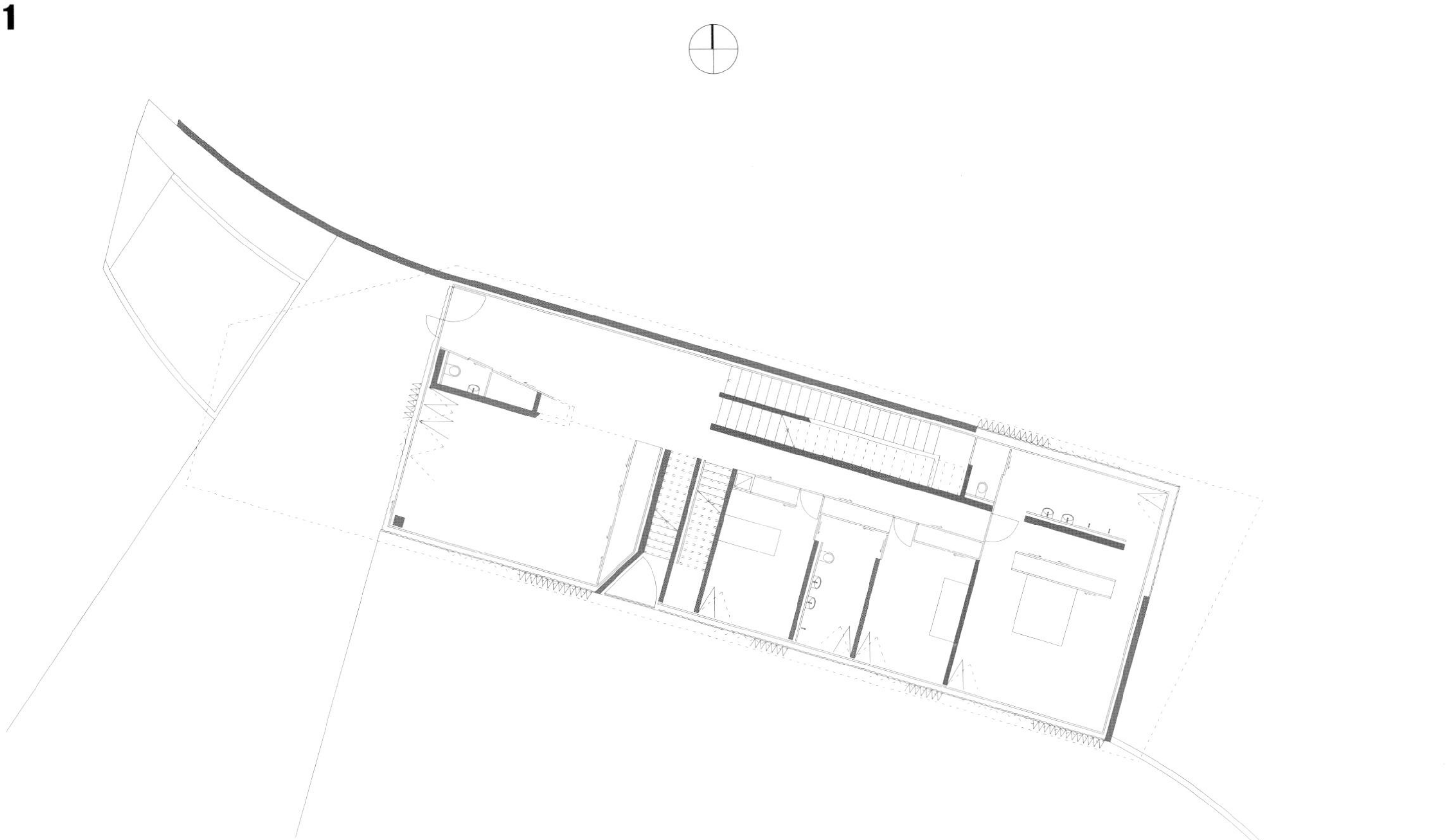

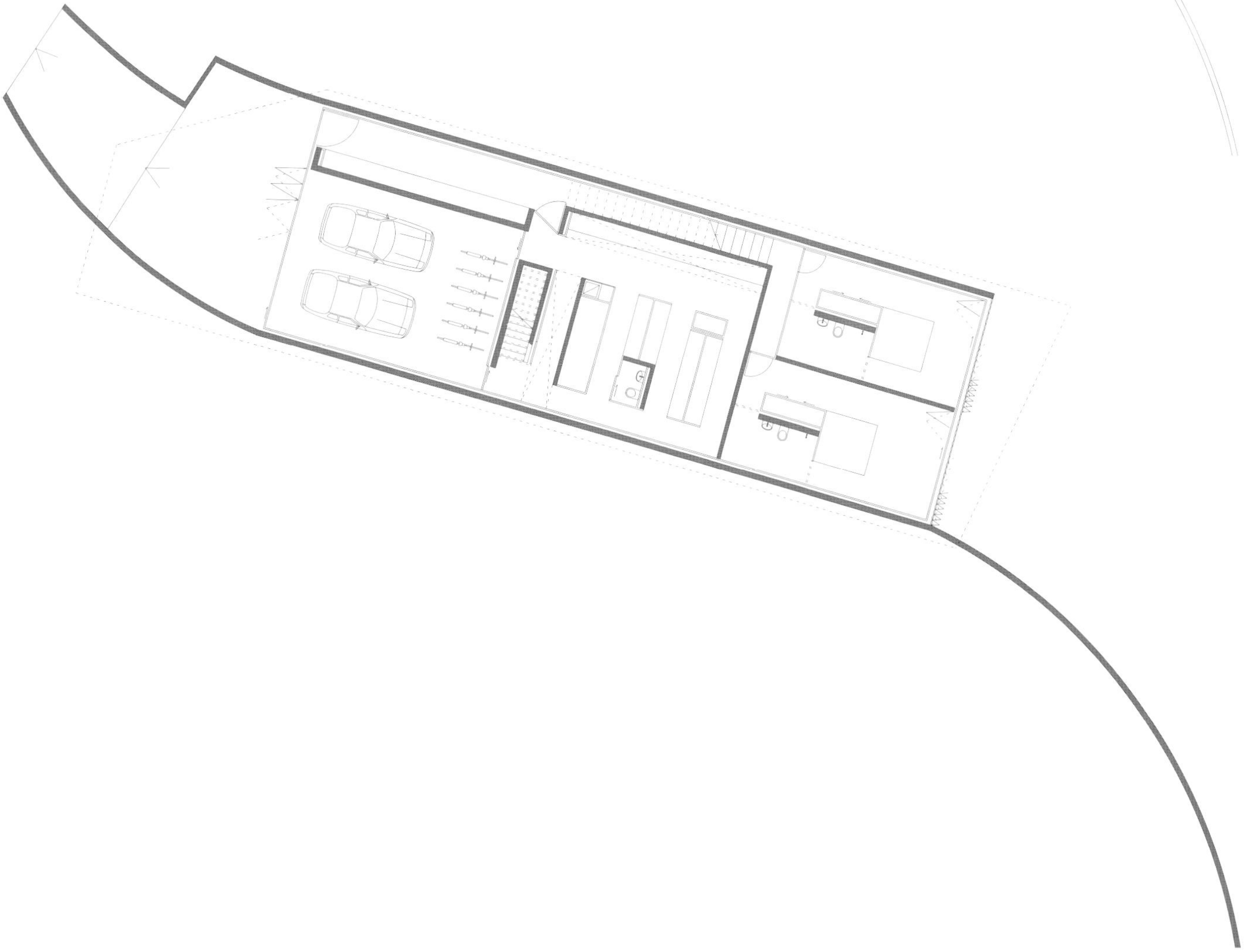

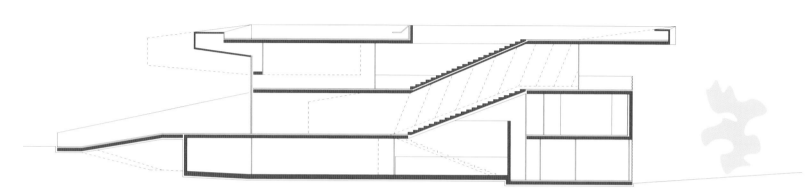

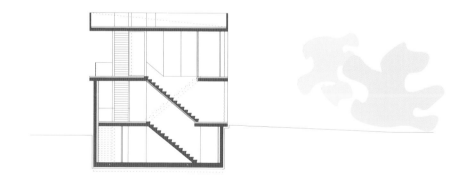

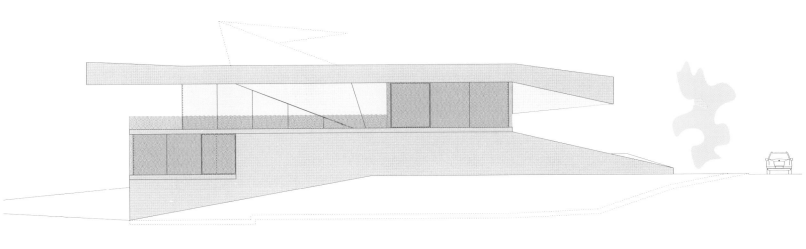

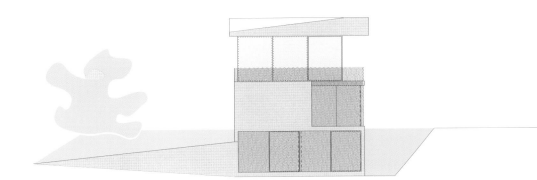

Arena Tower (086)
Amsterdam, 1999/2005

Adjacent to the Ajax Stadium, lying on the south-eastern outskirts of Amsterdam, the site of this tower terminates a major thoroughfare that leads from the nearby train station. Seen from the road, railway, or air, the tower becomes a significant urban landmark, reaching a height of 150 meters. Deep incisions into the volume of the building provide daylight and ventilation not only to apartments, but also to the public and semi-public circulation systems. Cutting into the building's mass results in a shift in floor plan and a deformation of its volumetric form, in accordance with the size and position of the voids. The void fluctuates, the plan is dislocated, the facade shuffled. Perceptions of scale are articulated in reference to our relative viewpoints — a singular massive tower from a distant glance, an articulated amalgamation of public and private entities. Vertiginous views frame the landscape without any point of orientation.

The tower emphasizes verticality and deep voids. Horizontal links between these voids define semi-public programs, distributed at various levels and at different orientations of the tower. The tower voids optimize light, space, air, and programs for the building's inhabitants, whereas at an urban scale they assist in articulating form and mass. The program differentiates public, semi-public and private zones. Apart from the residents' entrance to the tower, the first four levels and the roof level are designated for public and commercial uses. In between are the private apartments and the semi-public programs scattered throughout these levels. There are nine standard apartment types. Each apartment is a component of a volumetric puzzle. They twist and rotate, connecting to form a greater whole. Standardized units of concrete and glass combine to produce pre-fabricated modules of multiple combinations, generating a haphazard elevation to the building.

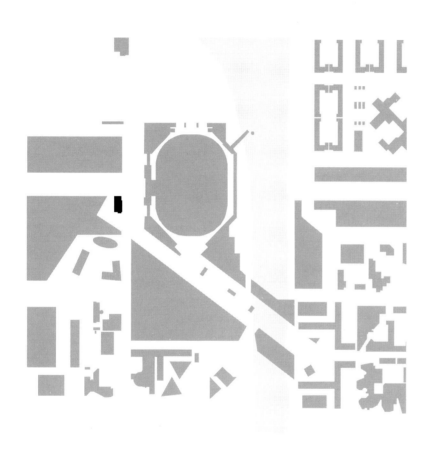

central Amsterdam

hiphol Airport

stadium

landscape

railway station

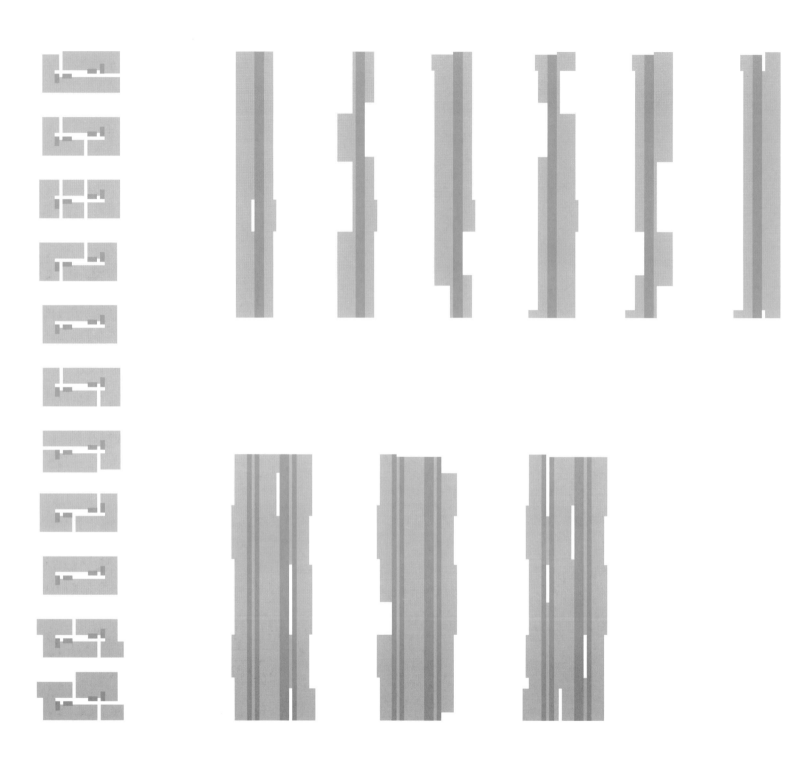

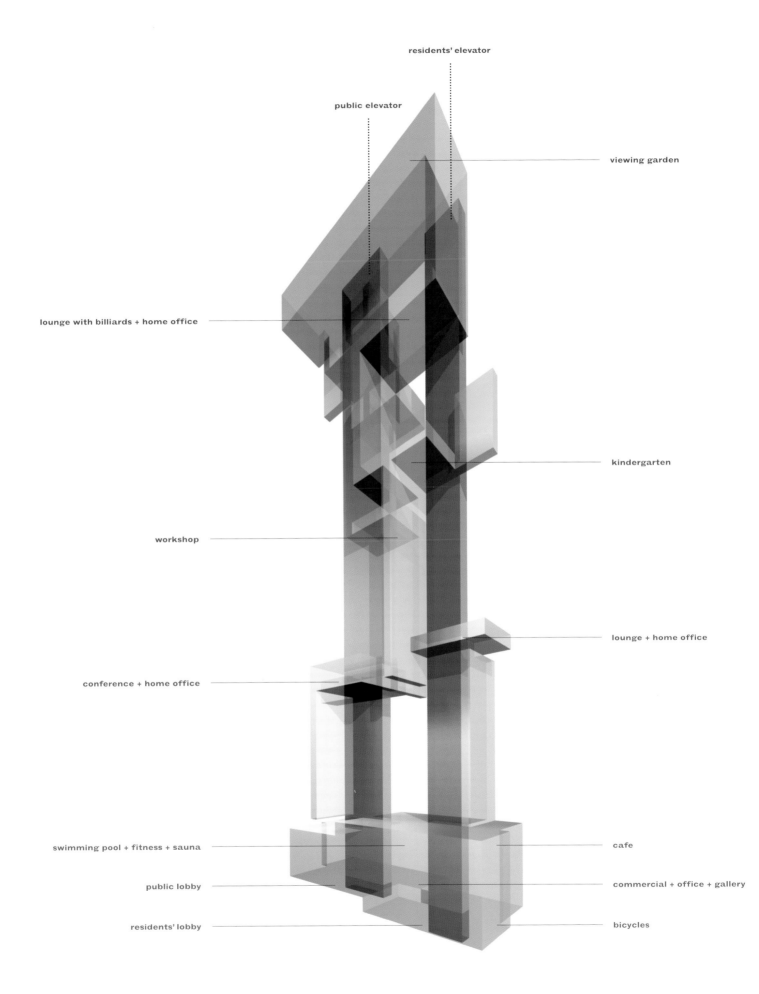

residents' elevator

public elevator

viewing garden

lounge with billiards + home office

kindergarten

workshop

lounge + home office

conference + home office

swimming pool + fitness + sauna

cafe

public lobby

commercial + office + gallery

residents' lobby

bicycles

0   30 m

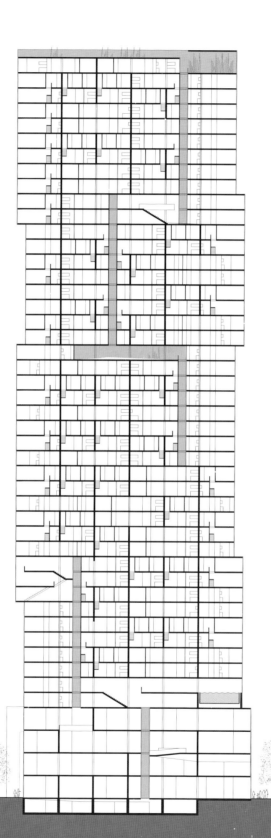

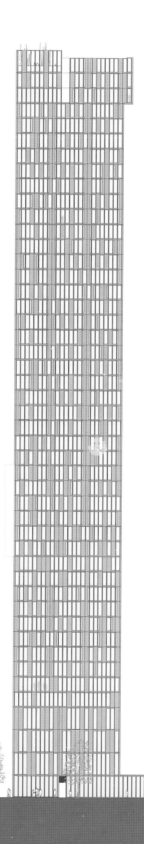

Bijenkorf Tower ⁽⁰⁸⁷⁾
Rotterdam, 1999/2000

The position and orientation of the tower are based on the urban context as well as on its program. The base of the tower is defined by the parking garage and the department store of De Bijenkorf. All new functions, such as apartments, offices and public facilities — restaurant and cafe — are rotated to meet the structure of the existing building block. The inside corner of the entrance to the apartments and offices offers a hint of the upper volume. Its geometrical deformation underlines the formal articulation of the different apartment types.

The architectural development of the apartments relates directly to the "tower-slap" by using both orientations of the tower within each apartment. The organisation of the apartments provides a system of different types, where each type defines its own city-perspective. The S-type perceives the extreme condition of the "tower-slap." The view of both sides is never obtained at once, but only by moving along stairs from one side to the other. The L-type forms both conditions of the "slap." In the penthouse, the inside patio adds a third view, a vertical connection to the outside. Each apartment is provided with an outside space, a balcony with a border defined by the inward movement of the facade.

0   30 m

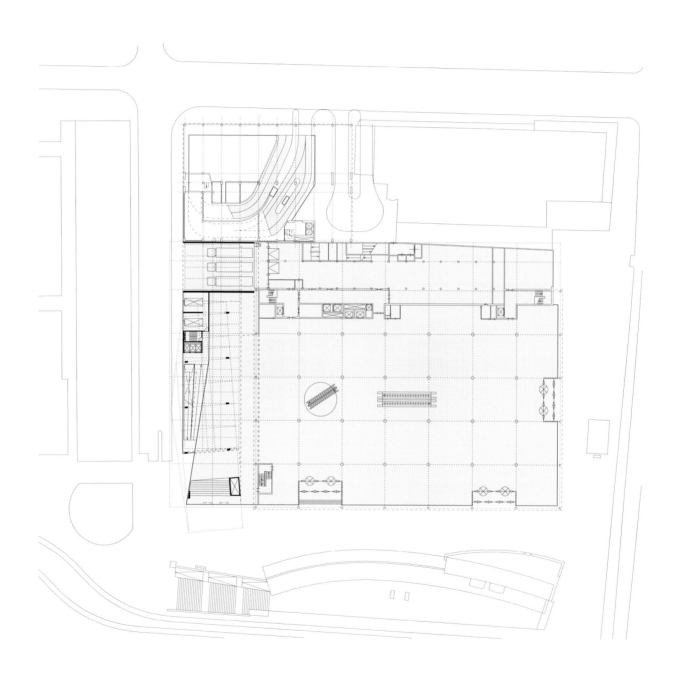

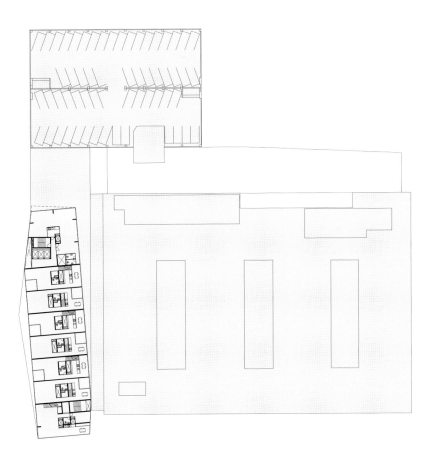

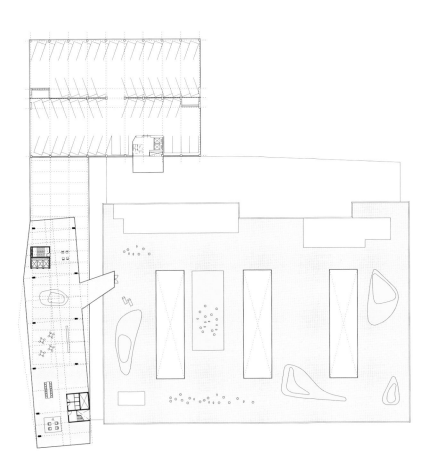

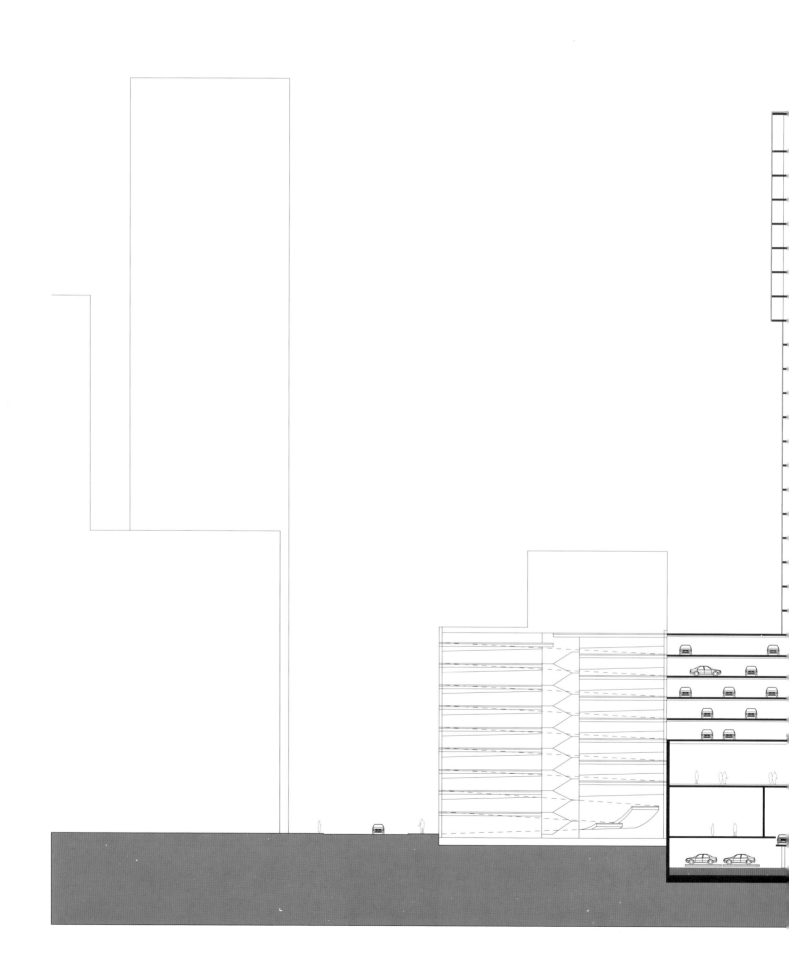

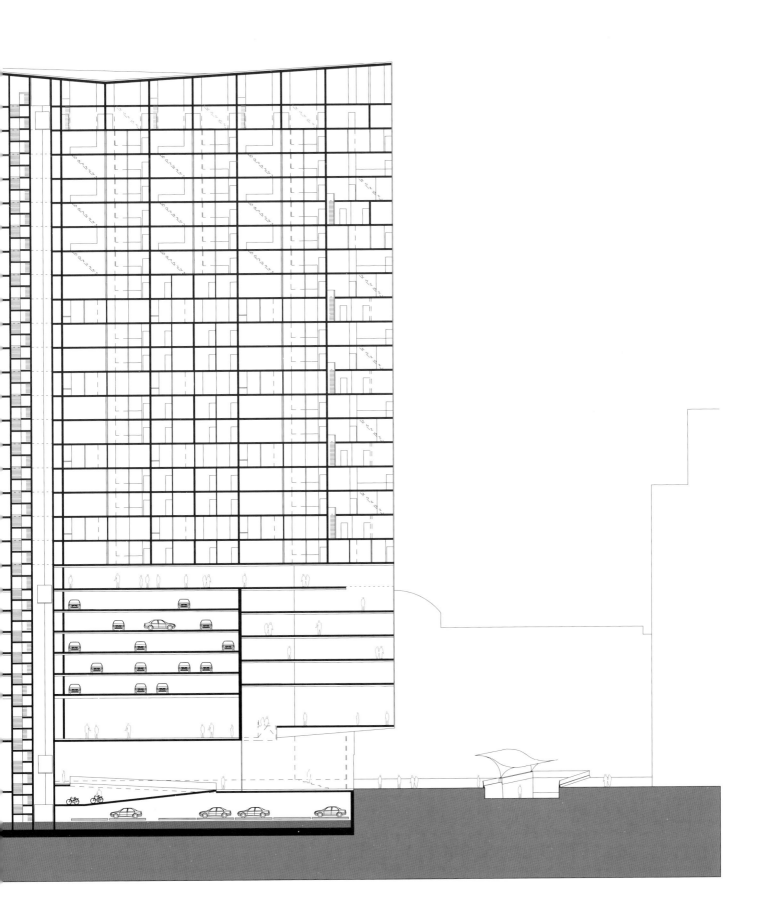

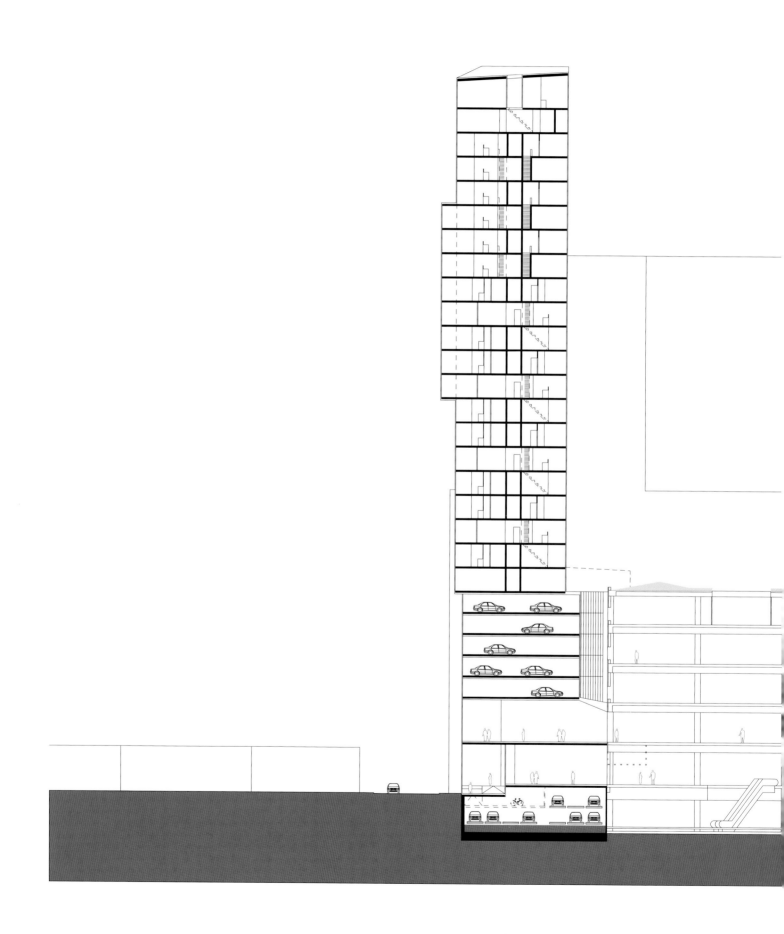

Kwakkel House (094)
Apeldoorn, 2000

The brief called for three main programs. These programs consisted of a single family house, a "museum" for storing restored automobiles, and a garden with a greenhouse structure. An existing stable and house occupy the north-eastern corner of the 1,000 m² site, which will be demolished and replaced by the proposed design. Due to strict council planning regulations for this area, the size and position of the new buildings is determined by the variables inherent in the buildings that will be replaced. In response to the vast size of the site, the concept lies in creating different private and sheltered exterior spaces by configuring the three programs.

A new driveway meanders through the garden in front of the house. In plan, the living areas are located in between the spaces reserved for the automobile collection, and the garden component, resulting in several spatial confrontations between these two programs.

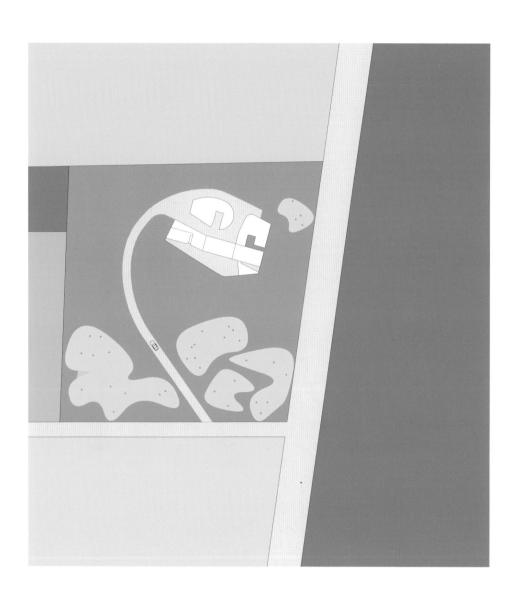

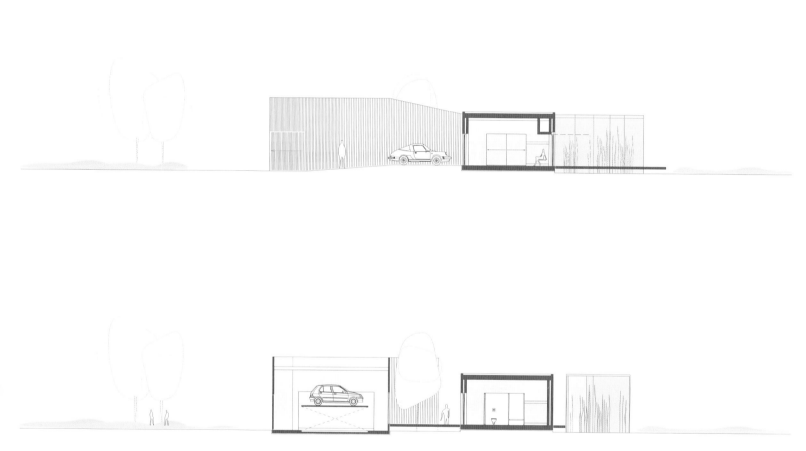

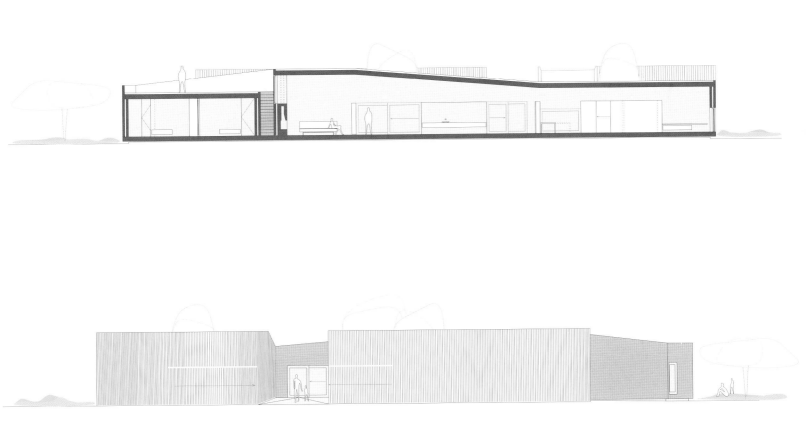

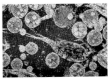

Algae

Pierrot le Fou (Jean Luc Godard)

Masai

Tula (Mexico)

Torres Satillitas (Mexico–Barragan/Goeritz)

Fireplace (Villa Malaparte–Capri)

Walled city (Hong Kong)

Wiel Arets

An Alabaster Skin[*]

Architecture may be considered a desire for purity, a striving for perfection. The principal color white marks a process in which the undecidable is respected; it is not a question of meaningful or meaningless.

The whiteness of newly fallen snow in the morning light, the white of perfect skin, the white of paper on which the design will be sketched — white is everywhere and may be considered the color of origin and beginning. White is the color of the between: between conception and execution, between unblemished and defiled, between innocence and seduction, between virginity and marriage.

Architecture is unblemished. Its entire logic risks something that is of only short duration. It appears only to disappear. It seduces through innocence, yet it loses that very innocence through seduction. It presents us briefly with freshness and untaintedness, only to lose those properties precisely by offering them to us.

Architecture is therefore a between, a membrane, an alabaster skin, at once opaque and transparent, meaningful and meaningless, real and unreal. To become itself, architecture must lose its innocence; it must accept a violent transgression. It can only become part of the world by entering into marriage with its surroundings. Therefore architecture is not only untainted but violent, and its violence once again has two sides. On one side architecture is violent because it resists having to be the victim of its surroundings; on the other it can distort those surroundings. This relationship lends it cunning.

Those who engage in architecture should keep their wits about them. This applies first to architects. Architecture bestows upon us not the pleasure but the fear of freedom. If we are to prosper, we must learn to see through its ambiguities and find a way of coping with its vagaries, for it inflicts incisions everywhere. Architecture cuts through the skin of the city; as an image, it graves images; itself defiled, it defiles others. However, we should not be intimidated by this. Too often it cuts itself, and seldom does it intend to cut off our retreat. It is more likely to cut to make something visible. It makes incisions to make life more comprehensible. Architecture with its surgical interventions parallels biology as a science representing life. As a virus can radically alter the human organism, so

....

[*] First Published in **An Alabaster Skin, Wiel Arets Architect,** Heerlen-Rotterdam, 1991. Lecture by Wiel Arets at Columbia University, 9 October 1991. Published in **Columbia Documents of Architecture and Theory,** Volume 2 (pp. 35–39), 1993.

can a building radically alter the organism of a city, and just as a body is a functioning assemblage of organs, a city is a functioning assemblage of buildings. It is appropriate to speak of traffic arteries and traffic streams, of the heart and lungs of a city, but the city can be compared to the human body in many other ways. Architecture is to the city what an artificial organ is to the human body. We all may agree that the city is sick and needs curing. It no longer functions spontaneously but calls for prosthetics and surgical operations. Wherever the city is functioning below standard, architecture takes action. It takes the place of the city's spontaneous and organic functioning; it is a prosthesis, architecture is always the place of, "in the place of."

Architecture is ephemeral due to the fact that it always takes the place of something. Though built of brick and concrete, architecture is temporary. In addition to the cuts of biology and surgery, it is subject to the cuts of film and cinematography. Through the rapid succession of images and the torrent of stimuli, architecture is cinematic. We experience the city through the car window, as if watching a film. Architecture is to the city what a film director is to the script he wants to make into a film. Film is a skin lit with images. The succession of these images is governed by a rhythm of intervals, incisions, "cuts". We are not aware of this when watching a film. It is the same with architecture — it introduces intervals into the urban fabric often without our awareness.

The space in the city is the artificial space for a scenario. The way in which we perceive a city has been structured beforehand by films, and so architecture introduces programmatic transformations into the urban structure without pretending to preserve its original character. Architecture is essentially incision.

To speak of film and architecture is not innocent; it suggests how the city and urban life are drastically altered by new media and technologies. Perceiving life as if it were a film is only the beginning of an altered reality. We are discovering how traditional ways of observing are being transformed into new strategies of perception.

Just as architecture of the modern movement attempted to respond to production techniques then in practice, so architecture today should provide an answer to the simulation techniques now emerging. Technology at the beginning of this century was largely a machine technology, geared towards making things; today's fabrication concerns the immaterial, particularly controlling and sending information, regulating and channeling images.

Fifty years ago technology brought us reality. Now it is destroying it. The design of the thirties already contributed to a series of man-machine communication; today architecture has reached the status of an interface. It is architecture's task to mediate between man and everything that befalls him.

Walled city (Hong Kong)

Scaffolding (Hong Kong)

Ryoanji Temple (Kyoto)

Mets stadium (New York)

Integrated circuit

Untitled (Richard Serra)

Wiel Arets

Transition: Beyond the cult of imagery, Boulevard Domburg[*]

Ours is a global age.

As technology starts to destroy reality, living today entails acceleration — or deceleration — in order to pass from one code to another, to translate one impulse into another and to engage different situations from different vantage points.

Architects do not believe in a conflict between mathematics and history. In the universal pictorial language in which the world unfolds, mathematics and geometry have become indispensable ingredients. Only since imaginary coordinates were drawn across the surface of the globe have we been able to chart the world and explore it. It is primarily through the creative power of mathematicians that we have made ourselves a place on earth, a place that we can share with others.

This project begins with the assumption that any application of mathematics to our view of the world brings the challenge of the grid. For architects, the grid is a way of spiritualizing the earth and freeing it from the burden of gravity. The planetary architecture thus advocated here has no other goal than to make the sea and the town of Domburg participate in this challenge.

By doing this our design converts a seaside resort into a social condenser, giving everyone the opportunity to relax as he or she chooses. Each can go his or her own way without disturbing the others. Those who wish to play golf can drive directly to the course; for those who want to swim or sunbathe, the sea will not be spiritualized, elevated to an object of meditation, as it is for those temporarily or permanently occupying the transparent tower blocks along the boulevard.

Traffic circulates along a kilometer-long boulevard. A ribbon of shops, swimming pools, galleries and restaurants is introduced between the traffic level and promenade area. Next to and above them are conference rooms, hotels and villas.

Domburg, while remaining as it is, will become imbedded, like a pearl in an oyster, in an elegant gridlike structure in which the sea's gray northern light dissolves everything material into a spatial state. This recreation can mean recreation.

The design is organized by four ideas: the grid, the social condenser, translucence and disorder.

The grid is the place where spirit and the material, intellect and the material, become harmonious. It is ethereal and incorporeal material and at the same time immaterial, a spiritual entity that

[*] Published in **An Alabaster Skin, Wiel Arets Architect**, Heerlen-Rotterdam, 1991.

has taken on palpable form. The grid today is ubiquitous: in television screen dots, on computer chips, as radiation in the air; it is all around us and passes though us. The grid is our destiny and our future.

In our desire to render the grid visible we frequently opt for translucent material; penetrating light is important. We have no secrets. We want the architecture to bathe in the transparent northern light of Domburg and the North Sea, making it truly a "place." And this is where the grid, stripped of all symbolism, comes in.

Our buildings are social condensers in that their identity derives from their function regarding circulation. Vehicles and pedestrians are led between buildings and then brought to a halt. This deceleration transforms and "sorts" the traffic so that everyone can seek the place of recreation that attracts him/her the most. The buildings are designed so that one may enter and leave quickly yet pass between them slowly to make one's choice and park one's car. The complex should therefore be understood as an intervention to which the traffic is subjected as a solution to traffic problems. It is not that the complex stands on the road; rather, the complex is the road. And as every road is a detour, so too is this complex.

The detour takes the form of a Z bend in which Domburg and then the sea swing into view. This detour is a disorder, not just a disorder of road and grid but a disorder of the road which becomes a detour, and a disorder of the road that becomes a disordered grid. This "disordered grid" is our way of criticizing the increasing tendency of our society in general and the modern movement in particular to have everything function free of friction and disorder.

Whereas modern architecture is primarily a hygienic architecture, pure, unblemished and imperturbable, we on the other hand accept imperfection, noise and disorder as an essential element of modern technology. Our ideas are not upset but, quite the reverse, stimulated by collisions with information and concepts, concepts that can be interpreted not simply as opposition but as accelerators or condensers of our ideas.

Technology, particularly information technology, consists in large part of translating codes: electronic impulses are turned into images, magnetic material is decoded into data. During the translation of these codes and the transformation of logistics and information, things are likely to go wrong at times. Equally, traffic involves not only acceleration but deceleration, not just orderly progress but bottlenecks and snarls.

Whereas much architecture usually is intended to keep things running smoothly, we advocate the rational acceptance of rhythm. We do not try to avoid conflict but welcome it as an indispensable element of communication.

Finally this design attempts to strip architecture of the cult of imagery and attain an "Architecture of Freedom". At present architecture does nothing other than attract and titillate its spectators is every way possible. It tries to create the most powerful images in conducive places, to draw the public into metropolitan life.

With these projects we wish to break this code of imagery. Instead of using architecture to endear a place to the public, people are relieved of their obligation to respond to architecture. That we are able to see Domburg and the sea from these buildings is not the only issue. Of far greater relevance is the fact that, aided by this project, Domburg itself should acquire the gift of sight, it is Domburg that should see the sea.

Perspective

Surrounding area

Long section

Model

Wiel Arets

Videre: Theater, body and brain, thought, Delft Theater

Our perception is subject to constant change. Not only visual perception but also how we perceive intellectually and how we accommodate this perception in our thinking. Biological engineering has been a major science since the mid-nineteenth century. Its technology has altered the way life is represented. In the twentieth century we have seen the total subordination of the human body to medical science. Leonardo explores the body in an abstract manner, indifferent to its organs. Artaud's body, featured in the Theater of Cruelty, does not require organs. Jacques Lacan addresses the body's absence. Within this context "cut" and "montage" are regarded as ways of thinking in which the body is (re)presented: "to cut a fine figure." Biological engineering enables us to change our bodies with artificial hearts, lungs and joints, but mental change has also become a reality in genetic manipulation. It is partly through these developments that electronics have influenced our perception; for example David Lynch's Eraserhead (1978) and David Cronenberg's Dead Ringers (1988). The influence on contemporary theater is undeniable.

This project addresses the challenge of treating the theater within the urban context of Delft as expressing our changing conditions of thought. In this respect the membrane of the city — not only the skin as a facade but as ground surface and as a cultural layer — is a key concept. The ideas of "current" and of "evocative program" also play major roles. "Current" means not only the electrical currents present in the urban context and within each building but also patterns of communication: everything connected with circuits, routes, tracks, circulation and with the relationship between people, between man and machine, in which every hierarchy is obstructed. The project cuts into Delft's skin, and the section may be regarded as an incision. The horizontal movements of the station, market and university towards the Delft Theater are of primary importance, as are the vertical lines of movement that cut through and skewer together the three layers of the design.

Those arriving at the theater by car, taxi or tram are led through an incision in the skin to an entrance below ground level. This is done on the one hand to create a pedestrian promenade on the ground floor and on the other as a practical answer to the question of where to locate traffic within the site. The building reacts to these two lines of movement. The pedestrian infiltrates the building from the square, from the city, and encounters visitors brought by vehicle in the entrance hall. A box office separates the entrance hall from the foyer like a large swing door. The visitor can deposit his/her coat (external skin) in the cloakroom tucked beneath the fly tower. The main auditorium is accessed via two ramps. Moving from the foyer's transparent features, the visitor is confronted by a translucent skin and then enters the auditorium, which is completely closed off from natural light. This movement turns the visitor into a member of the theater audience. The room, filled with people drinking, smoking and telephoning is transformed into a theater of the city, and when the final curtain falls, the public departs through the various layers of skin out of the theater (after donning coats and entering cars) and away from the area of Delft colored by its insertion, to return to ordinary life. The uppermost level of the project is enfolded in a black screen of perforated synthetic rubber that can be read as a skin, from which the theater opens the city and through which the city is open to the theater. This hospitable skin expresses the osmosis of the city and theater.

The artists enter the building as do the "civilians" along the eighty-three-degree axis, a direction that brings them immediately within the building's geometry, unlike the public, who follow a curved walkway. Once inside, the artists either make their way to a half sunken dressing room in the skin of the city to perform in the experimental theater on that level or ascend to the dressing room behind the main stage to play to the main auditorium. The artists exchange the code of their "public" faces for that of the masks that make them actors and actresses. After the final applause, the artists shower and retire to the "recovery bar" to regain, in a state of transition, their own identity: from dream to reality. The theater staff use the same entrance as the artists, taking the ramp to reach staff rooms overlooking the sculpture garden.

The equipment brought in through the skin's opening is moved from theater to theater, from city to city. Public circulation of artists, staff, vehicular traffic and equipment is not anonymous; all form part of the life of the theater and city, life that takes place between dream and reality.

The three components comprising the project are placed in parallel and related by function to an idea of neutral components within the logical conditions of a theater: foyer, cloakroom, bar, etc. None of the parts function fully autonomously, nor are they completely dependent upon each other. Here components are placed in parallel horizontally and vertically, neutral and independent, as sections through lines of movement to affect transitory relationships and produce moments of spatial intensity and interaction. Within these moments the concept of voyeurism is revealed and interpreted, as **videre** through which one can read this project as the **cinefaction** of the theater.

Perspective

Model

Presentation drawings

Urban, wood model

Wiel Arets

Body Invaders[1]

Wherever I present my work , I am always presented as a Dutch-man. We still think in those terms; you are born in the Netherlands, so therefore you are a Dutchman and because of this you have to evaluate your work through viewing Dutch architecture. In a recent article the architectural critic Greg Lynn[2] was trying again to raise the issue of comparing; you are Dutch and so therefore people start to dig into Dutch architectural history. I think this attitude is wrong.

I think that you are more a child of your time and not only born in a certain place, but that you travel around, you teach, you are influenced by things, which are going on all over the world. So I think, you should try to forget these placements, for example the De Stijl movement was impossible to describe as a Dutch style as many people coming from Russia such as Lissitzky were at least as important for De Stijl.

For me it is important that I studied physics for a while before studying architecture. I am still interested not only in physical issues but also in biological and biochemical processes. The way we work today in the studio is that we start from the abstract, in order to try to develop an architectural idea.

I am interested in "Flux," the turbulence which keeps planes in the air, logistics and traffic movements; things that influence architecture a great deal. We should not look at the architectural criteria only from within. In my projects you can see that I am fascinated by the skin, by its surface; in fact, the thickness of the surface and the porosity of that surface. What seduced me, in fact can be seen as an innocent artifact. In that sense, artificiality is something which interests me as well. I do not want to quote Martin Heidegger, however if you think about his philosophy and Japanese philosophy both have a lot in common with artificiality in the form of the untouchable, and the intellectual character.

When I went to Japan for the first time, I discovered a lot of things which I would summarize with the word "touching." Roland Barthes in his book about Japan also in fact talks about "touching," as the opposite of the physical incision. In that sense "touching" as a mental incision, physical incisions and particularly with respect to the body are issues that continually interest me. I like to look, I like to read, to be involved in as many different issues as

....

[1] Published in Arthur Kroker (ed.), **City Invasions**, Vienna, 1994 (pp. 41–54).
[2] Published in **"Maastricht ..."** Rotterdam: 010 Publishers.

possible. I like to be confronted by fashion, everything that stimulates my eye and my stomach. I like to read Scientific America, advertisements and newspapers. I am very interested in the media as another form of collectivity; millions of people looking simultaneously at one event, unlike Nero's Coliseum, where only a few thousand people could look at once. Collectivity is transforming our thoughts. It is quite interesting that in this sense collectivity is something other than the neighbourhood or the boundaries of a country. The question is, how will architecture react to these changes, how do these changes influence our architectural product?

The interference of art in my work is relevant. Mapplethorpe's body, Serra's weight, Klein's mediums' of fire, air and wind, Godard's cutting, and Valéry's white paper are all issues that stimulate my work. When a work is completed, I think it should have a certain amount of potentiality. Godard's movies are on the one hand very simple stories and on the other hand the complexity and the thickness of each frame create a potentiality, which I think, we can hardly find in any architectural place. We can learn a lot from other disciplines and other cultures.

We can learn a lot from the Masai, in so far as how they treat and change their bodies. It is interesting how Mapplethorpe's work also transforms the body. It is different from the Masai, as he makes the incisions in the body in a very different way.

Yves Klein's use of the body as a medium is interesting. He uses the body as medium, in the same way as he uses fire to make a painting. He employs the medium of painting and fire although he understands that it is impossible to control it, so the effect is something he can not foresee. He uses wind and rain for his painting. In short, he uses a manifestation of energy to make his artworks.

I am fascinated by the porous quality of Serra's drawings; you see the different layers and it is interesting how you see the weight in the work itself even though physically the painting is very thin. Even the paint looks very heavy on the one hand but very thin and translucent on the other hand. When a painting in the museum he is working in is positioned in a certain place, there is a confrontation between the city, the museum and the painting and in that sense what is fascinating about Serra's work is that he is performing space, and ultimately he is transforming the museum, the architectural space, by his paintings. In that sense it is a confrontation and dialogue with the surroundings, it is dealing with its context, and creating a completely different environment.

In the movie Pierrot le Fou, Godard starts with a scene in a bathroom, where Ferdinand, Pierrot, is reading "Velázquez" to his daughter. His wife is passing by and Godard is showing the confrontation between the real world and the surreal world as an advertisement. On the one hand Pierrot, played by Jean-Paul Belmondo, is the puppet and the man, who are both playing the figure of the fairy tale; on the other hand Ferdinand is a real person. They arrange a party and while there, people talk in terms of an advertisement to each other. He uses the colours red, yellow and blue to indicate the position people are in. Red is also used to describe the violent character of Paris, yellow the in-between of the countryside and blue is the colour of the south of France, the paradise. Ferdinand/Pierrot is balancing himself between violence and paradise. He cannot find his real identity. We as architects have to be confronted with violence and innocence and fear and tranquility. Finally, at the end of the movie he kills himself.

He uses the colour yellow to indicate the fact that he is blowing himself up as he is unable to choose between Pierrot and Ferdinand, reality and surreality, red and blue.

It is six forty-five in the evening, and the geishas in Kyoto are going to work. They leave home and walk in a group to their destination. They are exquisitely dressed and their faces and neck are painted white.

There are approximately one hundred geishas in Kyoto, where the whole cult of becoming a geisha and their special education is imbedded in the city's history. The importance of this is the fact that we perceive Japan through its technologies and modern architecture. However there is the second much less physical layer of tradition. It is real life on the one hand and on the other it is a fairy tale. Japan has a lot to do with this mental condition, and a lot to do with "touching." The Ryoanji temple in Kyoto is built on a site

Mapplethorpe

Serra

Klein

Godard

Masai

Geisha

where they first laid stones on the ground, and then put the floor one metre above the earth supported by pillars. The occupants walk barefoot on the floor; they sit, contemplating; they only touch the garden through the mental touch of meditation.

One of the reasons I am fascinated by Malaparte's work is the dialogue that Malaparte brings to us again between the real and the surreal world. The dialogue has, since the days of Plato, been a confrontation between the lay person and the specialist. Plato uses Socrates to let him say what he wants him to say. He does the same in Eupalinos in which the architect is talking. Cesare Cataneo wrote "Giuseppe e Giovanni" and it is the layman and the architect who talk, but through the voice of the architect. Cesare Cataneo is presenting his work. In that sense Malaparte's written works, La Pelle and Kaputt make us aware as architects that architecture has less to do with physical issues and physical examples that we should study, than a poetic quality which you can never gain solely from studying architecture. So what he is in fact doing in Villa Malaparte is using his history and his thoughts.

The staircase at Villa Malaparte refers to the stairs of the church in Lipari, where he was put into exile. The white curve of the roof refers to the sail of a boat. You can say it is a shipwrecked boat, but on the other hand, and this is the most interesting form for me, he is creating an underworld.

This is an underworld in which the people who visit him are treated very well, but they are dictated to by his layout of the plan. Getting to this place is a feat of endurance. You can go there by boat, by airplane, or on foot. It is one hour's walk to get there from Capri, but once you are there, you have the feeling that you are in a prison, and simultaneously in an incredible villa. The fireplace is something which intrigues me, for it is again confronts the opposites of inside and outside. The fire is not only used inside to warm the house, but also tells the fishermen in the boats that Punta Masulla is an extremely dangerous sea cliff. Villa Malaparte is a house which can be best explained by the term "An Alienation Machine."

A city which intrigues me constantly is Hong Kong, not because of the horse races or because of the Chinese food, both of which are incredible, but because it also has a double position, a kind of a mask. On the one hand the streets are built as facades, not unlike the architecture of some Italian cities, yet on the other hand, a mask is presented on these facades by bamboo scaffolding and their advertisements, creating a condition in which architecture during the day is characterized by the shape of the walls of the street, and by night it is the light of the advertisement itself that creates the architectural environment.

Fear is an extremely interesting and complex issue in Hong Kong. When the planes begin their descent over the city, above the top of the houses, you see the lights of the runway approach. The airport runway is built of stone, which they took from the wall which surrounded the so-called Walled City. This was a 600 by 400 metre area twenty-three stories high, where people flew when the British colonized Hong Kong. It was in fact a fortress where people started to live. In the beginning, fifty or hundred people lived there, but because of a political loophole it was the only Chinese property in Hong Kong; people sought sanctuary there from crime and started to live in the fortress.

They built their own houses, which grew into a huge precarious organic system that subsequently collapsed on a few occasions. It is demolished now, but I think it was one of the most interesting architectural places I knew. This was not in terms of its beauty, but in terms of its spatial diversity, the complexity of its program, the conditions of the community, which in fact was not a community at all, and the fact that it was so massive, that there was only one courtyard in the middle, which contained a school and a church. It was the only open air space in the whole city, where 20,000 people once lived. Of course you can say it was dangerous to live there, but on the other hand, these were spaces we can learn a lot from. Many of my projects are stimulated by this work.

I would not be a Dutchman if I did not mention Van der Vlugt and particularly his incredible house for Van der Leeuw. The reason why I talk about him is because he preempted the whole contemporary discussion on the body. The body in the 20s according to Le Corbusier, for example, was treated as a physical presence and the

Ryoanji temple

Ryoanji temple

Malaparte

Malaparte

Malaparte

Hong Kong

Hong Kong

Hong Kong

human being as someone who should be ideal and exercised. The exercise machine was an important icon in its day. Nowadays our body is changing in a different way. Through exercise you can change your body, but by technology we can also start to put devices **in** our bodies, which change them in a different way. We are now using artificial kidneys and we have ways to help our hearts. I saw a woman on TV once who was walking with a small car which was in fact her heart. It is quite intriguing how in an artificial way, we keep people alive, but even more interesting is the fact that we are now starting to change people, we are trying to manipulate their brains. As one philosopher said a few years ago, perhaps people will some day have only a big head and no limbs, and will use their computer by looking at it or making vocal sounds.

The computer rooms built in the 50s have now been replaced by a chip 8 by 8 millimeters, and that chip can store far more information. In the computer room of the 50s you could walk in and see, hear and smell the computers. The chip however has rendered these things almost undetectable.

Another issue which interests me is the skin of our earth, in fact the ground we are building on. For many years we have not thought about the earth. As previously mentioned, in Japan they put a stone on the ground and start building on top of the stone. We are not "touching" the ground. We make a foundation, but the earth we are building on is artificial. It is made by us. When this is the case, we should use the instruments to change the earth. What interests me about the quality of lava is its pliability. Lava does not create smoothness, for although we perceive the earth as smooth it is the opposite, like our skin, which is rough when seen through the microscope. In fact the pliable condition of the site we are building on is something we should take great care of. We live in a changing world and as architects we have to deal with it.

Van der Vlugt

Computer room

AHK aerial view

AHK perspective ground level

AHK perspective basement

AHK model

AHK model

AHK model

AHK model

AHK model

Wiel Arets
Grid and Rhizome^(*)

The new buildings for the Amsterdam Academy of the Arts need to accommodate a diversity of functions. The client wishes the complex to express the unity thus newly attained by the Academy, which at present is spread across several premises in the city. This unity is important, for the fusion of the various faculties should have a recognizable countenance. Diverging faculties in the fields of film and television, dance and theater, music, architecture, painting, sculpture and museology will enter into a collaborative context and the accommodation they share is to bear this out. This new unity, however, should be so achieved that the autonomy of each faculty is maintained. The crux of the matter, then, is unity in diversity, and this we have set out to express in our design.

While the Academy wishes its design to show unity in diversity, the city of Amsterdam, on the other hand, wants something to rivet the attention of its inhabitants, guests and tourists. It wants to offer its citizens and visitors something that adds harmoniously to the tradition so illustriously present at this location, but at the same time to show that Amsterdam is right in the middle of modern-day life. Hence investigations into the historical background and morphological structure of this place in the city are supplemented by analyses of the traffic streams that slice through it, and of today's patterns of communication which here must permit intelligent contact between people.

Traffic streams, communication patterns — everything to do with circuits, circulation and social contact is essential to the design. Indeed, this is where relationships between people find expression. Here it concerns an art institute for higher education, with its efficient operation as a binding element, and because of this, we have paid extra attention to developing routes and paths between the buildings which express nothing whatsoever of hierarchy and ensure that users have the space to meet each other at will, yet guaranteeing their ability to work in silence and seclusion on artistic activities. The issue of how organizational and managerial aspects of culture could best be combined with artistic inspiration and production has been the continual point of departure for our design.

As for the design itself the first step it takes is to demolish the "Maupoleum," one of Amsterdam's university premises. In its place will come an elongated, explicitly horizontal building that is only half the breadth of the Maupoleum. The new block is clad in an

....

(*) Published in **A+U**, vol. 2, 1994 (pp. 103–106).

mantle of stainless steel and is so designed that it appears to float; below it is a view through, which renders visible part of the concentric rings of canals, at present obscured by the Maupoleum. The harmony between the canal rings, Jodenbreestraat and the square (Mr. Visserplein) is thus restored. Below the building is a car park whose roof is a grid in glass block.

The strip parallel to the new building, between it and the canals, forms the main access to the locations on the square. One descends by one of several escalators to reach the entrances to the various blocks on the square from a number of moving walkways.

Projected to stand on the square and extending the line of the building on Jodenbreestraat are a pair of slabs; facing these are three towers. All differ in breadth, height and volume. Each is constructed in concrete with facades of glass block, clear glass in steel sections and corten steel. The latter material provides grids with shutters, behind which are frames containing clear glass which can be opened. The ensemble is split into two by Muiderstraat and Jodenbreestraat, which together form a perfectly straight axis; the sight line along these is graced by the Zuiderkerk.

The slabs and towers occupy inner courtyards off the square and each has its own surface level: the lowest floor of each is at a different height. All entrances, however, are at 14.40 m below ground level.

At the entrance level each tower has an inner courtyard which not only admits light and air but can function as an outdoor area. On reaching the entrance to one of the buildings by a moving walkway, one has a view though its glazed lobby of the inner courtyard bathed in light from above. Thus at the entrances one is welcomed by the materializing of a light that shines through the building and, seeming to continue into the earth, makes its transparent strength felt.

Besides our interpretation of the requirements relating to its setting in the city and the wishes of the client, three aspects played a prominent part when realizing the design: the location, the traffic and the complex's allocation as an institute for education and culture.

The location is a square (Mr. Visserplein) which might be considered the second heart of Amsterdam, after the Dam. Whereas at the Dam we commemorate the victims of the Second World War, here it is the February Strike (held in 1941 as a protest against mass arrests of Jews in Amsterdam) that we remember. It is in every respect a place of commemoration, of remembrance and of what is now no more.

Here once stood the bustling Jewish Quarter; now it houses the Jewish Historical Museum, and the Portuguese Synagogue. The museum shows us what has vanished, but the synagogue is still the place where the imageless God of Judaism is worshipped, the place where the Scriptures, the Book and the Law refer to a culture of absence. Both buildings represent the diaspora, the uprooting and dispersion of the Jewish people. What we have here, then, is a place of disappearance, of what was, of absence; not, however, in the sense of a thing consigned to obscurity, rather of something that lends direction to our culture and history.

In the present situation the mood this square should reflect has been tainted by the traffic that reduces the monuments standing there to the level of decor. In a certain sense the effect of traffic on this place is the same as that of the war and the demolition during the postwar period of reconstruction. In now addressing ourselves to restoring the square's monumentality and regrafting this area onto the city, we cannot simply ignore the traffic as if it did not exist. On the contrary — the issue is to integrate the traffic on the square into the monumentality of the place and see to it that the new school block amply reflects our culture's present as much as its past.

This is even more valid when considering the building's function. The Amsterdam Academy of the Arts wishes to house its dance, theater, film and television classes there. Film and video are particularly concerned with the modified conditions of our perception. These art forms are much more than the expression of our individual artist. Indeed film and television have so influenced our way of seeing and of interpreting what we see that it is safe to say that they have radically transformed our entire lifestyle.

Consequently the design for the new school block has to take into account the monumentality of the setting, its commemoration of what has departed, and departure itself. Nor must the present be overlooked, the accelerated perception generated by the traffic and the "cinematic effect." Moreover, also requiring consideration is the change in reality wrought by film as a medium. Film and video do not supplement reality as much as decide how we perceive that reality and how that reality appears to us.

In the final analysis this design has to do with making a statement about our culture, about what we understand by culture and how we experience it. The theater plays an important part here. We only need to think of Brecht and Artaud to realize the high expectations we have when drama is to be understood as a means of acquainting ourselves with our society and our ability to alter and improve that society. Traditionally the theater has been a vehicle for collective reflections about the nature of our culture; a place for reflecting on who we are and what we are doing. Culture is usually perceived as a medium for establishing sense and lending meaning and we consequently expect from it the indicative, expressive gesture. With the theater of the absurd in general and Beckett's plays in particular, however, it has become apparent that culture could well be something entirely different, something involving futility and loss of meaning, the concept of the void and disappearance, in short the depletion of the very essence of humanity.

We want our design to conform to the existing city and remain open to the dynamics of change taking place there. To this end we have carried out a historical-morphological investigation into the urban fabric and the present structure of the place in which our design is set. Two key concepts form the crux of our analysis; the grid and the rhizome.

The term rhizome was developed by the philosopher Gilles Deleuze and the psychoanalyst Félix Guattari to introduce a notion that does justice to the chaotic nature of modern life. Their point of departure is that the world cannot be reduced to a single entity nor thought to a single word, but that multiplicity and dispersal should be met by a new philosophy. In this philosophy there are no authorities and hierarchies, and democracy is characterized not only by the principles of equality, consultation and equal representation, but over and above that by the proliferation of interlinking strands of production, commerce and desire. For such a proliferation, for which there was no existing word, Deleuze and Guattari introduced the botanical term rhizome.

A rhizome is a root like stem that emits both roots and shoots without beginning or end, and without a centre. Unlike the more familiar formation of, say a tree with its roots in the soil and its crown in the sky, unlike the hieratic principle of origin and the vertical principle of authority, rhizome is emblematic of the irreducible nature of the plurality of our experiences, the uncertainty — rated a positive challenge — of life's surprises and the horizontal nature of the exchange, an aspect decisively important to democracy. For Deleuze and Guattari, Amsterdam is the example par excellence of a rhizome-city, because Amsterdam is the product not of a single idea, a single central perspective or a compulsive rationalism, but a proliferation of labyrinthine canals and alleyways, a combination of intense passions with the most calculating spirit of commerce.

While the rhizome concept does not so much emphasize the irrational as it does that which transcends reason and derives its right to exist from passion and desires, grid is a word that speaks of rationalism. Here it is an unoppressive rationalism which recognizes in the pattern of the grid a religious basis; the grid perceivable in the windows of the Portuguese Synagogue, in the windows of the Zuiderkerk by Hendrik de Keyzer, in the austere facades of the Zeemagazijn (the former arsenal) by Daniël Stalpaert, (now the Amsterdam Maritime Museum) and of the former Orphanage of Van der Hart, now an old people's home. Time and again this grid speaks of the materializing of a light emanating from God, though from a God who has withdrawn from the world and who by His absence has left man in the white, imageless asceticism of his commerce and his work. This is why Amsterdam, perhaps more than other city, was a meeting place for Jews and Protestants, people for whom God revealed himself not in images but in the Scriptures, for whom God was represented on earth not by reconciliation but the Law — people for whom belief was a matter of waiting.

Democracy, as it has developed in these societies of belief and commerce, knows no hierarchy, but unfolds in the transparency of the light. It is for these reasons that grid and rhizome are key concepts in our design.

And so during the realization of the design, reflections on the difference between above and below ground played a role. Building below ground is something very rarely resorted to in Amsterdam, because of the level of the water table. Here, however, we were faced with an existing tunnel with an underground square above it. This facility is utilized in the design by so choosing the surface level at which pedestrian activities take place, so that from it the underground section can be seen below and the above-ground section above. The ground datum for pedestrian activities is "vectorized," in other words it expresses a direction and a movement. This oval, this ellipse, is orbital — that is, it is comparable to the orbit of a moon around its planet and functions as much in time as in space. The resulting dynamics of the plan accommodate the dynamics of the traffic stream, accepting the existence of the hectic and chaotic traffic while at the same time expressing how the visual pathway and our way of seeing things, both of which have been modified by new media and technologies, are integrated in the design.

Traffic has been integrated in the design too. However, this does not mean that we expose the users of our buildings to it. On the contrary, the traffic here is accepted and the design conceived as something that latches onto its presence — the complex is treated as subordinate to the road rather than vice versa.

The buildings are so designed that they banish the noise of the traffic while retaining a view of it. So one can look at the traffic without it being disturbing. This means that the energy, normally employed to protect and arm the user against the momentum of traffic and city, against the confusion of the metropolis bombarding the retina, can be used for other purposes. By accepting that metropolitan reality for what it is, the design strives for a tranquility that will lead to the meditative and contemplative mood befitting an art academy and cultural institute.

For here peace and quiet is of the essence. Indeed, without it it is impossible to create art or exchange ideas. Should one need to meet others with the intention of creating art works, however, then the technological innovations and metropolitan reality must be confirmed, though at the same time kept at a distance.

Skin

Geisha

Masai

Lava

Hong Kong

Wiel Arets

A Virological Architecture [1]

Lately, architecture has been regarded as a means in which to criticise of urban development. More and more, one hears the metaphor that it is up to architecture to make the city healthy once again. If one accepts the metaphor that it is architecture's responsibility to help the city regain its health, what kind of medicine are we talking about and with what medical procedures can we compare architecture?

In the first case, an architectural intervention in the urban fabric is comparable to a surgical intervention. A dilapidated building or decaying neighborhood can be razed, the ground levelled and new buildings put up. This is in many ways comparable to a situation in which a wound or tumor (the old and decaying neighbourhood or building) is disinfected or excised (building demolition and levelling of the site) in order to allow new tissue growth (the renewal, the healing process).

Surgery is, however, not the only medical metaphor with which the architectural intervention can be compared. Not only is a comparison to a surgeon possible, but the architect can also be likened to a researcher in the pharmaceutical industry or to a chemist. The plan to make a city healthy again implies that one considers architecture as medicinal. Everyone has an idea of what surgery is: grab a knife and cut. But what is a medicine? If it works, the patient gets better. But medicine works where we can't see it.

The surgeon is visible with the naked eye, but when it comes to medicine, there are biological processes involved, at work out of sight, deep within the body. And the medicine itself, is that something different from the illness, or something actually related to the disease? And what is health? Does health mean never being sick, or is it the ability to recover from illness? What type of diseases afflict the city?

These questions are just marking time. Perhaps the metaphor is not a very good one. Maybe the city is not sick at all, and cannot be compared to a body. The body is, after all, a single unit, a whole, whereas the city is not. In contrast to the body, a city lacks limits or a contour. Normally, the practice of medicine assists the patient in recovery, it "repairs" (another metaphor!) the body and restores it to its original state. Architecture, in contrast, has no intention of restoring the city to its previous condition or original state, nor can it. The intervention of the physician or surgeon is verifiable;

....

[1] Published in **A+U**, vol. 2, 1994 (pp. 103–106).

that of the architect in the city is not. It is more a matter of effecting a process in the city with the assistance of the architectonic intervention whereby the result is unpredictable. Surgery concerns "repair," whereas architecture concerns the experiment.

The Masai are masters of cutting. They carve, for example, a figure in the ear and let an infection take place. Or they carve notches in the skin and stretch their necks with the use of rings made by silversmiths. Despite the pain, they transform their bodies into works of art and make life a celebration.

Reflections on the Masai and surgery have played a role in the creation of this text; so did considerations regarding virology. How can the design contribute to penetrating the city the way a virus does, consuming it and transforming it into something new? The fascination with the virus and things viral is a product of the fascination with the invisible. It would have been nice if the design for the projects displayed here had led to invisible architecture, a building which you could walk right through but could not see and which is the catalyst for unexpected meetings and events.[2] It is the unpredictable character of virology that makes this discipline such a fantastic source of inspiration. Virology confronts us with things that are of great importance for us but which we cannot understand.

What is a virus? A virus is a source of infection in humans, animals, plants and bacteria which for its reproduction is dependent on the metabolism of living host cells. A virus is therefore a parasite which causes an illness, cannot exist without a host and overpowers, infiltrates and imitates the genetic codes of the host in order to reproduce.

In terms of genetic information, a virus resembles the host to a significant degree and makes use of the host's codes to reproduce and multiply itself relentlessly; differing only slightly from the previous form each time. The original tissue does not disappear, but begins to repeat itself endlessly in a slightly different form, grows rampant and becomes disintegrated with respect to the rest of the organism.

What makes the study of viruses so fascinating is that material, especially living material, should continue to be interpreted as coded information (and therefore as consciousness) and that transformations in the codes are identical to transformations in the tissue. An architect is not only a surgeon and a chemist, but a virologist inasmuch as he recognises these processes in the urban tissue and has learned how to manipulate the codes to good use.

This brings us to a fundamental equivocalness, as many viruses can only be cured by the injection of the identical or a virtually identical virus in small homeopathic doses in order to mobilise the defense mechanisms. In this way, smallpox, deadly to humans, was eradicated by immunizing everyone or almost everyone through vaccinating against the cowpox virus. The human defense mechanisms are mobilised and the disease generated in a moderate form so that a dangerous variant of the disease is stripped of its chances. One gets a little sick so as not to get seriously ill.

This equivocalness of medicine, of the toxin capable of both poisoning and inducing an antitoxin, most eloquently expressed in the phenomenon of the toxin-antitoxin-, where a mixture of the two was formerly used as a vaccine, has presented virology with an important model in the study of the city and society which exists in the city. We offer two examples of the virological model in social theory. First a comment by Jean Baudrillard: "for me, the emergence of the virus is a theoretical happening because a remarkable aspect comes into play here which is no longer to be placed at the level of the subject or history, but at the level of the objective, and which at the same time occurs in every aspect of the economy, over politics and pathology going deep in the heart of biology." What fascinates him so much in this is "that no external criticism of the viral processes is possible. The subversion, the destabilisation appears to come from within the system itself because the system is exhausted. That is actually a whole new event."[3]

A second example is related to Baudrillard: the panic — viral

....

[2] "Transition: Beyond the cult of imaginary," in **An Alabaster Skin, Wiel Arets Architect,** Rotterdam, 1991, pp. 21–27.
[3] "Viralität und Virulenz." Jean Baudrillard im Gespräch mit Florian Rötzer (red.); **Digitaler Schein. Ästhetik der electronischen Medien,** Frankfurt a.M., 1991, p. 81. The subject of the interview is the book by Jean Baudrillard: La Transparence du Mal. Essai sur les phénomènes extrêmes, Paris, 1990.

theory of Arthur Kroker, a theory "which no longer is externally based from the position of an autonomous subject, but a theory which interprets itself as a viral agent which functions according to three rules of biology: invasion of the host, cloning of the genetic master code and copying of the virus with the aid of the waning power of the organism. And that not only in a parasitical fashion, but as viral theory which attempts to probe the deeper logic of the genetic code, forcing the host to relinquish its secrets. Viral utopia, in a way: the end of a post-politics of invasion, cloning and instantaneous copying."[4]

For both Baudrillard and Kroker, the power of attraction of the viral model is found in the social theory which is hidden within: the subject of its (supposed) autonomy is discarded and the aspiration of cultural criticism to omnipotence is done away with. It no longer makes any sense to test the social reality against political or other ideals and to subsequently devise processes of change.

They no longer dispute a social system which is considered to be static from the point of dynamic alternative models, but recognize the instability of that system and point out that on a microlevel the social system itself is constantly subject to changes and alterations in power relationships, and that this instability and insecurity, which characterise the system from within, are best recognised from the point of view of a virological model.

In terms of thoughts regarding the city, this means that one jettisons the idea of creating a perfect city and works on an imperfect perfection, an incomplete completeness. It comes down to creating space for the unpredictable and allowing there to be tension in the city: not that the unpredictable actually happens, but that it can happen.

One should be able to construct a virtual biotechnology in the city, an art of living which hands over the laws of existence as a living organism to the urban tissue, putting modern technology to use for the urban and architectural design and making it fruitful. In this way, architecture can become a chance game, a condition for chance meetings and a condition for letting things happen. If architecture is consciously prepared to take chances and to create room for the "unplannable," then it no longer has to strive for harmony or reconciliation, but can make a start with accepting the dysfunction which invariably accompanies the growing pains of the first applications of new media and technologies, and no longer look back nostalgically on times past. The urban fabric is then recovered or revitalised and regarded as a substratum, as a sick body which can be cured by combatting the virus in the city with the help of injections of the architect's antitoxin.

Perhaps the virological model is for some too negative due to associations of fear and insecurity. That is understandable. Many unknown and deadly viruses do exist, and AIDS has an acutely disintegrating grip on our society. When one recognises, however, that the architect is a kind of doctor, then one must also recognise that architecture has something in the way of virology and that fear must be conquered to recognize the problem.

A similar difficulty arises when one ponders the question of living space and reflects on the status of the interior in the information society. The architect is presented with a major dilemma. On the one hand, information technology makes it possible for us to be up to date on and take care of everything without leaving the home or workplace. But we also run the danger of locking ourselves up in that telematic home or workplace and not venturing outside any more. There is the risk of our own functioning becoming uncoupled from ourselves and spinning around us in prosthetic devices, while we ourselves hardly ever leave our desk with its computer screen or the living room with its television and viditel screen.

Paul Virilio has expressed this in rather cogent terms: "Instead of assigning various domestic functions to different spaces within the home which the resident comes into contact with in his movements, all activities are grouped together at one point and are concentrated, using remote controls the intention of which is to free the resident from 'the burden of' movement. 'Interacting with each other no matter where the other person is,' the paradox of com-

....

[4] Arthur Kroker, Marilouise Kroker and David Cook, **Panic Encyclopedia. The Definitive Guide to the Postmodern Scene,** London, 1989, p. 238.

puter communication or telemeeting, amounts to a 'summary of distant things in one place' in the interactive home. This point, or rather this center of lack of movement, is clearly the user — the resident of these places of absolute comfort which in no way resemble the classic distribution of the normal home lay-out." Virilio adds to this: "Finally, man is not so much **in** the architec ture, rather the architecture of the electronic system is in him and invades man himself."[5]

This invasion of the architecture in people again confronts us with the virological model. The interior is no longer the exterior of our inner being, no longer the expression of our souls and the interpretation of our moods and feelings in the room arrangements and placing of furniture. Information technology has led to the virtual space which belongs to technology, claiming us and making us forget our own physical surroundings.[6]

With this, new light is shed on the controversy surrounding living. For Loos, it was matter of separating the interior and the exterior from each other. The exterior articulates the home to the city and does not maintain a forced relationship with the interior, which in the first place is a protective shell, a cocoon for the inhabitants. For Le Corbusier, it was a matter of abolishing the division between inside and outside and interpreting the living functions as akin to installing a machine in the home. Bachelard thought in terms of a poetic architecture: the home is an oyster and the people living in it slumbering pearls. And Deleuze opted for a nomadic way of thinking where homelessness is confirmed as a part of the freedom of longing. For Heidegger, living is the repose in the footsteps of the once — present gods and the withstanding of a namelessness which perhaps once again will bring man closer to being. Finally, uprooting and displacement are necessary conditions according to Deconstructivism. These conditions should be made visible through a planetary architecture.

It seems, therefore, that architecture is no longer a question of windows and walls, doors and thresholds, and that it is necessary to ask ourselves how architecture can contribute to the realization of a new balance between man and technology and how architecture can give shape and form to technology without sacrificing itself to it. Protecting people from technology will definitely become a task of architecture, as well as articulating the difference between the physical and the technical in an ergonomically responsible manner. Architecture will be responsible for preventing the physical aspect from being completely undermined and for creating an alternative in which the physical aspects of the human condition are done justice. However much telematics is on the move and however immaterial our lives may become, there will always be a physical dimension of the body with all its pains and pleasures. When I drink a glass of wine, what does the table on which I set the glass look like?

....

[5] Paul Virilio, **L'inertie polaire,** Paris, 1990.
[6] According to the recently published study by Arthur Koker, **The Possessed Individual. Technology and the French Postmodern,** New York, 1992.

Built Work

Beltgens Fashion Shop (013)
Maastricht, 1986/1987

This fashion shop for men, designed
as an exhibition space, is an architecture set within the structure of Maastricht, a city with Roman origins. It is
intended as a rather stark intervention, and is to be interpreted in this
context as a contrasting idea. The
space, governed by light, gives the
impression of having been specially
designed for what is being shown
there. The show window, entrance area,
and sales department connect the St.
Amorsplein with the inner courtyard,
while vertically, by way of the open
stairwell, the sales area is linked to the
three layers above it. The 1.70 m-high
wall containing stainless steel display
cases, and interrupted by three changing cubicles, accentuates the horizontal movement from the entrance to
the inner courtyard. Constructed of
corten steel, the facade is opened up
by a window and a door that measure
1.70 m and 3.40 m in height respectively.

The articulation of the interior
space follows the dictate of shaping
light for the purpose of displaying the
clothes and shop items. Within the
scale and modulation of the historic
center of the city, this shop explores
transparency, the direct relationship
between the public domain of the
street, the interior of the shop itself
and the courtyard. The logic of perception and display permeates the entire
design, its material definition, and its
relationship to the urban context.
A window is — both literally and
metaphorically — open at the heart
of Maastricht.

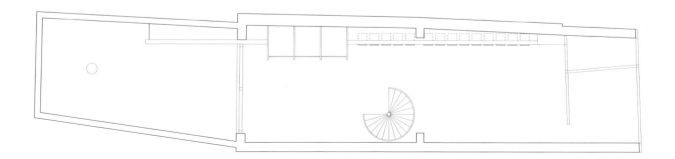

Academy for the Arts and Architecture [025]
Maastricht, 1989/1993

Conceived as an extension to the existing Rijkshogeschool, the Maastricht Academy for the Arts provides new spaces for the school of visual arts and architectural design. The building is an incision into the body of the city, an entirely new and foreign organism invading its urban context; a process akin to the operation of a virus. Yet it is set in a discreet, almost camouflaged relation to the city, providing an enclosed public space that achieves an intimate and secluded condition from the main areas of urban activity. The project includes the renewal of the existing Academy for the Arts, together with the extension effected by two buildings. Adjacent to the old building is the new structure that contains the auditorium, the library, an exhibition room, a bar and a roof garden. The connecting footbridge with translucent glass brick floor and ceiling leads one through the tree tops into the workshop building that accommodates wood and steel workshops. To follow Kenneth Frampton's interpretation, this element recalls the design of the Dessau Bauhaus, spanning between the two volumes of the workshop and the four-story public core.

To encourage a continuous dialogue, the design dwelt more on creating an environment that would be conducive to social interaction among the users of the building. This is effected through the circulation system which dominates the plan. There is only one entrance to the entire complex, and only one ramp leading into the newly constructed auditorium, library, and bar. The aerial bridge through the tree-tops is also the only linkage to the other part of the extension. The adjoining patio is designed as a sculpture garden. Both students and professors are made to walk along the same route through the different faculties: Architecture, Fashion, Painting and Sculpture. The entire complex becomes an environment for continuous communication between students and professors.

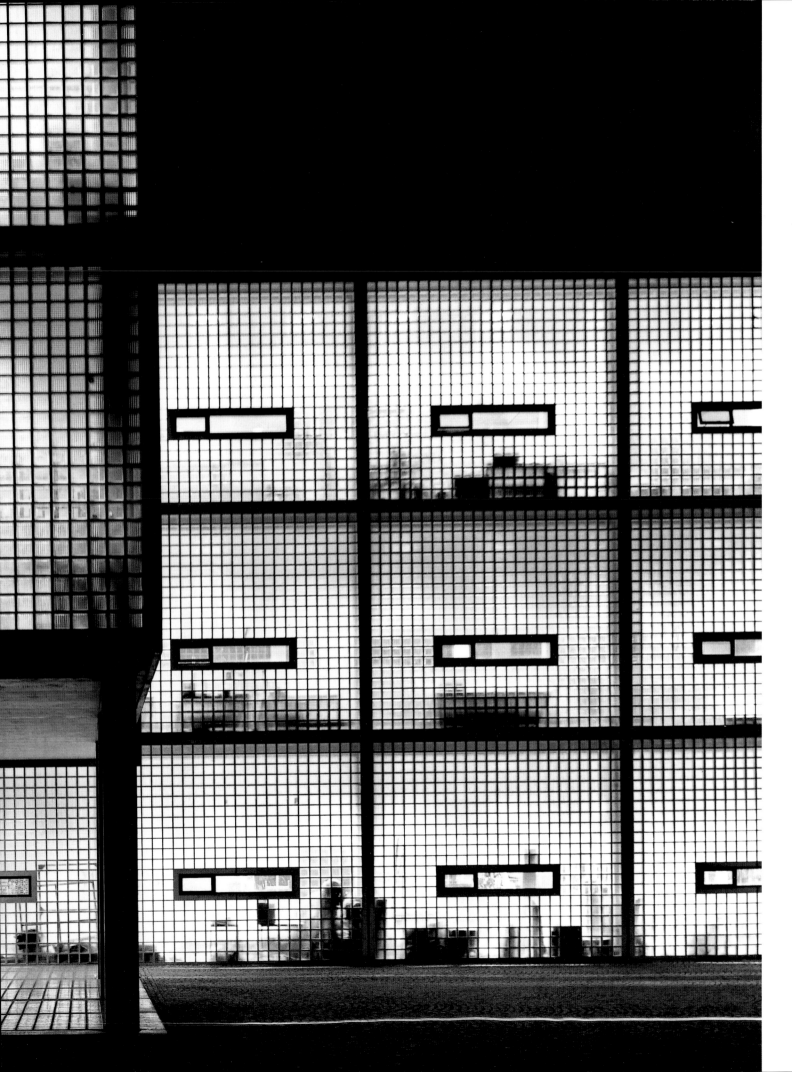

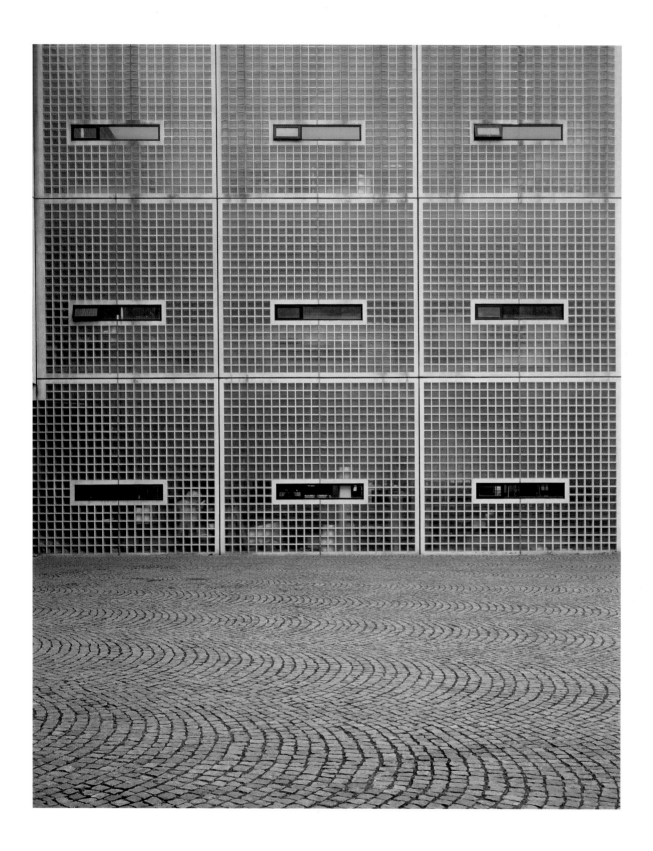

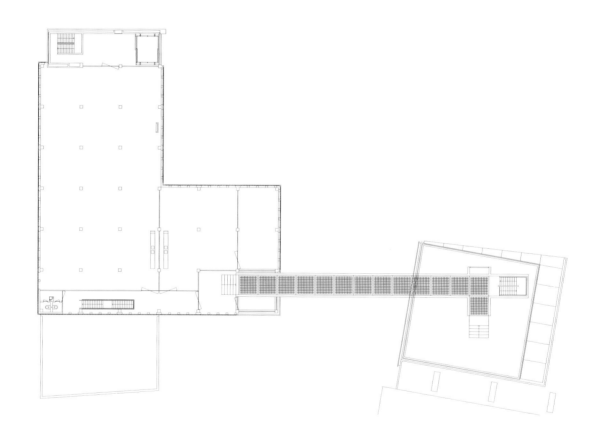

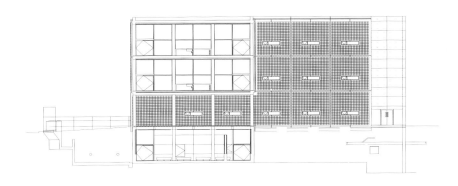

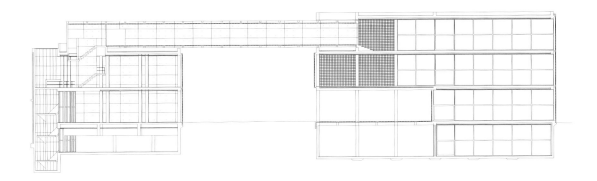

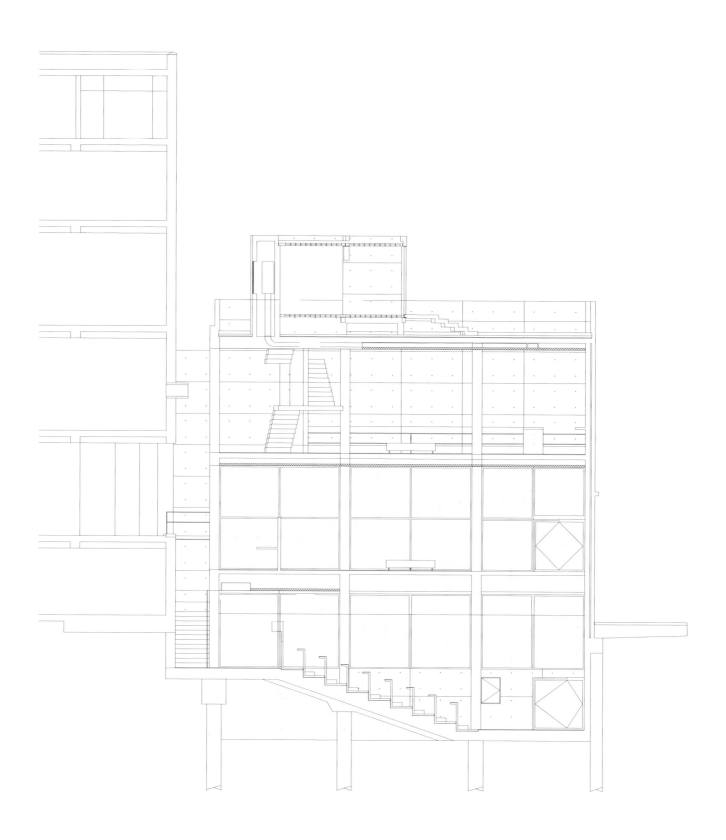

Apartment-Tower, KNSM-Island [(026)]
Amsterdam, 1990/1996

The design consists of four elements: four separate but closely grouped towers. The unit has twenty-one floors. Each floor contains five apartments. The tower block, standing on the island formerly occupied by the Royal Netherlands Steamboat Company, has a view of Amsterdam in one direction and of the waters of Ijsselmeer in the other.

The four elements comprising the tower block come into confrontation with the ground plane at different heights. Fluctuating in height with regard to the ground floor level, the elements are designed so as to create a skyline, as it were, at ground floor level. Views are afforded through the indoor car park from this level as well. The facade is made of a skin of concrete element poured into a rubber mould to create a "continuous" skin line appearance.

The colossal volumes of the tower complex become particularly striking through the solution of the towers' stylobate: the massive towers are suspended before touching the ground, in what Jos Bosman has perceptively termed as an "inverted skyline", so as to allow for a horizontal slice, a framed panoramic view of the Y of the river. The ground floor thus becomes an equivalent of the terrace. Such an interplay between different architectural components is also echoed in the pavement-like treatment of the vertical cladding.

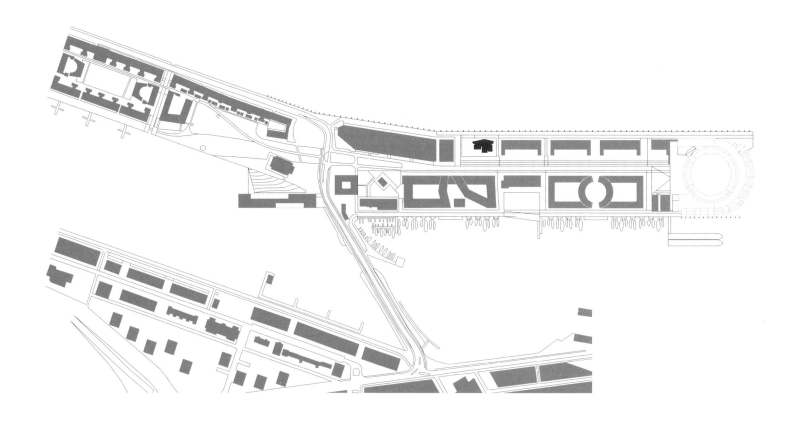

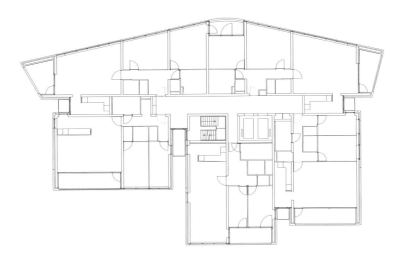

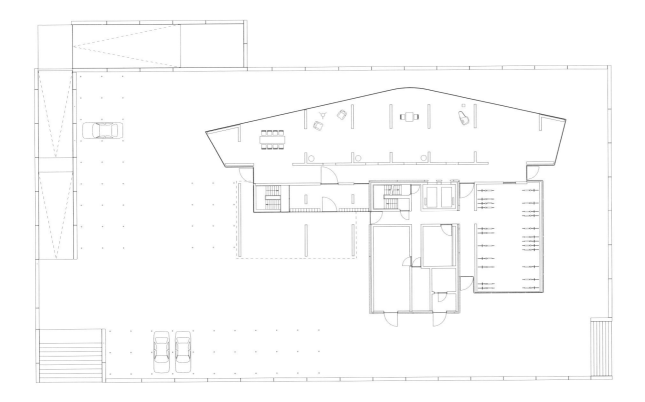

Headquarters AZL Pension Fund ⁽⁰²⁹⁾
Heerlen, 1991/1995

The AZL Beheer headquarters is an extension to an existing office building dating from the 1940s in the central area of Heerlen. This a project that investigates new conditions for working spaces, paying particular attention to visual relationships and to communal areas, in a design that manages to combine a sophisticated spatial articulation with a stark and restrained material definition that relies mostly on concrete, black steel, and black birchwood.

The site of the new building connects two different streets and it therefore has two different means of access. The program includes office space for 230 people, 23 private offices and a variety of open-plan and team office spaces, conference rooms, a restaurant, a car park and other areas related to the firm's work. The conceptual theme that governed the project's development was the idea of "grafting" or "plugging", the latter being a key component of the firm's activities, which become the direct conceptual route into the project's complex brief and site conditions. In effect, the new building components are literally plugged into the existing situation. The perpendicular extensions are attached to the rear side of the buildings and are inserted (plugged) into the existing units. Conversely, the traffic pattern is a reversal of the concept. The traffic is "unplugged" (from the street) and moves underground to be further hidden.

The major parts of the new facilities are housed in the elongated volume, made up of thin slab volumes clad in concrete and stainless steel. These slide upon each other and float above a large lineal space carved into the ground. The floating effect provides a perception of weightlessness, of defying gravity, and at the same time is an effective energy-saving double membrane. The hewn ground extends into the space left between the existing buildings, plugging the present condition into the newly created one. The carved volumes operate as a geometry-adjusting device, accommodating the entire complex to the subtle misalignment of the streets that define the AZL site.

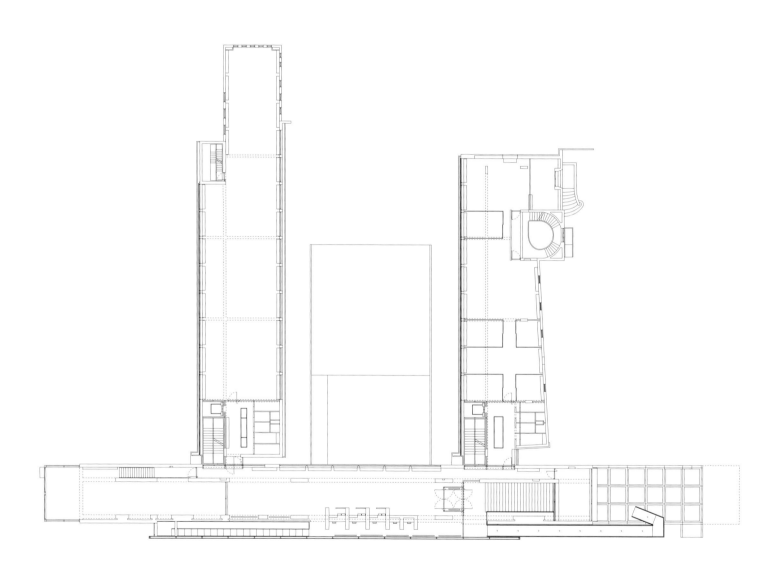

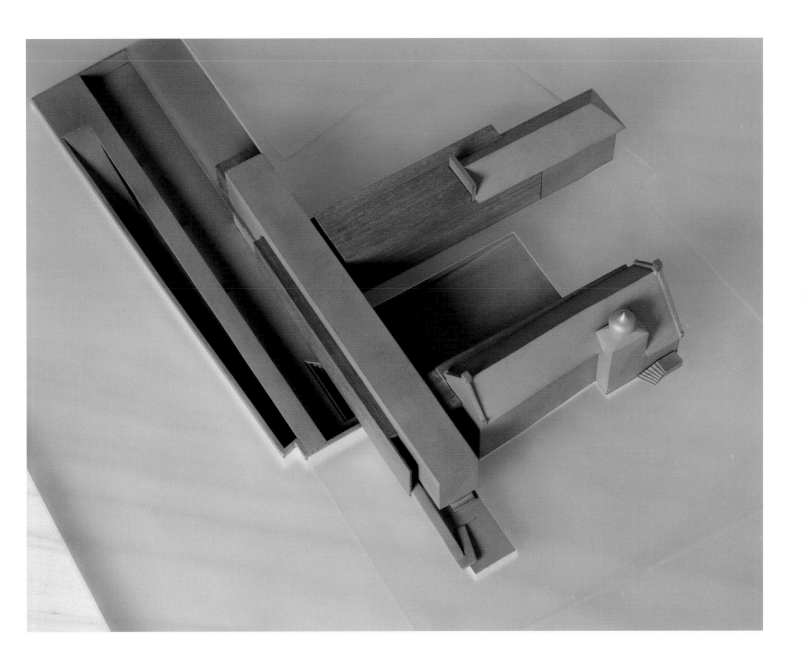

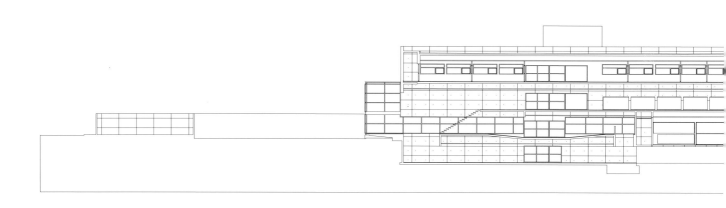

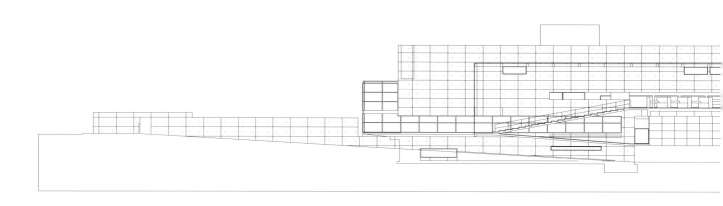

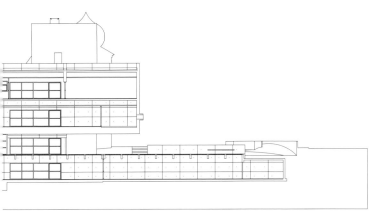

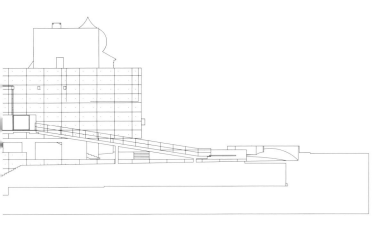

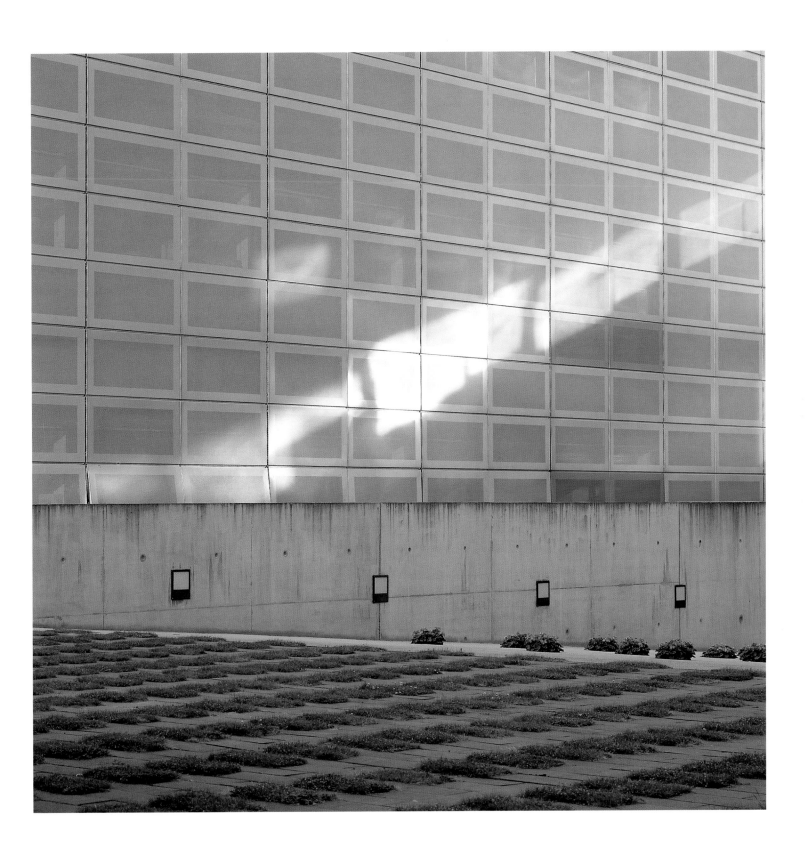

Police Station [041]
Vaals, 1993/1995

The Vaals Police Station is based on a reflection on the relationship between architecture and landscape, a trait common to a number of other works, and yet particularly central in the design of this building. The role of the landscape is present not only in the relationship between the building and the site topography, but also in the articulating presence of the ramps and other elements of mobility and access, and the construction of the visual directions as well. The Police Station seems therefore to be primarily structured according to a sequence of movements and views.

The design consciously stresses the ethereal character of the unit, discouraging the gap created between police officers and the public, and also bringing different materials side by side in complete harmony. The construction of the whole from the three connecting "boxes" is meant to strengthen the lightness of the building. The public pedestrian path that traverses the entire length of the complex leads passers-by out of the city but not without first drawing them closer to the kennels, the prison block, the reception and the entrance. Each of the three boxes that form the complex whole is constructed out of different materials: zinc, wood and concrete. The public path is linked to the zinc volume that houses the detention cells, the interrogation rooms and the police cap display room. The wooden structure not only links the two other structures together into a complex whole but also houses the administration and technical spaces. The concrete volume is designed to house the work and meeting areas of the police.

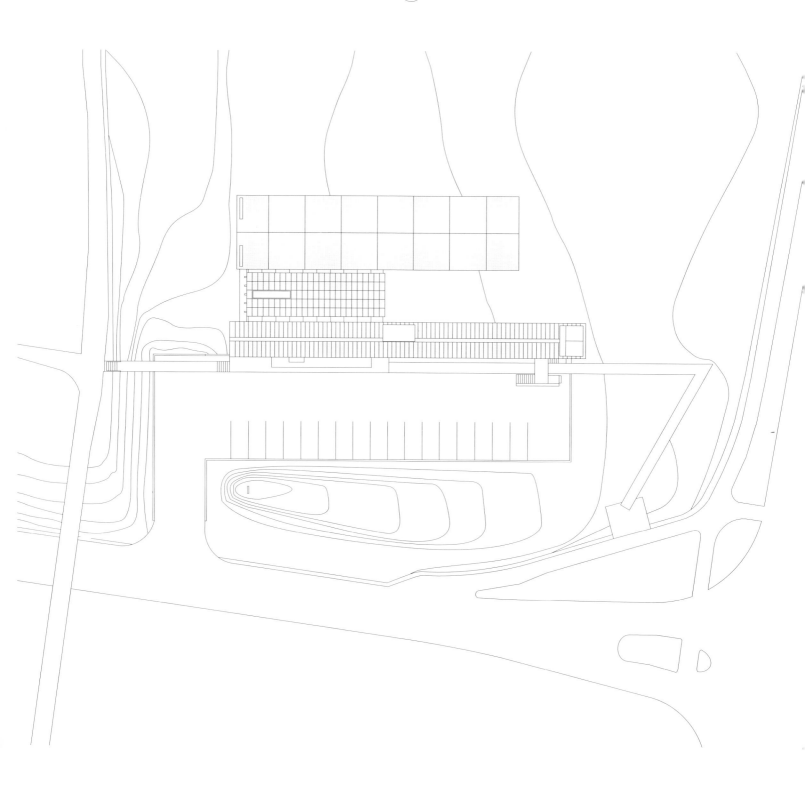

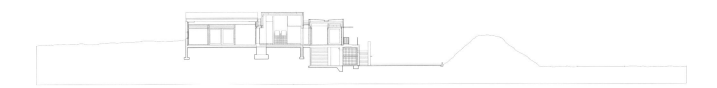

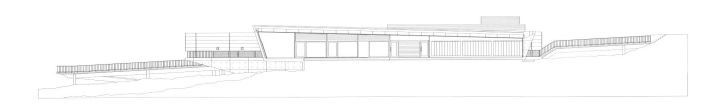

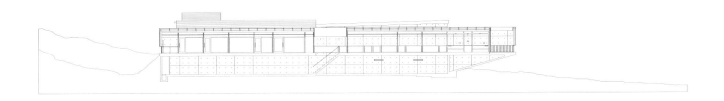

Arets-Sijstermans House/Studio [042]
Maastricht, 1993/1997

Set in an area of Maastricht dominated by villas and suburban houses, the Arets-Sijstermans House/Studio appears, when seen from a distance, as a rectangular wooden box implanted into the ground. It is the experience of its immediate surroundings and interior that unveils its complexity. The complex nature of the building is due to the architectural manipulation but within a host of restrictive laws imposed on constructional projects at the site. Its richness is brought to light by the complex arrangement of the terrain and the interior spaces.

The term "ground floor" is abstract in this design since half of the volume of the three floors is below the ground. In place of the ground level, it is appropriate to use the term "garden level." Thus, the levels include the top level, the garden level and the lower level. Not only is the building vertically divided by the technical spaces into house and studio, but horizontally it is also divided into two equal halves by the street level. The top floor contains the sleeping spaces of the villa and the architect's office, the administration space and the meeting hall of the studio. The living areas and the kitchen of the house, designed to capture the view of the garden, the swimming pool and the terrace, occupy half of the garden level floor.

The other half of the garden level contains the office space, which is connected to the walled court and the garden by the transparent glass facades. The distinct features of the walled court include its translucent glass brick floor that allows light into the lower level and its openness to fresh air and the surroundings while remaining enclosed. The lower level includes the workshop, the archive, the preparation areas and the drawing room lit by skylights through the translucent glass brick floor, as well as a children's playroom and sauna.

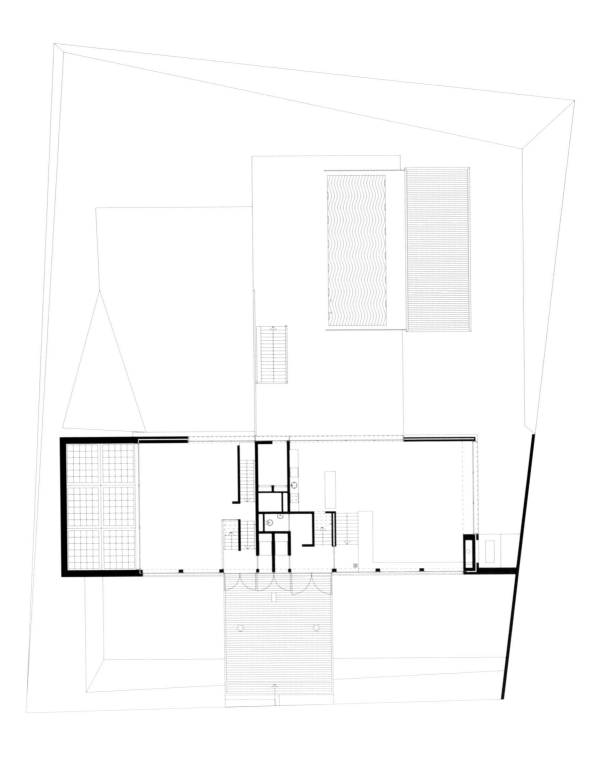

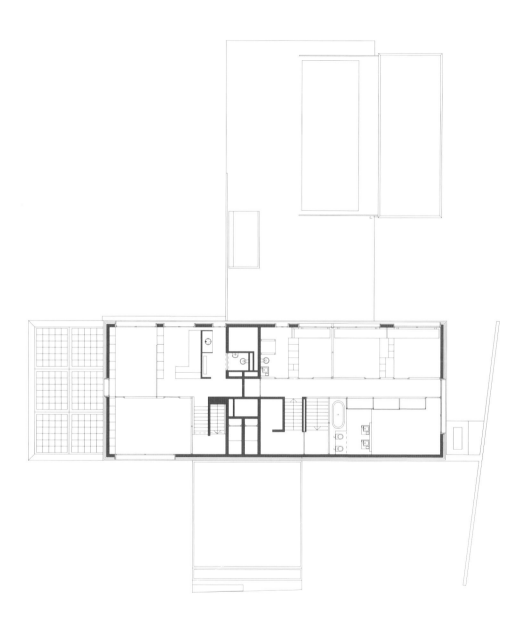

0 ___ 3 m

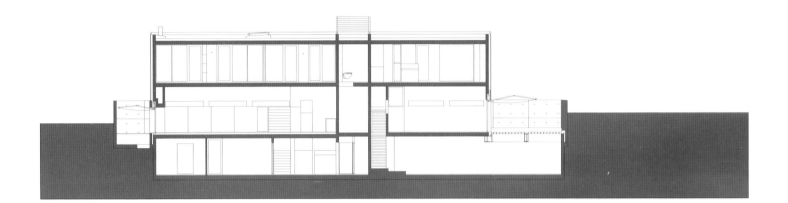

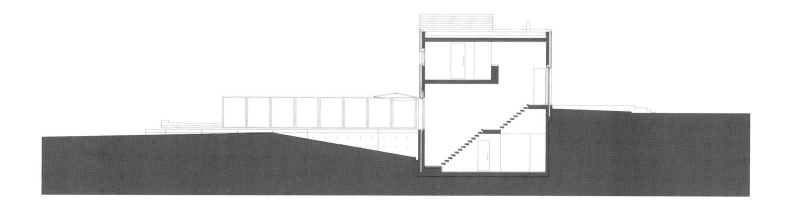

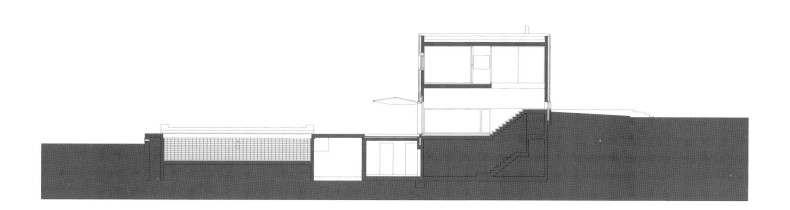

De Waag Pharmacy (044)
Breda, 1993/1994

The De Waag Pharmacy in Breda occupies a ground floor as a typical retail space. The relationship between the interior of the pharmacy and the exterior, urban space is defined by its facade, which is made of large, thick steel-framed glazed panels. The dominant role of transparency suggests an evident relationship with other retail outlets by Arets, such as the Maastricht fashion shop.

A brick pier lies behind the facade panels. The design of this pier introduces a sense of sliding mobility. In a text that builds on his studies on architectural transparency, Robert Slutzky has described the sequence of discovering the interior space of the pharmacy in this way: "To enter this chemist's is to submit to a ritualistic promenade, which culminates in being seated in one of five, webbed-steel chairs — certainly hygienic if not entirely comfortable — that face a metal service counter. The seats have their backs turned to the protective barrier of the glass wall, tenuously isolating them from the impurities of the urban environment. Those who are seated await the dispensation of curative medication calibrated and measured on the apothecary's scale, like architecture, a balancing beam symmetrically defining the twin conditions of ethos and pathos."

APOTHEEK   DE WAAG

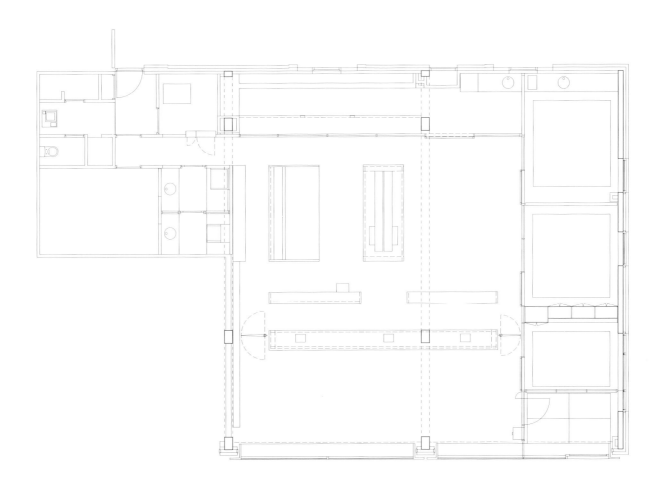

Police Station [045]
Boxtel, 1994/1997

The Boxtel building was commissioned by the Dutch regional police force and its design responds to the aim of the police to redefine their relationship with the general public and also within the police force through a process of "openness". This openness is sought at the institutional level, yet it is also to be represented in its new buildings. Such an objective requires architectural research into combining the needs of security with a design conveying this sense of permeability.

The Police Station is sculptured, enabling its users to traverse the building through a series of spatial thresholds creating a cinematic oscillation between the garden and the interior, between the served and serving spaces. Its form creates an ambiguity in scale which fluctuates between the industrial scale of its materials and the domestic scale found in the surrounding housing. A raised block creates an entrance void below allowing a momentary glimpse from the road and passing cars.

The building is enclosed in a homogenous skin of standardized, narrow, industrial profiled panels of matt, translucent glass connected to the main structure by an aluminum frame. Where required, differentiation is handled in a more subtle manipulation of the elements, producing the seemingly severe appearance of a gleaming, icy, alien body. In addition, the restrictive sun transmission regulations were reconciled with the skin by interpreting them as a percentage of the complete facade. This gave a freedom to manipulate the facade into a seemingly random arrangement of opaque, translucent and transparent areas depending on the functional requirements and the reconciliation of the conflict between openness and security.

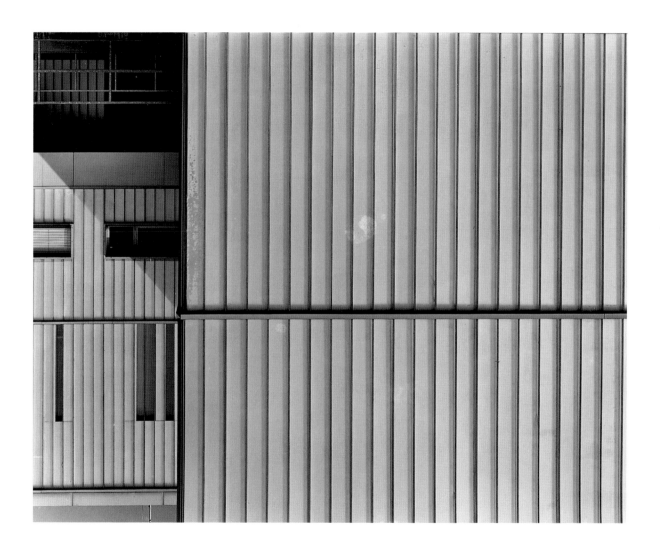

0 15 m

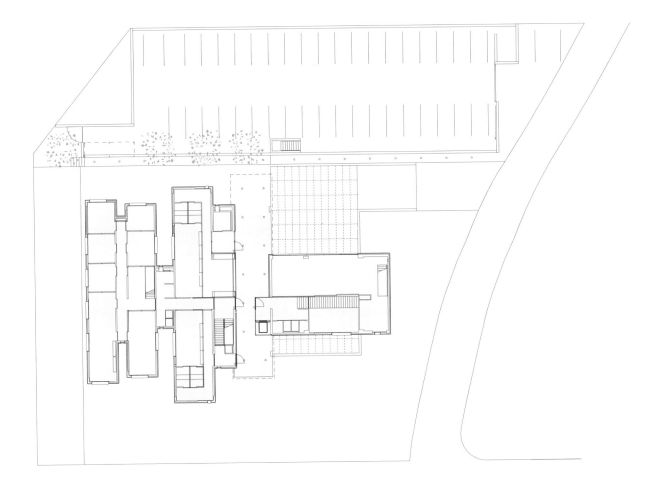

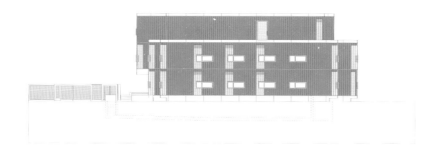

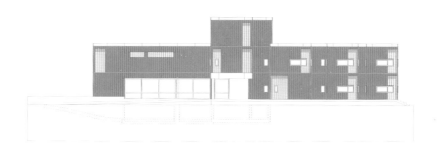

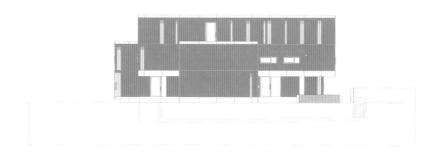

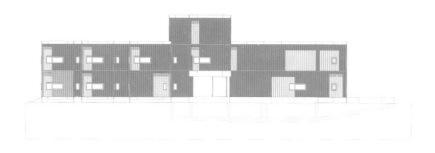

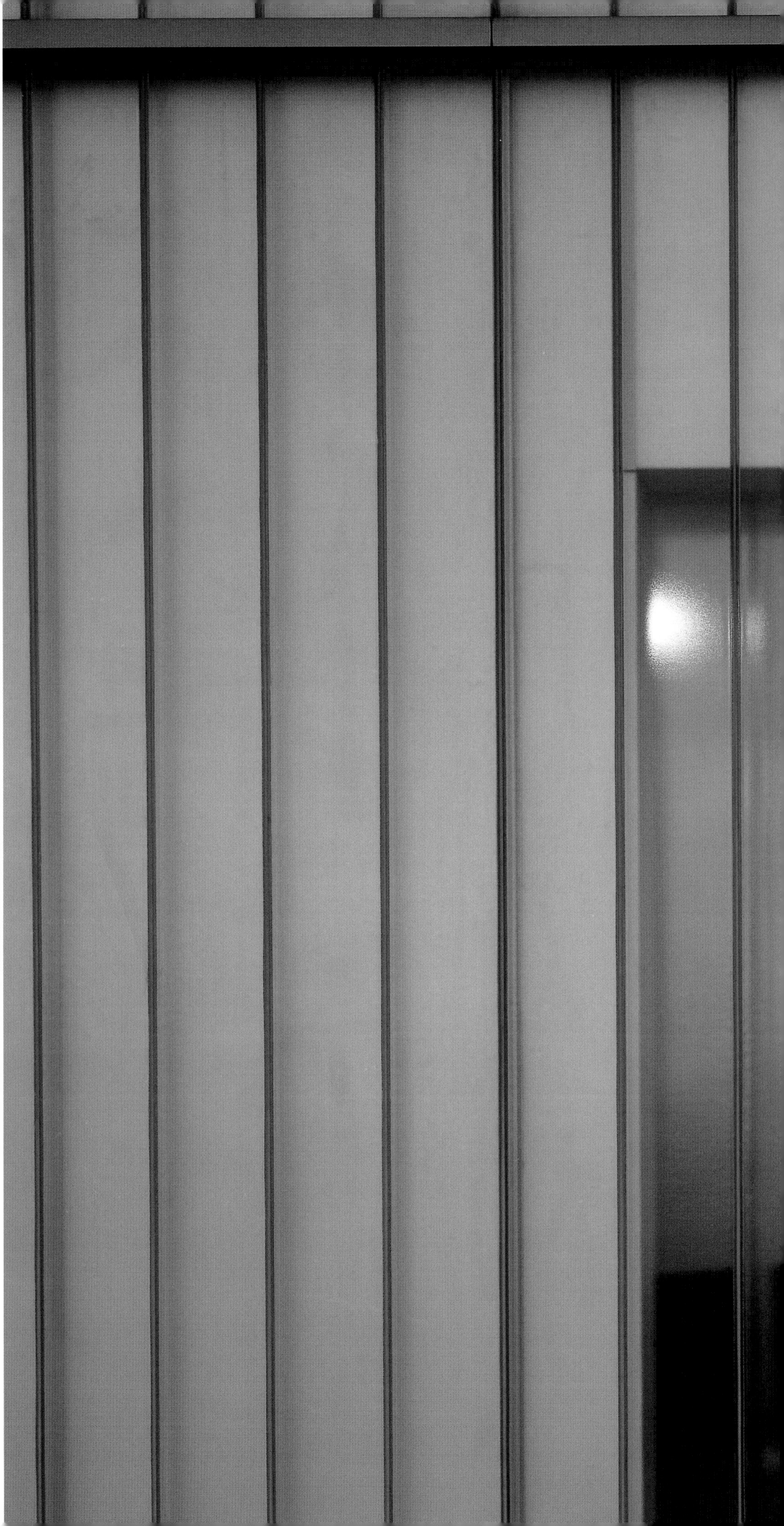

Headquarters Regional Police for South Limburg
Heerlen, 1994/1998

The police station is situated east of the Heerlen railway station and is split into two buildings that straddle both sides of the railway tracks. Occupying thin slices of marginalised land on each side, the building volumes are influenced by the contour of the street. The main District Police office building is entered via a ramp that follows the edge of the road to arrive under a central cantilevering volume. This building also contains the restaurant; a collective function that serves the whole complex. The design reflects the most recent developments in information technology and office management. This is achieved through the concept of the "Lean Office" which increases the efficiency of the organization and use of office space. In this concept, the employees no longer have their own office spaces, thereby eliminating redundant space vacated as a result of external meetings. This maximizes occupancy throughout the day and reduces floor area by as much as one third.

Small individual cells of 5.5 m^2 are used only for tasks requiring concentration, while a larger collective space is created for group tasks and communication. The ambition was to create a conglomeration of volumes where the railway is no longer seen as a barrier but acts as the dynamic part of the entire complex. The train is seen to move through the building. The connection between the buildings is physically made through the re-utilization of an existing pedestrian tunnel. The material treatment also unites the composition, where volumes of zinc protrude out of a "piano nobile" of in-situ concrete. Finally the buildings are marked by large openings at the entrance level, visually connecting the two streets, the buildings, and the passing trains, incorporating them into the urban conglomeration.

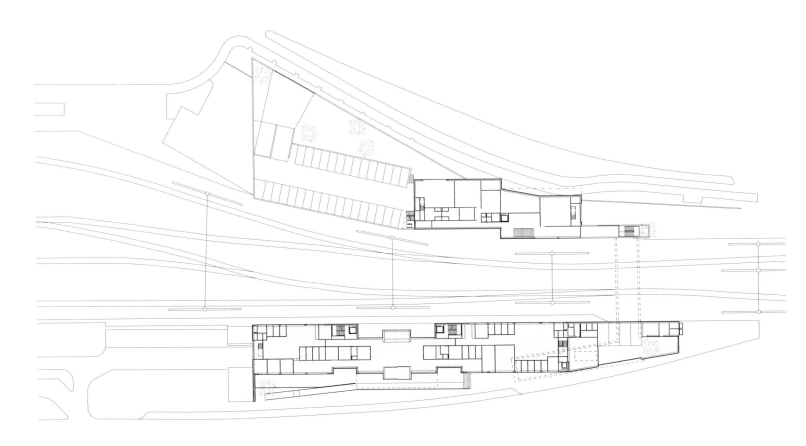

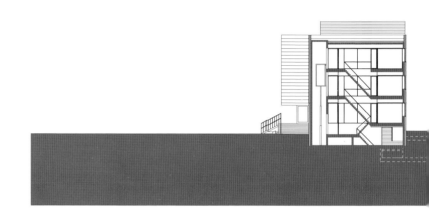

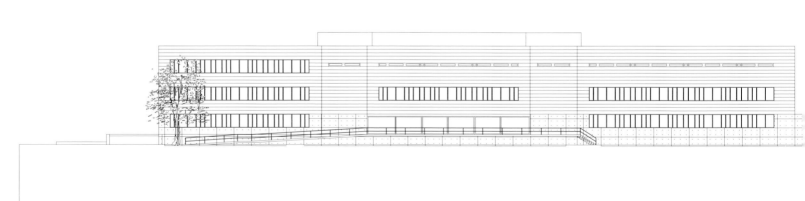

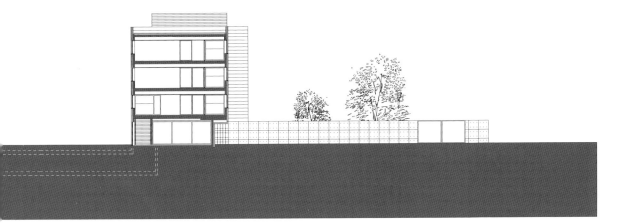

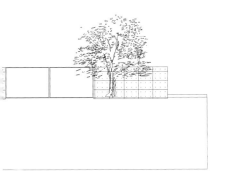

Lensvelt Offices and Factory Building
Breda, 1995/1999

The Lensvelt complex is designed for a furniture factory and its offices. It is located in a flat landscape facing a network of roads. The architecture responds to this stark, horizontal landscape with an equally taut volume that echoes the lines and flatness of its setting. Unlike most industrial architecture that tends to produce opaque containers, the Lensvelt complex develops a facade which, when lit from inside, becomes a screen offering a blurred view of its interior, a ghostly perception for those in passing vehicles who catch a brief glimpse of it. This spectacular effect is achieved through a facade built with translucent glass strips.

The West 8 landscape office was invited to collaborate in the entrance and interior gardens. Their work included the mound of jagged slates located in the interior courtyard, which is paved with wooden decking and includes a group of gingko trees. The landscaping project also includes a pair of ogive-shaped mounds and depressions in the parking area.

The complex that houses the offices and the factory is a longitudinal structure that has a north-south orientation. Protruding out from each side of this rectangular volume is a box-shaped structure that hovers above the ground. The eastern protruding box hangs 2.5 m high above a large entrance for pedestrians, whereas the western box which floats slightly above the ground serves as the main entrance into the interior of the building and contains the lobby overlooking the highway. The eastern facade of the building is incised with rectangular openings that serve as entrances for vehicles.

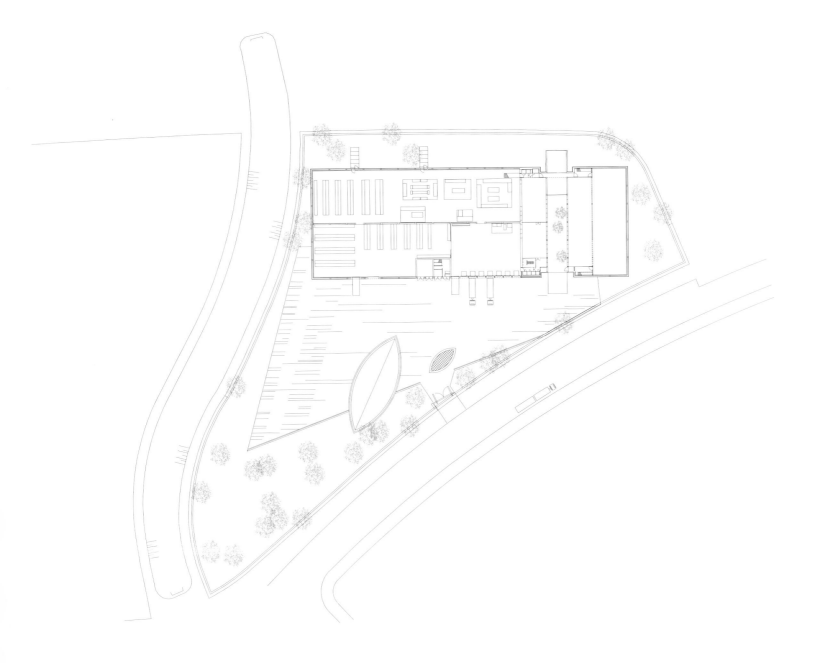

0   30 m

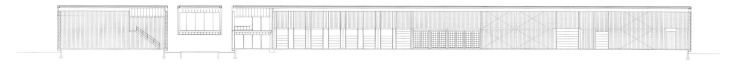

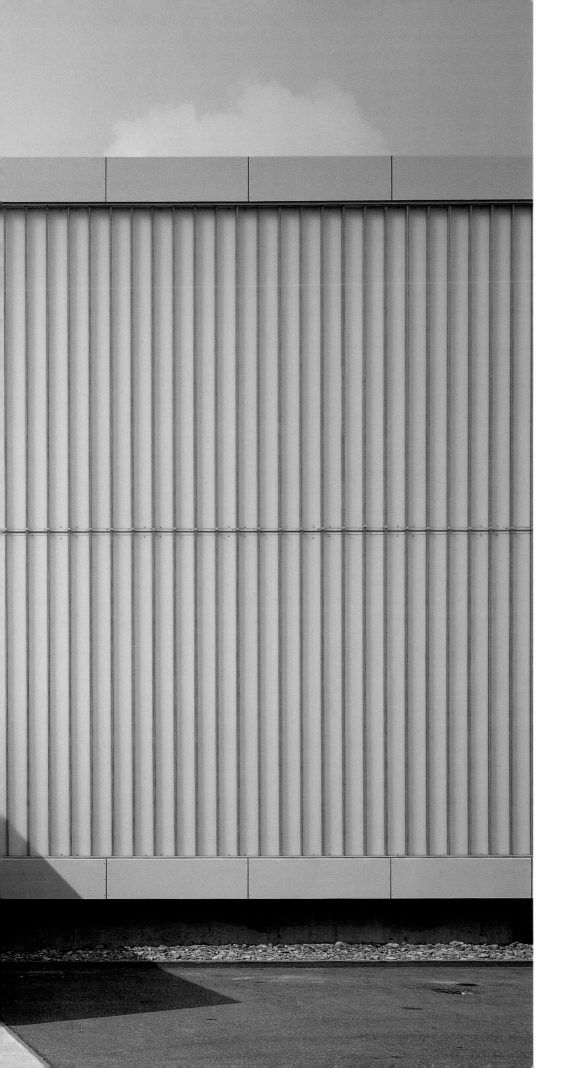

Villa Van Zanten (075)
Lisse, 1997/2000

The concept behind the "Body House" takes domestic space in a contemporary landscape beyond its suburban setting. The house achieves this aim by allowing a multiplicity of itineraries to permeate and characterize the villa, thus creating an ongoing relationship between the "bodies" of the house, and the "bodies" of its inhabitants.

Split into three volumes that occupy the middle of the site, the house reconfigures the terrain into two equal yet distinct gardens. One is located in a lower and flat setting, the other one is on a slope in relation to the street level. Wrapped around the circumference and the roof, a continuous envelope of glass allows the treatment of the material itself to modify the level of privacy, enclosure, use and movement. The two massive hovering zinc volumes bear down on the glass envelope. The private domain of the family occupies this level divided between the parents' and children's quarters.

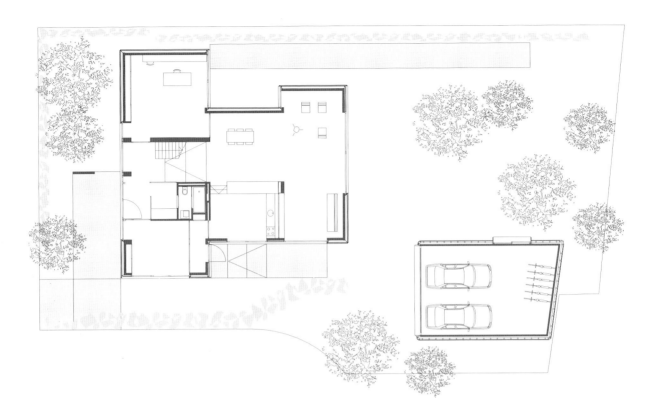

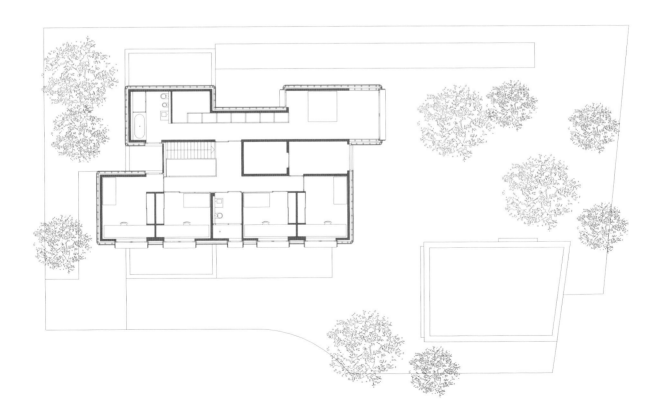

001 (000)

project: Housing Kruisplein (competition)
location: Kruisplein in Rotterdam, the Netherlands
project team: Wiel Arets, Wim van den Bergh, Bert ter Haar
date of design: 1982
models: Wiel Arets, Wim van den Bergh, Bert ter Haar
photographs: Wiel Arets, Wim van den Bergh, Bert ter Haar
client: DROS Huisvesting
program: housing for adolescents

bibliography
▸ W. Arets, B ter Haar en W. v.d. Bergh, "Leven en stad," **Plan** 13 (1982) 7/8, pp. 6–8.
▸ An., "Overzicht tekeningen Kruisplein," **Mededelingen Bouwkunde THE** (1982) 11, p. 6.

....

002 (002)

project: Dentists Practice
location: Burgemeester Joostenlaan in Roermond, the Netherlands
project team: Wiel Arets
date of design: 1983
date of completion: 1984
photographs: Wiel Arets
client: Mr. M. Willemsen
program: renovation dentists practice
building contractor: Smeets/Verhaegh
structural engineer: Jacobs bv

bibliography
▸ W. Arets, "Tandartsenpraktijk in Roermond," **Plan** (1984) 6/7, pp. 20–21.

....

003 (008)

project: House & Pharmacy Schoonbroodt
location: Rumpenerstraat 112 in Brunssum, the Netherlands
project team: Wiel Arets, Mathieu Bruls, Piet Grouls, J. Stoeldrager, Jeroen v.d. Ven
date of design: 1985
date of completion: 1989
photographs: Kim Zwarts
client: Mr. L. Schoonbroodt
program: single-family house and pharmacy
buiding contractor: Hub Keulers bv
building physics consultant: Cauberg-Huygen Raadgevende Ingenieurs bv
structural engineer: Jacobs bv

bibliography
▸ W. Arets, A. Vidler, **Wiel Arets, architect,** 010 Publishers, Rotterdam, 1989, pp. 30–35.
▸ M. Bock, **Wiel Arets, architect,** 010 Publishers, Rotterdam, 1998, pp. 26–31.

....

004 (009)

project: A Style for the Year 2001: 82 Glass Towerhouses for Tokyo Metropolis
location: harbor site in Tokyo, Japan
project team: Wiel Arets, Wim van den Bergh
date of design: 1985
models: Wiel Arets, Wim van den Bergh
photographs: Wiel Arets, Wim van den Bergh
client: Shinkenchiku-sha co.
program: apartments, shops, subway station, gardens, piers for boats, museum

bibliography
▸ T. Ishido, **A style for the Year 2001 [JA-A+U joint ed.],** Tokyo, 1985, pp. 56, 235.
▸ W. Arets, W. v.d. Bergh, "Tokyo style," **Wiederhall** (1986) 1, pp. 2–7.
▸ J. Meuwissen, "Urban blocks," **Wiederhall** (1986) 1, pp. 16–19.
▸ An., "A Wining Team," **Limburg International 7** (1986) 5, pp. 34–37.
▸ W. Arets, W. v.d. Bergh, "De architect als kolonist," **Het Bassin 2** (1987) 4, pp. 8–13.

....

005 (010)

project: Tower Villa Hotel: A Bulkwark of Resistance (competition)
location: site in the center of Moscow, Russia
project team: Wiel Arets, Wim van den Bergh
date of design: 1985
models: Wiel Arets, Wim van den Bergh
photographs: Wiel Arets, Wim van den Bergh
client: Shinkenchiku-sha co.
program: tower villa hotel for Russian dissidents

bibliography
▸ W. Arets, W.v.d. Bergh, "Moscow Resistance," **Wiederhall** (1986) 1, pp. 8–9.
▸ J. Meuwissen, "Urban blocks," **Wiederhall** (1986) 1, pp. 16–19.
▸ An., "A Wining Team," **Limburg International 7** (1986) 5, pp. 34–37.
▸ W. Arets, W.v.d. Bergh, "De architect als kolonist," **Het Bassin 2** (1987) 4, pp. 8–13.

....

006 (011)

project: Garden for Villa Farsetti: Progretto Venezia (competition)
location: Villa Farsetti, Veneto, Italy
project team: Wiel Arets, Wim van den Bergh
date of design: 1985
models: Wiel Arets, Wim van den Bergh
photographs: Wiel Arets, Wim van den Bergh
client: Biennale di Venezia
program: garden

bibliography
▸ An., "Villa Farsetti: Wiel Arets, Wim van den Burgh," in C. Pirovano, **Terza Mostra Internazionale di Architettura,** Venice, 1985, p. 145.
▸ Wiel Arets, Wim van den Burgh, "Veneto Narrative," **Wiederhall** (1986) 1, pp. 10–11.
▸ An., "A Winning Team," **Limburg International 7** (1986) 5, pp. 34–37.
▸ W. Arets, W. v.d. Bergh, "De architect als kolonist," **Het Bassin 2** (1987) 4, pp. 8–13.

....

007 (013)

project: Foreign Student Hotel: Je Vous Salue (competition)
location: site next to the Rijn-Schie canal in Delft, the Netherlands
project team: Wiel Arets, Wim van den Bergh
collaborator: Gonard Vleugels
date of design: 1985
models: Wiel Arets, Wim van den Bergh
photographs: Wiel Arets, Wim van den Bergh
client: City of Delft
program: hotel for foreign students

bibliography
▸ Wiel Arets, Wim van den Burgh, "Delft Fragment," **Wiederhall** (1986) 1, pp. 12–15.
▸ J. Meuwissen, "Urban blocks," **Wiederhall** (1986) 1, pp. 16–19.
▸ An., "A Wining Team," **Limburg International 7** (1986) 5, pp. 34–37.
▸ W. Arets, W. v.d. Bergh, "De architect als kolonist," **Het Bassin 2** (1987) 4, pp. 8–13.

....

008 (014)

project: Barbershop & Mayntz House
location: Heerlerbaan 179 in Heerlen, the Netherlands
project team: Wiel Arets
collaborators: Piet Grouls, Gonard Vleugels
date of design: 1986
date of completion: 1987
photographs: Kim Zwarts
client: Mrs. Marlies & Mr. W. Mayntz
program: barbershop and single-family house
area: 72 m^2
building contractor: Piet Jacobs bv
building physics consultant: Van Oosterhout

bibliography
▸ N. Bisscheroux et al., **Architektuurkaart van Heerlen,** Delft, 1987.
▸ W. Arets, A. Vidler, **Wiel Arets, architect,** 010 Publishers, Rotterdam, 1989, pp. 28–29.
▸ M. Bock, **Wiel Arets, architect,** 010 Publishers, Rotterdam, 1998, pp. 32–35.

....

009 (016)

project: Ca'Venier dei Leoni (competition)
location: Ca'Venier dei Leoni Peggy-Guggenheim Museum
on the Grand Canal in Venice, Italy
project team: Wiel Arets, Joost Meuwissen
collaborator: Gonard Vleugels
date of design: 1985
models: Wiel Arets, Joost Meuwissen
photographs: Wiel Arets, Joost Meuwissen
client: Biennale di Venezia
program: extention of the museum, apartments, small theater

bibliography
▸ An., "Ca'Venier dei Leoni: Wiel Arets, Joost Meuwissen," in C. Pirovano, **Terza Mostra Internazionale di Architettura,** Venice, 1985, p. 499.
▸ W. Arets, J. Meuwissen, "collector's," **Wiederhall** (1986) 2, pp. 30–35.

....

010 (020)

project: Albert & Bergsma Medical Center
location: Boshoverweg 90 in Weert-Boshoven, the Netherlands
project team: Wiel Arets
collaborator: Mathieu Bruls
date of design: 1987
date of completion: 1989
photographs: Kim Zwarts
clients: Mr. J.A.G. Albert & R. Bergsma
program: doctors practice and pharmacy
area: 100 m^2
building contractor: Hub Keulers bv
structural engineer: Van Oosterhout

bibliography
▸ H. Kerkdijk, "Een idee van zuivere architectuur," **Forum** 32 (1988) 02, pp. 42–47.
▸ M. Kloos, "Le goût des choses simples," **L'Architecture d'Aujourd'hui** (1988) 257, pp. 48–71.
▸ An., "Artsenpraktijk en apotheek," in H. v. Dijk (red.), **Jaarboek Architectuur in Nederland 1987/1988,** Deventer, 1988, p. 30.
▸ W. Arets, "Daglicht bepaalt architectuur," **Architectuur/Bouwen** 5 (1989) 2, pp. 24–25.
▸ W. Arets, A. Vidler, **Wiel Arets, architect,** 010 Publishers, Rotterdam, 1989, pp. 20–25.
▸ H. de Beer, "Autonomie en differentiatie. Contrasten tussen vijf praktijkruimten," **Architectuur/Bouwen** (1989) 2, pp. 28–29.
▸ E. Hubeli, "Architekt: Wiel Arets. Artzpraxis mit Apotheke in Weert-Boshoven, 1986–1987," **Werk, Bauen + Wohnen** (1990) 1/2, pp. 56–59.
▸ W. Arets, "Apotek og klinik," **Arkitektur B** (1991) 47/48, pp. 170–171.
▸ E. Schossig et al., **Arztpraxen,** Leinfelden-Echterdingen, 1995, pp. 150–151.
▸ M. Bock, **Wiel Arets, architect,** 010 Publishers, Rotterdam, 1998, pp. 36–41.

....

011 (026)
project: Mourmans House
location: Bessemerstraat in Lanaken, Belgium
project team: Wiel Arets, Max van Beers
collaborator: Gonard Vleugels
date of design: 1986
date of completion: 1987
client: Fam. Mourmans
program: renovation of house
structural engeneer: Jacobs bv

....

012 (028)
project: Sijstermans Pharmacy
location: Dr. v. Kleefstraat in Maastricht, the Netherlands
project team: Wiel Arets, Lars van Es, Maurice Paulussen
date of design: 1986
date of completion: 1987
photographs: Kim Zwarts
client: Mrs. A.W. Sijstermans
program: pharmacy and apartment
constructor: Hub Keulers bv
structural engeneer: Jacobs bv

bibliography
▸ W. Arets, A. Vidler, **Wiel Arets, architect,** Rotterdam, 1989, p 60.

....

013 (030)
p. 130   **project:** Beltgens Fashionshop
location: St. Amorsplein 14, square in the center of Maastricht, the Netherlands
project team: Wiel Arets
collaborators: Piet Grouls, Max van Beers
date of design: 1986
date of completion: 1987
photographs: Hélène Binet, Kim Zwarts
client: Mr. G. Beltgens
program: fashion shop for men clothes
area: 55 m^2
building contractor: Hub Keulers bv
structural engineer: Jacobs bv

bibliography
▸ W. Arets, "Cortenstalen gevel in historische omgeving," **Architectuur/Bouwen** 3 (1987) 1, pp. 26–27.
▸ W. Arets, "Idea. Fashionshop For Men," **Wiederhall** (1987) 5, pp. 2–3.
▸ An., "Ontwerpersprofiel," **Eigen huis & interieur** (1989) 10, p. 127.
▸ W. Arets, A. Vidler, **Wiel Arets, architect,** 010 Publishers, Rotterdam, 1989, pp. 54–57.
▸ W. Arets, "Maastricht Fashion Shop," **A+U** (1994) 02, no. 281, pp. 126–131.
▸ M. Bock, **Wiel Arets, architect,** 010 Publishers, Rotterdam, 1998, pp. 42–45.

....

014 (032)
project: Lamens Pharmacy
location: Oranjeplein 245 in Weert/Keent-Moesel, the Netherlands
project team: Wiel Arets
collaborator: Mathieu Bruls
date of design: 1986
date of completion: 1987
photographs: Kim Zwarts
client: Mr. F. v. Looy
program: pharmacy
building contractor: H. Keulers bv
structural engineer: Van Oosterhout

bibliography
▸ W. Arets, A. Vidler, **Wiel Arets, architect,** 010 Publishers, Rotterdam, 1989, pp. 38–43.
▸ M. Bock, **Wiel Arets, architect,** 010 Publishers, Rotterdam, 1998, pp. 46–51.
▸ S. Damaschke, B. Scheffer, **Apotheken: Planen, Gestalten und Einrichten,** Leinfelden-Echterdingen, 2000, pp. 136–137.

....

015 (039)
project: Columbusworld, a timemachine
location: Lisbon, Portugal
project team: Wiel Arets, Wim v.d. Bergh
date of design: 1988
models: Wiel Arets, Wim v.d. Bergh
client: Mr. J. Perestrella
program: international resort / theme park

bibliography
▸ An., "Architecten" in S. Ex (red.), **Stipendia '85–'86,** Amsterdam, 1987, pp. 96–97. (catalogue)
▸ W. Arets, W. v.d. Bergh, "Columbusworld: een tijdmachine," **Forum** 32 (1988) 03, pp. 42–45.
▸ J. Rodermond, "Biennale jonge Nederlandse architecten 1987," **de Architect** 19 (1988) 1, pp. 24–31.
▸ W. Arets, W. v.d. Bergh, "Colombusworld," **Wiederhall** (1989) 9, pp. 22–25.

....

016 (043)
project: Ofi-Sportcenter
location: Heraklion on the island of Crete, Greece
project team: Wiel Arets, Wim v.d. Bergh
date of design: 1988
models: Wiel Arets, Wim v.d. Bergh
photograph: Helfering
client: OFI Football club
program: sports grounds, sports-hotel, home for complex keeper, gardens

bibliography
▸ W. Arets, W. v.d. Bergh, "OFI-sportscenter: een competitie-machine," **Forum** 32 (1988) 03, pp. 46–49.

....

017 (044)
project: Villa Romanoff
location: Key West, Miami, United States of America
project team: Wiel Arets, Wendy Bakker, Isabel Martinez Stolche
date of design: 1987
clients: C. Romanoff and C. King
program: house

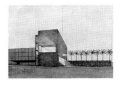

bibliography
▸ W. Arets, A. Vidler, **Wiel Arets, architect,** 010 Publishers, Rotterdam, 1989, pp. 26–27.

....

018/019 (045/046)
project: Vissers Medical Center & House
location: street corner Oude Provincialeweg and Lindenstraat in Hapert, the Netherlands
project team: Wiel Arets, Annette Marx, Jeroen v.d. Ven
furniture design: Wiel Arets
date of design: 1987
date of completion: 1990
photographs: Kim Zwarts
client: Mr. J. Vissers
program: home, medical center, dental practice, pharmacy, midwife-center
area: 2,000 m^2
building contractor: Boerenkamp bv;
structural consultant: Jacobs bv, Maastricht

bibliography
▸ W. Arets, A. Vidler, **Wiel Arets, architect,** 010 Publishers, Rotterdam, 1989, pp. 46–51.
▸ E. Mik, "Tot achter de oren gewassen architectuur," **de Volkskrant,** 22 June 1990.
▸ A. Vidler, "Wiel Arets. Centro medico e casa d'abtazione, Hapert/Olanda," **Domus** (1990) 715 [Apr.], pp. 38–45.
▸ B. Lootsma en M. v. Stralen, "Ingewikkelde eenvoud," in R. Brouwers (hoofdred.), **Jaarboek Architectuur in Nederland 1989/1990,** Deventer, 1990, pp. 34-37.
▸ An., "Wiel Arets," in R. Brouwers (red.), **Modernisme zonder dogma,** Rotterdam, 1991, pp. 11–13. [Eng. Transl.: Modernism without dogma].
▸ W. Arets, "Hapert Medical Center and House," **A+U** (1994) 02, no. 281, pp. 132–137.
▸ M. Bock, **Wiel Arets, architect,** 010 Publishers, Rotterdam, 1998, pp. 52–57.

....

020 (048)
project: Penthouse King
location: Miami, United States of America
project team: Wiel Arets,
collaborator: Jeroen v.d. Ven
date of design: 1988
date of completion: 1989
models: Lars van Es
clients: C. Romanoff and C. King
program: penthouse renovation

bibliography
▸ W. Arets, A. Vidler, **Wiel Arets, architect,** 010 Publishers, Rotterdam, 1989, pp. 52–53.

....

021 (050)
project: Air-Festival, Tracé Spoortunnel
location: Railway track Binnenrolte till Hefbrug Rotterdam, the Netherlands
project team: Wiel Arets, Wim v.d. Bergh
collaborators: Wendy Bakker, Jo Janssen
date of design: 1988
models: Wim v.d. Bergh
client: OBR
program: offices, housing, theater, parking, swimming pool

bibliography
▸ W. Arets en W. v.d. Bergh, "City in Noord: Translucent City," in A.M. Devolder, **Tracé Spoortunnel: negen concepten,** Rotterdam, 1988, pp. 52–57.
▸ W. Arets, A. Vidler, **Wiel Arets, architect,** Rotterdam 1989, pp. 36–37.
▸ M. C. Loriers, "Appel d'air pour un tunnel: consultation de concepteurs à Rotterdam," **Techniques & Architecture,** (1989) 382, pp. 98–101.
▸ H. Kerkdijk en T. Goossens, "Keerpunt / Turning point," **Forum** 33 (1990) 4, pp. 29–35.
▸ A. Devolder, "The city as a stage. Architectural initiatives in Rotterdam," in G. Hansen, H. Welling (red.), **Holland. Moderne arkitektur,** Arhus, 1991, pp. 78–86.

....

022 (051)
project: Jan van Eyck Academy
location: Academieplein in Maastricht, the Netherlands
project team: Wiel Arets, Wim v.d. Bergh
collaborators: Wendy Bakker, Jo Janssen
date of design: 1988
models: Math Cortlever
photographs: Frank van Helferen, Kim Zwarts
client: Mr. William Greelfma, director Jan van Eyck Academy
program: Jan van Eyck Academy

bibliography
▸ W.P.A.R.S Graatsma, **Macchina Arte,** Maastricht, 1992.
▸ H. Ibelings, "Inhoud als ornament. Ontwerp Arets & Van den Bergh voor Jan van Eyck Academie Maastricht," **Archis** (1989) 11, pp. 6–7.
▸ An., "Wiel Arets," in R. Brouwers (red.), **Modernisme zonder dogma,** Rotterdam, 1991, pp. 11–13 [Engl.transl.: Modernism without Dogma].

....

023 (058)

project: Jürgens House
location: Spaanshof in Ransdaal, the Netherlands
architect: Wiel Arets, Wim v.d. Bergh
project team: Wiel Arets, Wim v.d. Bergh
date of design: 1990
date of completion: 1991
models: Lars van Es
photographs: Kim Zwarts
client: family J. Jürgens
program: single-family house
area: building area 130 m^2
contractor: Eusen bv
structural consultant: Jacobs bv

....

024 (059)

project: Study for Boulevard Development
location: dune between the village of Domburg and the North-Sea, the Netherlands
project team: Wiel Arets, Charlotte Greub
collaborators: Paul Draaijer, Lars van Es, René Holten, Maurice Paulussen
date of design: 1990
models: Charlotte Greub
photographs: J. Derwig, Kim Zwarts
client: Cultural Department Zeeland
program: beach boulevard for the village of Domburg
area: building area 113,000 m^2

bibliography
▸ D. Camp, "Ontwerpen tussen droom en daad," **de Architect** 21 (1990) 11, pp. 44–47.
▸ A. Wortmann, "De architect als joker. Tentoonstelling in Domburg," **Archis** (1990) 9, pp. 4–5.
▸ W. Arets, "Transition. Beyond the cult of Imagery," **Wiederhal** (1993) 13, pp. 12–15.
▸ J. Meuwissen, "Pier and ocean," **Wiederhall** (1993) 13, pp. 21–33.
▸ W. Arets, "Domburg Boulevard," **A+U** (1994) 02, no. 281, pp. 110–113.
▸ An., "Boulevard Domburg / Domburg boulevard," **ViA arquitectura** (1997) 01.V–2, pp. 92–97.

....

025 (060)

p. 138 **project:** Academy for the Arts and Architecture
location: Herdenkingsplein 12, a square in de center of Maastricht, the Netherlands
project team: Wiel Arets, Jo Janssen
collaborators: Lars van Es, Anita Morandini, René Holten, Maurice Paulussen
date of design: 1989
date of completion: 1993
models: Paulus Egers
photographs: Kim Zwarts, Hélène Binet
client: Rijkshogeschool Maastricht
program: renovation and extension of the existing Academy for the Arts and Architecture
with studios and general facilities
area: building area 1,300 m^2; room area 4,000 m^2; circulation area 550 m^2
structural consultant: Grabowsky & Poort engineers
lightning consultant: Ir. F.M.J.L. van de Wetering
contractor: Laudy Bouw & Planontwikkeling bv

bibliography
▸ An., "Treffpunkt Weg/Meeting-point On-the-way," **Daidalos** (1993) 47 [15 March], pp. 36–39.
▸ C. Boekraad, "Consequentie tot het uiterste," **Architectuur/Bouwen** 9 (1993) 8, pp. 6–7.
▸ R. v. Toorn, "Leven in architectonische rituelen," **Archis** (1993) 11, pp. 17–27.
▸ B. Lootsma, "Bouwen aan cultuur," **de Architect** (1993) 11, pp. 30–51.
▸ M. Dubois, "Accademia delli Arti e dell'Architettura a Maastricht, Olanda / Academy of Arts and Architecture in Maastricht," Holland, **Domus** (1994) 757 [Feb.], pp. 23–29.
▸ G. A. Joas, "Ein raster für die Kunst," **Bauwelt** 85 (1994) 15 [15 Apr.], pp. 820–827.
▸ An., "Wiel Arets; académie des arts et de l'architecture, Maastricht," **L'Architecture d'Aujourd'hui** (1994) 293, pp. 52–57.
▸ An., "Academie van Beeldende Kunsten," in R. Brouwers (hoofdred.), **Jaarboek Architectuur in Nederland 1993/1994,** Rotterdam, 1994, pp. 28–33.
▸ R. Ryan, "Maastricht's School of hard Edges," **Blueprint** (1994) 110 [Sept.], pp. 42–43.
▸ W. Arets, "Expresión concentrada," **Arquitectura Viva** (1994) 38 [Sept.–Oct.], pp. 62–67.
▸ J. H. Kohne, "Abstractie als bron van inspanning," **Cement** 46 (1994) 2 [themanr.: Bedrijfsvloeren van beton], pp. 42–49.
▸ M. Canonico, "Academy of Fine Arts," **Controspazio** 2, pp. 62–67.
▸ W. Arets, "Maastricht Academy for the Arts and Architecture," **A+U** (1994) 02, no. 281, pp. 44–77.
▸ H. Hertzberger, "Académie Beeldende Kunsten, Maastricht," in S. Lebesque, **Voor Hedy d'Ancona, Minister van Cultuur 1989–1994,** Amsterdam, 1994, pp. 26–27.
▸ An., "Wiel Arets. Académie des arts et de l'architecture, Maastricht," **L'Architecture d'Aujourd'hui** (1994) 293, pp. 52–57.
▸ W. Arets, "Architectuur zonder verhaal," in Gemeente Maastricht, **Herdenkingsplein Maastricht,** Maastricht s.a. [map met projectbeschrijving n.a.v. de opening in 1994].
▸ D. Gray, "Maastricht. Academy for the Arts and Architecture," in **Mies van der Rohe Pavilion Award for European Architecture 1994,** s.l. 1995, pp. 12–23.
▸ W. Arets, G. Lynn, **Maastricht Academy for the Arts and Architecture,** Rotterdam, 1994.
▸ An., "Modern Departures," **P/A (Progressive Architecture)** (1995) June, pp. 96–105.
▸ K. Frampton, "Intentions in Architecture: An Appraisal of the 1994 Award," in H. Hortet, **Europäische Architektur/European Architecture 1984–1994,** s.l./s.a. [catalogue].
▸ R. Ryan, "Plastic Arts," **The Architectural Review** (1995) 1183 [Sept. 9], pp. 48–52.
▸ W. Arets, "Transluzid," **Werk, Bauen + Wohnen** (1995) 11, pp. 60–61.
▸ A. Lapuzina, "Academy Maastricht & AZL Pensionfund Heerlen," **Projeto** (1995) 192, pp. 32–40.
▸ An., "Wiel Arets. Uitbreiding Kunstacademie Maastricht," **Bouwen met Beton** 1995, pp. 12–23.
▸ An., "Selearchitettura," **Architettura** (1995) 472, pp. 122–123
▸ R. Miyake, S. Muramatsu, M. Fuchigami, **581 Architects in the World,** Tokyo, 1995, p. 111.
▸ An., "W. Arets: Erweiterung der Kunstakademie in Maastricht," **Bauen in Beton** 1995, pp. 12–23.
▸ Betonvereniging, **Betonprijs 1995,** Delft 1995, pp. 12–13
▸ W. Arets, "Stadtarchitektur II: Maastricht," in U. Schwarz, **Risiko Stadt: Perspektiven der Urbanität,** Hamburg, 1995, pp. 126–137.
▸ S. Allen, "Wiel Arets; Accademia delle Arti e dell'Architettura a Maastricht," **Archint, Architettura Intersezioni** (1996) 3, pp. 12–17.
▸ An., "Kunstakademie / Academy of Arts in Maastricht," **Detail** (1996) 4, pp. 548–552.
▸ M. Santacesaria, "The new Building for the Academy of Arts and Architecture in Maastricht, the Netherlands," **L'Industria italiana del Cemento** (1997) 725 [Oct.], pp. 732–743.
▸ R. C. Levene, F. Márquez Cecilia (red.), "Wiel Arets 1993–1997," **El Croquis** (1997) 85, pp. 44–61.
▸ Gemeente Maastricht, **De keuze voor kwaliteit; Nota architectuur-, monumenten- en welstandsbeleid,** Maastricht, 1998, pp. 17, 20–21, 38–39.
▸ F. Migsch, "Academy of Fine Arts, Maastricht," in K. Battista en F. Migsch, **The Netherlands; a guide to recent architecture,** London, 1998, pp. 210–213.
▸ M. Bock, **Wiel Arets, architect,** 010 Rotterdam 1998, pp. 58–71.
▸ H. Hertzberger, "Academie van Beeldende Kunsten en Academie van Bouwkunst, Maastricht," in H. Hertzberger, **De ruimte van de architect. Lessen in architectuur 2,** Rotterdam, 1999, p. 189.
▸ W. Arets, K. Frampton, R. v. Toorn, "Wiel Arets," **Context 3** (1999) 04, pp. 144–167.
▸ F. Kaltenbach, "Über den Dächern von…- Wiel Arets über sein Konzept der Stadt / On the roofs of…- Wiel Arets on his Concept for the City," **Detail** (2000) 5, pp. 806–810.
▸ H. Ibelings, F. Strauven, **Hedendaagse architecten in Nederland en Vlaanderen,** Rekkem, 2000, pp. 50–55.

▸ B. Lootsma, **SuperDutch: De tweede moderiteit van de Nederlandse architectuur,** Nijmegen, 2000, pp. 26–49.
▸ F. Nicotra, "Wiel Arets. Academy for the Arts and Architecture," **Materia** (2001) 34, pp. 60–71.
▸ A. Ilonen, "Alankomaiden wosituhannan askkistehtuwia," **Betonin** (1993) 3, pp. 36–41.
▸ An., "Academie van Beeldende Kunst, Maastricht," in M. Eckhort et al., Plandocumentatic productie + Vitvoering, Delft, 2000, pp. 48–53.

....

026 (061)

p. 158   **project:** Apartment-Tower KNSM-Island
       location: KNSM-Island, eastern harbor area of Amsterdam, the Netherlands
       project team: Wiel Arets, Elmar Kleuters, Paul Kuitenbrouwer, René Thijssen
       collaborators: Anca Arenz, Ivo Daniëls, Jo Janssen, Maurice Paulussen, Henrik Vuust
       date of design: 1990
       date of completion: 1996
       models: Paul Egers
       photographs: Hélène Binet, Kim Zwarts
       client: Wilma Bouw bv Amsterdam
       program: 100 apartments, lobby, parking garage
       area: building area 2,100 m^2; room area 650 m^2 (each apartment level)
       building physics consultant: Cauberg & Huijgen Raadgevende Ingenieurs bv
       building contractor: Wilma Bouw, Amsterdam
       prefab concrete façade: Loveld, Aalter (Belgium)

bibliography
▸ T. Dijkstra, "KNSM: un nuovo quartiere per il porto di Amsterdam," **Casabella** (1994) 616 [Oct.], pp. 6–19.
▸ W. Arets, "Amsterdam Residential Tower Block," **A+U** (1994) 02, no. 281, pp. 118–121.
▸ M. Kloos en B. de Maar, "The hesitant high-rise of Amsterdam," in M. Kloos (red.), **Amsterdam's High-Rise,** Amsterdam, 1995, pp. 62, 80–81.
▸ O. Koekebakker, "Adelaarsnesten: de opmars van de woontoren," **Items** 14 (1995) 3, pp. 26–32.
▸ J. Bosman, "Tower and Block," **Wiederhall** (1995) 18, pp. 34–37.
▸ H. Ibelings, "Woontorens: zicht op uitkijk," in A. Oosterman, **Woningbouw in Nederland / Housing in the Netherlands,** Rotterdam, 1996, pp. 42–47.
▸ J. Bosman, "Die Tektonik der Landschaft und der neue Wiel Arets," **Werk, Bauen + Wohnen** (1996) 4 [April], p. 62.
▸ An., "Geënsceneerde massa ontkend, KNSM Toren," **de Architect** (1996) 27, pp. 80–83.
▸ An., "Torre de apartementos / Apartment tower," **Quaderns** (1997) 214 [2 Forum International], pp. 92–97.
▸ R. C. Levene, F. Márquez Cecilia (red.), "Wiel Arets 1993–1997," **El Croquis** (1997) 85, pp. 108–115.
▸ An., "Atalaya habitada; Torre de viviendas en la KNSM-Eiland, Amsterdam," **Arquitectura Viva** (1997)54 [May/June], pp. 50–53.
▸ An., "Housing Skydome," in M. Kloos, **Amsterdam Architecture 1994–96,** Amsterdam, 1997, pp. 80–81.
▸ V. van Rossem, "Hoogbouw, bouwkunst en stedebouw / High-rise, architecture and urban design," "Woontoren KNSM-toren,"
  in E. Koster en T. van Oeffelt (red.), **Hoogbouw in Nederland 1990–2000,** Rotterdam, 1997, pp. 24, 54–55.
▸ M. Bock, **Wiel Arets, architect,** 010 Publishers, Rotterdam, 1998, pp. 72–75.
▸ An., "Apartment Tower KNSM-eiland," **SD (Space Design)** (1999) 02, pp. 57–60.
▸ W. Arets, K. Frampton, R. v. Toorn, "Wiel Arets," **Context 3** (1999) 04, pp. 220–225.
▸ H. Ibelings, F. Strauven, **Hedendaagse architecten in Nederland en Vlaanderen,** Rekkem, 2000, pp. 50–55.
▸ M. Koivisto, "Arkkitehti Wiel Arets," **Betoni** (2001) 1, pp. 22–29.

....

027 (063)

  project: Hopmans-Gielen House and Doctor's Office
  location: Le Corbusierstraat 16 / Altostraat in Amersfoort, the Netherlands
  architect: Wiel Arets, Wim v.d. Bergh
  project team: Wiel Arets, Wim v.d. Bergh, Lars van Es, Charlotte Greub,
  Maurice Paulussen, Neda Todorovic
  date of design: 1990
  date of completion: 1991
  models: Lars van Es
  photographs: Kim Zwarts
  clients: Mr. Hopmans and Mrs. Gielen
  program: home and psychologists practice
  area: building area 950 m^2; room area 275 m^2
  constructor: Janson bv
  structural consultant: Jacobs bv

bibliography
▸ M. Kuperus en S. v.d Berg (red.), **De villa's van Zielhorst: maatwerk in architectuur,** Amersfoort, 1993, pp. 22–23.
▸ B. Lootsma, "Gebaselte Biographien und erfundene Traditionen," **Arch+** (1999) 146 pp. 40–42.

....

028 (064)

  project: Indigo Office Building
  location: Limburglaan 5, Sphinx-Ceramique Area in Maastricht, the Netherlands
  project team: Wiel Arets, Ivo Daniëls, Elmar Kleuters, Paul Kuitenbrouwer
  collaborators: Jo Janssen, Anita Morandini
  date of design: 1990–94
  date of completion: 1995
  models: Paulus Egers
  photographs: Kim Zwarts
  clients: Wilma Vastgoed bv Nieuwegein / ABP Heerlen
  program: offices
  area: building area 1,300 m^2; room area 4,000 m^2; circulation area 550 m^2
  installations and building physics consultant: Coman raadgevende Ingenieurs bv
  structural consultant: Brekelmans advisory agents
  building contractor: Wilma Bouw Maastricht

bibliography
▸ W. Arets, "Kantoorgebouw Maastricht," in W. Arets, **An Alabaster Skin,** 1992.
▸ W. Arets, "Maastricht Commercial Office," **A+U** (1994) 02, no. 281, pp. 122–125.
▸ An., "Kantoorgebouw Céramique Maastricht," **de Architect** (1995) 11, p. 65.
▸ R. C. Levene, F. Márquez Cecilia (red.), "Wiel Arets 1993–1997," **El Croquis** (1997) 85, pp. 100–107.
▸ Gemeente Maastricht, **De keuze voor kwaliteit; Nota architectuur-, monumenten- en welstandsbeleid,** Maastricht, 1998, pp. 17, 20–21, 38–39.
▸ M. Bock, **Wiel Arets, architect,** 010 Publishers, Rotterdam, 1998, pp. 76–79.
▸ W. Arets, K. Frampton, R. v. Toorn, "Wiel Arets," **Context 3** (1999) 04, pp. 168–171.

....

029 (065)

p. 170   **project:** Headquarters AZL Pension Fund
location: Akerstraat 92, site with historical buildings between two roads in Heerlen, the Netherlands.
project team: Wiel Arets, Dominic Papa, Ani Velez
collaborators: Lars van Es, Malin Johanson, Maurice Paulussen, Joanna Tang, René Thijssen, Richard Welten
site supervisors: Hein Urlings
furniture design: Wiel Arets, Hans Lensvelt
garden architect: Wiel Arets, Pieter Kromwijk (Eerenbeemt & Kromwijk), Dominic Papa
date of design: 1991
date of completion: 1995
models: Paul Egers, Joanna Tang
photographs: Hélène Binet, Kim Zwarts
client: Pensionfund AZL Beheer Heerlen
program: administration building for 220 people for the AZL Pension Fund Beheer Heerlen
area: building area 5,400 m^2; room area 3,600 m^2
management consultant: Veldhoen Facility Consultants bv
structural consultant: Ingenieursbureau Grabowsky & Poort bv
mechanical, electrical consultant: Tema Ingenieurs bv
building physics consultant: Cauberg & Huygen Raadgevende Ingenieurs bv
buildingcontractor: Laudy Bouw & Planontwikkeling bv

bibliography
▸ W. Arets, "Heerlen Headquarters for the AZL," **A+U** (1994) 02, no. 281, pp. 114–117.
▸ An., "Hoofdkantoor AZL Heerlen," **de Architect** (1995) 11, pp. 56–64.
▸ A. Lapuzina, "Academy Maastricht & AZL Pensionfund Heerlen," **Projeto** (1995) 192, pp. 32–40.
▸ J. Meuwissen, "Plug-in-Field," **Casabella** (1995) 628, pp. 54–63.
▸ R. Ryan, "Rationalist Representation," **The Architectural Review** (1996) 1190 [April], pp. 50–53.
▸ S. Schneider, "Verwaltungsgebäude in Heerlen," **Baumeister** (1996) 5, pp. 32–37.
▸ An., "Wiel Arets. Politistation I Vaals," "Kontorbygning I Heerlen," **Arkitekten magasin** 98 (1996) 11, pp. 28–30, 29–33.
▸ An., "Kantoorgebouw / Office Building," in R. Brouwers (hoofdred.), **Jaarboek Architectuur in Nederland 1995/1996,** Rotterdam, 1996, pp. 80–83.
▸ A. Lapunzina, "Wiel Arets; Headquarter for the AZL Pensionfund," **GA Document** (1996) 48, pp. 46–55.
▸ B. Lootsma, "Une tradition de l'innovation," **L'Architecture d'Aujourdhui** (1996) 306 [Sept.], pp. 50–57.
▸ W. Arets, "AZL Pension Fund Directional Center," in G. Keller (hoofd. red.), **6th International Architecture Exhibition: Sensing the future-The Architect as seismograph,** Venice, 1996, pp. 16–19.
▸ J. Rodermond, "Beeld en bodem; Strategieën voor en dynamisch contextualisme," **de Architect** 28 (1997) 3, pp. 58–69.
▸ R. C. Levene, F. Márquez Cecilia (red.), "Wiel Arets 1993–1997," **El Croquis** (1997) 85, pp. 82–99.
▸ T. Henning, "Nieuwbouw AZL Beheer Heerlen heeft interne cultuuromslag 'n handje geholpen," **Limburg Management** 9 (1997) 2, pp. 28–29.
▸ P. Jodidio, "Wiel Arets; AZL Headquarters," in P. Jodidio, **Contemporary European Architects; Volume V,** Köln, 1997, pp. 52–59.
▸ An., "Kantoorgebouw in Heerlen / Immeuble administratif à Heerlen," **Bouwen met beton** 1998, pp. 28–35.
▸ R. Barke, C. Wieacker, "Transluzente Körper," **Tain** (1998) 3, pp. 6–13.
▸ F. Migsch, "Academy of Fine Arts, Maastricht," "Police station, Vaals," "AZL office, Heerlen," in K. Battista en F. Migsch, **The Netherlands; a guide to recent architecture,** London 1998, pp. 210–213, 220–223, 224–229.
▸ M. Bock, **Wiel Arets, architect,** 010 Rotterdam, 1998, pp. 80–93.
▸ An., "Wiel Arets," in B. Lootsma, M v. Stralen (red.), **Het verlangen naar architectuur en de beslommeringen van alledag,** Bussum, 1999, pp. 20–29.
▸ S. Allen, **Wiel Arets; AZL Heerlen,** Rotterdam, 1999.
▸ W. Arets, K. Frampton, R. v. Toorn, "Wiel Arets," **Context 3** (1999) 04, pp. 172–195.
▸ F. Kaltenbach, "Über den Dächern von…- Wiel Arets über sein Konzept der Stadt / On the roofs of…- Wiel Arets on his Concept for the City," **Detail** (2000) 5, pp. 806–810.
▸ B. Lootsma, **SuperDutch: De tweede moderiteit van de Nederlandse architectuur,** Nijmegen, 2000, pp. 26–49.
▸ A. Ilonen, "Alankomaiden wosituhannen arkkiteht wia," **Betonin** (1993) 3, pp. 36–41.
▸ M. Koivisto, "Julkinen Piha, Heerlen - Kivipuutarha," in M. Koivisto, **Betonin Ja Luonnonkiven…,** Forssa, 2000, pp. 56–57.

....

030 (066)

project: Stealth Office Furniture Line
location: Produced by Lensvelt, Breda
project team: Wiel Arets
date of design: 1994
date of dcompletion: 1995
photographs: Kim Zwarts, Datema & Mulder
client: Pensionfund AZL Beheer Heerlen
program: tables, cupboards, front desk

bibliography
▸ J. Smeets, **Stealth,** Tilburg, 1995.
▸ An., "Orgatec: 48 nuovi mobili per l'ufficio," **Abitare** (1997) 360 [March], p. 111.

....

031 (067)

project: Academy of the Arts (competition, first prize)
location: Mr. Visserplein, a square in the center of Amsterdam, the Netherlands
project team: Wiel Arets, Harald Straatveit, Anita Morandini
collaborators: Eric Bolle, Paul Draaijer, Lars van Es, René Holten, Jo Janssen, Maurice Paulussen
date of design: 1990
models: Paul Egers, Lars van Es, Maurice Paulussen
photographs: Kim Zwarts
client: Amsterdamse Hogeschool voor Kunsten
program: academy for the arts, film and television, theater, architecture, music, fashion and administration building
area: room area 48,600 m^2
structural consultant: Ingenieursbureau Grabowsky & Poort bv
mechanical, electrical consultant: Tema Ingenieurs bv
building physics consultant: Cauberg & Huygen Raadgevende Ingenieurs bv

bibliography
▸ J. Rodermond, "Architectuur van het verdwijnen," **de Architect** 21 (1990) 12, pp. 42–47.
▸ B. Lootsma, "Bouwen aan cultuur. Ideeën en werk van Wiel Arets," **de Architect** (1993) 11, pp. 30–51.
▸ W. Arets, "Amsterdam Academy for the Arts," **A+U** (1994) 02, no. 281, pp. 102–109.
▸ M. Kloos en B. de Maar, "The hesitant high-rise of Amsterdam," in M. Kloos (red.), **Amsterdam's High-Rise,** Amsterdam, 1995, pp. 62.
▸ W. Arets, K. Frampton, R. v. Toorn, "Wiel Arets," **Context 3** (1999) 04, pp. 196–199.

....

032 (069)

project: Theater (competition, first prize)
location: Plein Zuidpoort, a square near the center of Delft, the Netherlands
project team: Wiel Arets, Henri Rueda-Coronel, Victor Wong
collaborators: René Holten, Jo Janssen, Elmar Kleuters, Maurice Paulussen
date of design: 1991
models: Henri Rueda-Coronel, Victor Wong
photographs: Kim Zwarts
client: Municipality Delft
program: lobby, auditoria for 550 and for 200 seats, offices for administration
area: room area 1,800 m²; circulation area 200 m²
building physics consultant: Cauberg–Huygen Raadgevende Ingenieurs bv

bibliography
▸ C. Boekraad, "5 ontwerpenvoor Delfts Stadstheater," **Architectuur/Bouwen** (1991) 8, pp. 14–18.
▸ J. v. Eldonk en H. de Koning, "Vijf theaters voor Delft," **Archis** (1991) 9, pp. 4–5.
▸ H. Moscoviter, "Vijf architecten tekenen stadstheater voor Delft," **Bouw** (1991) 12/13, p. 3.
▸ S. Allen, "Wiel Arets. Dance Theater, Delft," **Assemblage** (1992) 17, pp. 38–51.
▸ B. Lootsma, "Bouwen aan cultuur. Ideeën en werk van Wiel Arets," **de Architect** (1993) 11, pp. 30–51.
▸ W. Arets, "Delft Theater," **A+U** (1994) 02, no. 281, pp. 86–95.
▸ An., "Una austeridad retórica / A Rhetorical Austerity," **AV Monografías** (1998) 73, pp. 44–53.
▸ W. Arets, K. Frampton, R. v. Toorn, "Wiel Arets," **Context 3** (1999) 04, pp. 200–201.

033 (070)

project: Law Court (competition, first prize)
location: Guyotplein, on the north side of the center of Groningen, the Netherlands
project team: Wiel Arets, Lise- Anne Couture and Hani Rashid, John Cleater, Scott Devere, Kevin Estrada, Marianne Geers, Nadim Khattar, Rick Maund, Dominic Papa, Ani Velez
collaborators: William H. Deegan, Paulus Egers, Jo Janssen, Maurice Paulussen
date of design: 1991
models: Scott Devere, Paulus Egers
photographs: Kim Zwarts
clients: Municipality Groningen, Department of Justice and RGD
program: law court, with offices for administration
building physics consultant: Cauberg-Huygen Raadgevende Ingenieurs bv

bibliography
▸ J. Rodermond, "Theo Bosch ontwerpt gerechtsgebouw Groningen," **de Architect** (1992) 3, pp. 23–24.
▸ H. Kerkdijk, "Prijsvraag gerechtsgebouw Groningen," **Archis** (1992) 4, pp. 10–11.
▸ B. Lootsma, "Bouwen aan cultuur. Ideeën en werk van Wiel Arets," **de Architect** (1993) 11, pp. 30–51.
▸ M. Schijve, "Huisvesting nieuwe rechterlijke macht," **Contour** (1993) 30, pp. 12–18.
▸ W. Arets, "Groningen Court Building," **A+U** (1994) 02, no. 281, pp. 78–85.
▸ An., "Modern Departures," **P/A (Progressive Architecture)** (1995) June, pp. 96–105.
▸ R. Miyake, S. Muramatsu, M. Fuchigami, **581 Architects in the World,** Tokyo, 1995, p. 111.
▸ W. Arets, K. Frampton, R. v. Toorn, "Wiel Arets," **Context 3** (1999) 04, pp. 206–207.

034 (071)

project: 67 Apartments for the Elderly
location: Kuiperstraat/Tjeuke Timmermanspad in Tilburg, the Netherlands
project team: Wiel Arets, Michel Melenhorst
collaborators: Reina Bos, Tina Brandt, René Holten, Andrea Wallrath
date of design: 1993
date of completion: 1995
models: Paulus Egers
photographs: Kim Zwarts
client: Stichting Verenigde Woningcorporaties SVW
program: 67 apartments
area: building area 3,450 m²; room area 7,560 m²
structural consultant: Goudstikker-de Vries's Hertogenbosch
building contractor: Alphons Coolen bv Tilburg

bibliography
▸ H. Grünhagen, "Serene schoonheid op oud fabrieksterrein," **Woningraad** (1995) 21 [18 Oct.], pp. 24–27.
▸ J. Meuwissen, "Plug-in-Field," **Casabella** (1995) 628, pp. 54–63.
▸ An., "Viviendas en ángulo / Dwellings at an Angle, Tilburg. Wiel Arets," **AV** (1995) 56, pp. 52–55.
▸ M. Steinmann, "76 [sic!] senioren woningen bij het De Pont museum te Tilburg," in A. Smeulders en A Oxenaar, **Nominaties Architectuurprijs 1996 regio midden-Brabant,** s.l. 1996, p. 10.
▸ An., "Tilburg Apartments," in F. Asensio Cerver, **The Architecture of Multiresidential Buildings,** New York, 1997, pp. 84–93.
▸ R.C. Levene, F. Márquez Cecilia (red.), "Wiel Arets 1993–1997," **El Croquis** (1997) 85, pp. 62–73.
▸ M. Bock, **Wiel Arets, architect,** 010 Publishers, Rotterdam, 1998, pp. 94–99.
▸ W. Arets, K. Frampton, R. v. Toorn, "Wiel Arets," **Context 3** (1999) 04, pp. 226–237.

035 (073)

project: 290 Apartments, Zalmhaven Towers
location: Zalmhaven, site nearby the river the Maas in Rotterdam, The Netherlands
project team: Wiel Arets, René Thijssen, Henrik Vuust
collaborators: Harold Aspers, Paul van Dongen, Lars Dreessen, Harold Hermans, Michel Melenhorst, Michiel Vrehen
site supervisors: PRC Bouwcentrum
date of design: 1993
date of completion: 2001
models: Paulus Egers
photographs: Hélène Binet, Kim Zwarts
clients: ABP / Vesteda
program: 290 Apartments, grand cafe, parking, swimming pool, sauna, fitness center, lobby
building physics consultant: Cauberg-Huygen Raadgevende Ingenieurs bv
structural engineer: C. van Ruitenberg bv
building contractor: Wilma Bom bv, Rotterdam
prefab facade: Loveld

bibliography
▸ W. Arets, "Rotterdam Two Residential Tower Blocks," **A+U** (1994) 02, no. 281, pp. 96–97.
▸ An., "Woontorens Zalmhaven," in E. Koster en T. van Oeffelt (red.), **Hoogbouw in Nederland 1990–2000,** Rotterdam, 1997, pp. 104–105.

▸ An.,"Plannen en projecten: appartementen," **Bouw** 54 (1999) 5, p. 51.
▸ W. Arets, K. Frampton, R. v. Toorn, "Wiel Arets," **Context 3** (1999) 04, pp. 244–247.
▸ An., "De Hoge Heren," in Zuiderlicht Bureau, **Koninklijke Mosa,** Nuth s.a.

....

036 (074)
project: Social Housing (competition)
location: Helmond, the Netherlands
project team: Wiel Arets, Jo Janssen, Frank van der Linden, Dominic Papa
date of design: 1992
models: Frank van der Linden
client: Projectbureau Helmond
program: housing

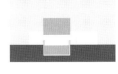

....

037 (075)
project: House Lückers
location: Caumerveld/De Erk in Heerlen, the Netherlands
project team: Wiel Arets, Jo Janssen, Dominic Papa, Richard Welten
garden architect: Buro van den Eerenbeemt en Kromwijk
date of design: 1992
client: C. Lückers family
program: single-family house and practice
structural consultant: Ingenieursbureau Palte bv
building contractor: Gubbels Bouwbedrijf

....

038 (076)
project: 20 Apartments for the Elderly
location: Fons Olterdissenstraat in Maastricht, the Netherlands
project team: Wiel Arets, Michel Melenhorst
collaborators: Ramun Capaul, Rhea Harbers, René Holten, Katharina Lundeberg
garden architect: Buro van den Eerenbeemt en Kromwijk, Maastricht
date of design: 1993
date of completion: 1995
models: Paulus Egers
photographs: Kim Zwarts
client: Maastrichtse woningbouwvereniging "Beter Wonen"
program: 20 3-room apartments, semi public garden
structural consultant: Ingenieursbureau Palte bv
building contractor: Coppelmans Bouwbedrijven bv Eindhoven

bibliography
▸ Woningbouwvereniging Beter Wonen, **Jaarverslag 1994,** Maastricht, 1994.
▸ R. Christiaans, "Wiel Arets," **Beter Wonen** 13 (1994) 3, pp. 6–8.
▸ G. Bergers, "Kleinood in vijf grenzen," **Woningraad** (1995) 4 [22 Feb.], pp. 10–13.
▸ J. Rodermond, "Herwaardering van het grote woongebouw," "Uitwisseling van functies," **de Architect** (1995) 5, pp. 66–73, 110–113.
▸ An., "Ir. Wiel Arets architect & associates," in An., **In vorm: projecten en bijbehorende kosten 1994/1995,** The Hague, 1995, p. 246.
▸ An., "Ir. Wiel Arets architect & associates," in An., **Nederlandse Architecten 2 / Dutch Architects 2,** Amsterdam, 1996, pp. 18–19.
▸ H. Ibelings, "Seniorenhuisvesting," "Woontorens: zicht op uitkijk," "Seniorenwoningen," in A. Oosterman, **Woningbouw in Nederland / Housing in the Netherlands,** Rotterdam, 1996, pp. 38–41, 42–47, 60–61.
▸ R. C. Levene, F. Márquez Cecilia (red.), "Wiel Arets 1993–1997," **El Croquis** (1997) 85, pp. 74–81.
▸ Gemeente Maastricht, **De keuze voor kwaliteit; Nota architectuur-, monumenten- en welstandsbeleid,** Maastricht, 1998, pp. 17, 20–21, 38–39.
▸ R. Barke, C. Wieacker, "Transluzente Körper," **Tain** (1998) 3, pp. 6–13.
▸ M. Bock, **Wiel Arets, architect,** 010 Rotterdam, 1998, pp. 100–105.
▸ An., "Luchtstraat met roosters," in Projectgroep VerStek, **Culturele identiteiten; woonvormen voor oudere migranten,** Rotterdam, 1999.
▸ W. Arets, K. Frampton, R. v. Toorn, "Wiel Arets," **Context 3** (1999) 04, pp. 238–243.
▸ An., "20 Apartamentos para Ancianos / 20 Apartments for the Elderly," **Quaderns** (2000) 227, pp. 102–105.

....

039 (081)
project: "A White Tower for Atuatuca Tungrorum" installation
location: Tongeren, the Netherlands
project team: Wiel Arets, Dominic Papa, Dorte Jensen, Michel Melenhorst
date of design: 1994 (temporary project)
date of completion: 1994
photographs: Kim Zwarts
client: Municipality Tongeren
program: Installation commemorating Roman history

bibliography
▸ G. Bekaert, "Tongeren en zijn gallo-romeinse ruïnes," **Archis** (1993) 7, pp. 2–3.

....

040 (082)
project: Cuijk Police Station
location: street corner Beersebaan/Heeswijksestraat at the edge of the city of Cuijk, the Netherlands
project team: Wiel Arets, Dorte Jensen, Ralph van Mameren, René Thijssen
collaborators: Paul van Dongen, Harold Hermans, Michel Melenhorst
site supervisors: Hein Urlings
furniture design: Doris Annen, Wiel Arets , René Thijssen
date of design: 1994
date of completion: 1997
photographs: Kim Zwarts
client: Politie Brabant Noord
program: Basiseenheid Politie Brabant Noord
building contractor: Giesbers Bouw bv
installation consultant: TEMA Ingenieurs bv

bibliography
▸ R. C. Levene, F. Márquez Cecilia (red.), "Wiel Arets 1993–1997," **El Croquis** (1997) 85, pp. 140–149.
▸ An., "Una austeridad retórica / A Rhetorical Austerity," **AV Monografías** (1998) 73, pp. 44–53.

▸ X. González, "Envoltura versus fachada: el concepto epidérmico / Envelope versus façade: the epidermal concept," "Envoltura autónoma: Comisarías de Policía en Boxtel y Cuijk, Holanda," **A + T (Arquitectura + Tecnología)** (1998) 11, pp. 10–25, 26.
▸ W. Arets, K. Frampton, R. v. Toorn, "Wiel Arets," **Context 3** (1999) 04, pp. 28–41.
▸ W. Arets, "Estaciones de Policía Boxtel y Cuijk, Holanda / Police stations Boxtel & Cuijk, Netherlands," **ViA arquitectura** (2000) 07.V–2, pp. 86–91.
▸ H. Ibelings, F. Strauven, **Hedendaagse architecten in Nederland en Vlaanderen,** Rekkem, 2000, pp. 50–55.
▸ B. Lootsma, **SuperDutch: De tweede moderiteit van de Nederlandse architectuur,** Nijmegen, 2000, pp. 26–49.

....

041 (083)

p. 194   **project:** Vaals Police Station
location: street corner Maastrichterlaan / Randweg in Vaals, the Netherlands
project team: Wiel Arets, Rhea Harbers
collaborators: Delphine Clavien, Michel Melenhorst
site supervisor: VFC bv
date of design: 1993–94
date of completion: 1995
models: Paulus Egers
photographs: Hélène Binet, Kim Zwarts
client: Politieregio Limburg Zuid, Cadler & Keer
program: police station for 35 employees
management consultant: Veldhoen Facility Consultants bv
structural consultant: Ingenieursburo Palte bv
mechanical consultant: TEMA Ingenieurs bv
electrical consultant: Huygen bv
building physics consultant: Cauberg-Huygen Raadgevende Ingenieurs bv
building contractor: Van Zandvoort bv

bibliography
▸ An., "Politieburo Vaals," **de Architect** (1995) 11, pp. 66–71.
▸ E. Melet, "Dubbele bodems van Wiel Arets," **de Architect** (1995) 11, pp. 51–55.
▸ Greg Lynn, "Police Station, Vaals (1993–95)," in J. Bosman (red.), **Wiel Arets. Strange Bodies/Fremdkörper,** Basel, 1996, pp. 19–33.
▸ B. Lootsma, "Police Station Vaals," **Domus** (1996) 718, pp. 30–35.
▸ I. Bravo, "Comisaría de policía en Vaals / Police Headquarter in Vaals," **Diseño interior** (1996) 53, pp. 76–83.
▸ An., "Wiel Arets. Politistation I Vaals," **Arkitekten magasin** 98 (1996) 11, pp. 28–30.
▸ B. Lootsma, "Police Station, Vaals," **OZ** (1996) 18, pp. 24–29.
▸ An., "Politiebureau / Police Station," in R. Brouwers (hoofdred.), **Jaarboek Architectuur in Nederland 1995/1996,** Rotterdam, 1996, pp. 80–83.
▸ O. Koekebakker, "Archi-textuur," **Items** (1996) 6, pp. 23–29.
▸ An., "Vaals als voorbeeld," **Vrij Nederland** (1996) 40.
▸ J. Rodermond, "Verkenningen van nieuwe kantoortypologieën," **de Architect** (1996) 63 [themanr.: Werkomgeving], pp. 26–30.
▸ B. Kraft, "Gefährlich schön," **DBZ [Deutsche Bauzeitschrift]** 44 (1996) 12, pp. 32–33.
▸ An., " Comisaria de policía / Police headquarters," **Quaderns** (1997) 214 [2 Forum International], pp. 100–109.
▸ J. Bosman, "Ein New Yorker Konzept landet auf einer südniederländischen Wiese," **Architese** (1997) 3, pp. 30–33.
▸ R.C. Levene, F. Márquez Cecilia (red.), "Wiel Arets 1993–1997," **El Croquis** (1997) 85, pp. 116–127.
▸ An., "Police Station Vaals," in D. Gray, **5th Mies van der Rohe Pavilion Award for European Architecture,** Milan, 1997, pp. 24–27.
▸ O. Winkler, "Polizeistation in Vaals," **Baumeister** 95 (1998) 3, pp. 18–25.
▸ R. Spetz, "Det dekorativa som arrangemang," **MAMA Divan** (1998) Feb., pp. 82–89.
▸ F. Migsch, "Police station, Vaals," in K. Battista en F. Migsch, **The Netherlands; a guide to recent architecture,** London, 1998, pp. 220–223.
▸ M. Bock, **Wiel Arets, architect,** Rotterdam, 1998, pp. 106–115.
▸ An., "Wiel Arets," in B. Lootsma, M v. Stralen (red.), **Het verlangen naar architectuur en de beslommeringen van alledag,** Bussum, 1999, pp. 20–29.
▸ M. Hageman, "Grijze groepring," **Chapeau!** 3 (1999) 11, pp. 76–78.
▸ W. Arets, K. Frampton, R. v. Toorn, "Wiel Arets," **Context 3** (1999) 04, pp. 208–219.
▸ F. Kaltenbach, "Über den Dächern von…- Wiel Arets über sein Konzept der Stadt / On the roofs of…- Wiel Arets on his Concept for the City," **Detail** (2000) 5, pp. 806–810.
▸ H. Ibelings (red.), **Het kunstmatig landschap: Hedendaagse architectuur, stedenbouw en landschapsarchitectuur in Nederland,** Rotterdam 2000, pp. 33–37.
▸ B. Lootsma, **SuperDutch: De tweede moderiteit van de Nederlandse architectuur,** Nijmegen, 2000, pp. 26–49.
▸ C. Slessor, **Concrete regionalism,** London, 2000, pp. 72–95.

....

042 (084)

p. 210   **project:** Arets-Sijstermans House/Studio
location: D'Artagnanlaan 29/31 in Maastricht, the Netherlands, sloping corner site in a suburban residential area
on the edge of the historic center of Maastricht
project team: Wiel Arets, Richard Welten
collaborators: Jo Janssen, Dominic Papa
site supervisors: Hein Urlings, Richard Welten
date of design: 1993
date of completion: 1997
models: Kees Lemmens, Roel v.d Linden
photographs: Hélène Binet, Kim Zwarts
client: Mr. and Mrs. Arets-Sijstermans
program: home and studio
structural consultant: Ingenieursbureau Palthe bv
building contractor: Coppelmans Bouwbedrijven bv
building physics consultant: Cauberg-Huygen Raadgevende Ingenieurs bv

bibliography
▸ R.C. Levene, F. Márquez Cecilia (red.), "Wiel Arets 1993–1997," **El Croquis** (1997) 85, pp. 164–175.
▸ W. Arets, K. Frampton, R. v. Toorn, "Wiel Arets," **Context 3** (1999) 04, pp. 42–55.

....

043 (085)

project: Hubert Sijstermans Gravestone
location: Kerkrade, the Netherlands
project team: Wiel Arets
collaborator: Charlotte Greub
date of design: 1993
date of completion: 1993
models: Charlotte Greub
photographs: Kim Zwarts
client: Mrs. A. Sijstermans
program: gravestone
building contractor: Moonen-Wanders bv

....

044 (086)

p. 234   **project:** De Waag Pharmacy
location: Heksenkruid 6, at the shopping center "Heksenwiel" in Breda, the Netherlands
collaborators: Wiel Arets, Sven Dyckhoff, Jo Janssen, Richard Welten
date of design: 1993
date of completion: 1994
photographs: Hélène Binet, Kim Zwarts
client: T. Cremers
program: exterior elevations and interior of a pharmacy containing offices, shop, laboratory
project management: Into Rotterdam bv

bibliography
▸ R. Slutzky, "Pharmacy "De Waag', Breda (1994)," in J. Bosman (red.), **Wiel Arets. Strange Bodies/ Fremdkörper,** Basel, 1996, pp. 12–17.
▸ S. Damaschke, B. Scheffer, **Apotheken: Planen, Gestalten und Einrichten,** Leinfelden-Echterdingen, 2000, pp. 136–137, 160–161.

....

045 (088)

p. 242   **project:** Boxtel Police Station
location: Bosscheweg, streetcorner at the edge of Boxtel, the Netherlands
architect: Wiel Arets
project team: Wiel Arets, Dorte Jensen, René Thijssen
collaborators: Lars Dreesen, Rhea Harbers, Harold Hermans, Ralph van Mameren, Dominic Papa
site supervisors: Hein Urlings
furniture design: Wiel Arets, Doris Annen
date of design: 1994
date of completion: 1997
photographs: Hélène Binet, Kim Zwarts
client: Politie Brabant Noord
program: Basiseenheid Politie Brabant Noord
building contractor: Bouwbedrijf van der Pas Oss bv
installation consultant: TEMA Ingenieurs bv

bibliography
▸ R. C. Levene, F. Márquez Cecilia (red.), "Wiel Arets 1993–1997," **El Croquis** (1997) 85, pp. 128–139.
▸ An., "Una austeridad retórica / A Rhetorical Austerity," **AV Monografías** (1998) 73, pp. 44–53.
▸ R. Barke, C. Wieacker, "Transluzente Körper," **Tain** (1998) 3, pp. 6–13.
▸ X. González, "Envoltura versus fachada: el concepto epidérmico / Envelope versus façade: the epidermal concept," "Envoltura autónoma: Comisarías de Policía en Boxtel y Cuijk, Holanda," **A + T (Arquitectura + Tecnologia)** (1998) 11, pp. 10–25, 26.
▸ An., "Police Station Boxtel," **SD (Space Design)** (1999) 02, pp. 57–60.
▸ W. Arets, K. Frampton, R. v. Toorn, "Wiel Arets," **Context 3** (1999) 04, pp. 14–27.
▸ W. Arets, "Estaciones de Policía Boxtel y Cuijk, Holanda / Police stations Boxtel & Cuijk, Netherlands," **ViA arquitectura** (2000) 07.V–2, pp. 86–91.
▸ H. Ibelings (red.), **Het kunstmatig landschap: Hedendaagse architectuur, stedenbouw en landschapsarchitectuur in Nederland,** Rotterdam, 2000, pp. 33–37.
▸ M. Kovisto, "Arkkitehti Wiel Arets," **Betoni** (2001) 1, pp. 22–29.

....

046 (089)

p. 260   **project:** Headquarters of Regional Police for South Limburg
location: Stationsstraat/Spoorwegsingel, north and south side of the railway tracks at the railwaystation in Heerlen, the Netherlands
project team: Wiel Arets, Pauline Bremmer, Richard Welten
collaborators: Pedro Anão, Buro Hoen bv, Dominic Papa
site supervisors: Peter de Graaf
date of design: 1994
date of completion: 1999
models: Ralph Blättler, Delphine Clavien, Paulus Egers, Kees Lemmens
photographs: Hélène Binet, Kim Zwarts
client: Politie Regio Limburg-Zuid
program: administration building for 260 people for the Headquarters for Politie Regio Limburg-Zuid, the investigation building is situated on the north side of the tracks, regional and local police on the south side of the tracks
area: building area 9,400 m^2; room area 7,920 m^2
management consultant: Veldhoen Facility Consultants bv
structural consultant: Aronsohn Raadgevend Ingenieurs bv
mechanical, electrical consultant: Huygen bv Installatie Adviseurs
building physics consultant: Cauberg-Huygen Raadgevende Ingenieurs bv
building contractor: M&M Bouw Sittard bv

bibliography
▸ R. C. Levene, F. Márquez Cecilia (red.), "Wiel Arets 1993–1997," **El Croquis** (1997) 85, pp. 150–155.
▸ W. Arets, K. Frampton, R. v. Toorn, "Wiel Arets," **Context 3** (1999) 04, pp. 108–113.

....

047 (091)

project: Gallery for Contemporary Art (competition, third prize)
location: Leipzig, Germany
project team: Wiel Arets, Anca Arenz, Dorte Jensen, Dominic Papa, Harold Schout
date of design: 1994
models: Paulus Egers
photographs: Kim Zwarts
client: Förderkreis der Leipziger Galerie für zeitgenössische Kunst Leipzig
program: exhibition space, auditorium, library, offices, cafe, videotheque

bibliography
▸ P. Guth, "Galerie für Zeitgenössische Kunst Leipzig," **Bauwelt** 85 (1994) 44 [18 Nov.], pp. 2430–2431.
▸ An., "Ideenwettbewerb Leipziger Galerie für Zeitgenössische Kunst," **Wettbewerbe Aktuell** 24 (1994) 11, pp. 51–62.
▸ An., "Leipziger Galerie für zeitgenössische Kunst," **Architektur + Wettbewerbe** (1995) 164 [Dec.], pp. 40–41.

....

048 (094)

project: Urban Plan
location: Doetinchem, the Netherlands
project team: Wiel Arets, Dominic Papa
collaborator: Anca Arenz
date of design: 1994–1997
models: Paul Egers
client: Van Wijnen Projectgroep Oost bv
program: housing, offices, cinema

bibliography
▸ J. Rodermond, "Uitwisseling van functies," **de Architect** (1995) 5, pp. 110–113.

....

049 (095)
project: Office Building
location: Doetinchem, the Netherlands
project team: Wiel Arets, Dominic Papa
collaborator: Anca Arenz
date of design: 1994–1997
models: Paul Egers
client: Van Wijnen Projectgroep Oost bv
program: office

bibliography
▸ J. Rodermond, "Uitwisseling van functies," **de Architect** (1995) 5, pp. 110–113.

....

050 (096)
project: 20 Apartments
location: Doetinchem, the Netherlands
project team: Wiel Arets, Dominic Papa
collaborator: Anca Arenz
date of design: 1994–1997
models: Paul Egers
client: Van Wijnen Projectgroep Oost bv
program: housing

bibliography
▸ J. Rodermond, "Uitwisseling van functies," **de Architect** (1995) 5, pp. 110–113.

....

051 (099)
project: Social Housing (competition)
location: Indische Buurt in Amsterdam, the Netherlands
project team: Wiel Arets
collaborator: Michel Melenhorst
date of design: 1994
client: Woningbouwvereniging Ons Belang
program: 100 apartments

bibliography
▸ J. Rodermond, "Van volkshuisvesting naar woonmarketing," **de Architect** (1995) 5, pp. 28–41.

....

052 (100)
project: 71 Apartments and Shops
location: Leipzig, Germany
architect: Wiel Arets,
project team: Wiel Arets, Dominic Papa, Henrik Vuust
date of design: 1994
client: Heagen Projekte
program: apartments and shops

....

053 (101)
p. 272 **project:** Offices & Factory Building Lensvelt
location: Hoogeind, an industrial area in Breda, the Netherlands
project team: Wiel Arets, Ivo Daniëls, René Thijssen
collaborator: Paul van Dongen
garden architect: West 8
date of design: 1995
date of completion: 1999
photographs: Hélène Binet, Kim Zwarts
client: Lensvelt B.V.
program: production hall, showroom and offices for the Lensvelt furniture company
area: building area 6,230 m^2; room area 5,710 m^2
management consultant: Traject Vastgoed & Advies Groep bv Holthuis bouwbegeleiding
structural consultant: Ingenieursbureau A. Palte bv
building physics consultant: Cauberg - Huygen Raadgevende Ingenieurs bv
building contractor: Korteweg Bouw bv

bibliography
▸ R. Thiemann, **Lensvelt 1999**, Breda, 1998.
▸ P. McGuire, "Life through a lens," **The Architectural Review** (1999) 1225 [March], pp. 68–70.
▸ C. Grafe, "The shed undecorated; Bedrijfsgebouw voor Lensvelt bij Breda door Arets," **de Architect** (1999) 7/8 [Jul.–Aug.], pp. 46–49.
▸ J. R. Krause, "Grüner Magnet," **AIT (Architektur-Innenarchitektur-Technischer Ausbau)** (1999) 10, pp. 78–81.
▸ An., "Gläserne Möbel-Box," **DBZ (DeutscheBauZeitschrift)** 47 (1999) 11, p. 86.
▸ W. Arets, K. Frampton, R. v. Toorn, "Wiel Arets," **Context 3** (1999) 04, pp. 56–61.
▸ W. Arets, "Lensvelt," in An., **Lensvelt,** Breda, 2000.
▸ M. G. Zunino, "Fabbrica, uffici e showroom Lensvelt / Lensvelt factory, offices and showroom," **Abitare** (2000) 392, pp. 92–95.
▸ J. Rodermond, "Design & interieur: De wereld volgens Hans Lensvelt," **de Architect** (2000) 4, pp. 91–95.
▸ H. Ibelings, F. Strauven, **Hedendaagse architecten in Nederland en Vlaanderen,** Rekkem, 2000, pp. 50–55.
▸ An., "Wiel Arets; Opslag-kantoor / Storage-Office," in H. Ibelings (hoofdred.), **Jaarboek architectuur in Nederland 1999/2000,** Rotterdam, 2000, pp. 46–51.
▸ R. Uhde, "Lensvelt-Gebäude in Breda; Mätherische Möbel-Box," **Leonardo-online** (2000) 5, pp. 14–19.
▸ A. Mostaedi, "Wiel Arets: Offices and Factory Building Lensvelt," in A. Mostaedi, **New working spaces: Architectural Design,** Barcelona, 2000, pp. 10–19.
▸ M. Koivisto, "Arkkitehti Wiel Arets," **Betoni** (2000) 1, pp. 22–29.
▸ P. Jodidio, "Wiel Arets: Lensvelt Factory and Offices," in P. Jodidio, **Architecture now! [Architektur heute / L'architecture d'aujourd'hui],** Cologne, 2001, pp. 92–89.
▸ Antonello Boschi, "Offices & factory building Lensvelt 1999," in **Schowroom,** Florence, 2001, pp. 32–37.

....

054 (102)
project: 48 Apartments
location: Eupen, Belgium
project team: Wiel Arets, Dominic Papa, Henrik Vuust
collaborators: Delphine Clavien, Michel Melenhorst
date of design: 1994
models: Delphine Clavien
clients: Werner Hanneman, PAN-Brasilia the Netherlands bv
program: housing
management consultant: Velhoen Facility Consultants bv

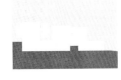

....

055 (104)
project: Hofplein 420 Apartments & Shops
location: Rotterdam, the Netherlands
project team: Wiel Arets, Henrik Vuust
collaborators: Dominic Papa, Sibylle Thomke
date of design: 1995
models: Paul Egers
client: NS Vastgoed
program: apartments, commercial space, parking

bibliography
▸ R. Uhde, "Lensvelt-Gebäude in Breda; Mätherische Möbel-Box," **Leonardo-online** (2000) 5, pp. 14–19.
▸ A. Mostaedi, "Wiel Arets: Offices and Factory Building Lensvelt," in A. Mostaedi, **New working spaces: Architectural Design,** Barcelona, 2000, pp. 10–19.
▸ M. Koivisto, "Arkkitehti Wiel Arets," **Betoni** (2000) 1, pp. 22–29.
▸ P. Jodidio, "Wiel Arets: Lensvelt Factory and Offices," in P. Jodidio, **Architecture now! [Architektur heute / L'architecture d'aujourd'hui],** Cologne 2001, pp. 92–89.
▸ Antonello Boschi, "Offices & factory building Lensvelt 1999," in **Schowroom,** Florence, 2001, pp. 32–37.

056 (105)
project: Study for Rotterdam 2045
location: Laurenskwartier in Rotterdam, the Netherlands
project team: Wiel Arets, Michel Melenhorst, Dominic Papa, René Thijssen, Sibylle Thomke, Henrik Vuust
date of design: 1995
models: Paul Egers, Lonnie Koken, Caroline Krogh Andersen
photographs: Kim Zwarts
client: city of Rotterdam

bibliography
▸ H. Tilman, "Haastwerk voor de komende vijftig jaar. Visies op de toekomst van Rotterdam," **de Architect** (1995) 11, pp. 80–93.
▸ W. Arets, "Unpredictable repetition of strange bodies," in **Rotterdam 2045. Visies op de toekomst van stad, haven en regio,** Rotterdam, 1995, pp. 35–37.
▸ H. Moscoviter, "Stedebouw: van Olympus naar maaiveld," **Bouw** 51 (1996) 2, pp. 43–46.
▸ J. Bosman (ed.), **Strange Bodies / Fremkörper,** Basel, 1996, pp. 112–113.

057 (106)
project: Railway Station (competition)
location: Erfurt, Germany
project team: Wiel Arets, Delphine Clavien, Andrea Gustafson, Dominic Papa, Maurice Paulussen, Sibylle Thomke, Henrik Vuust
date of design: 1995
models: Paulus Egers
photographs: Kim Zwarts
client: Deutsche Bahn AG, Frankfurt
program: railway station, cinema, offices, exhibition garden, shops, bus station, parking

bibliography
▸ An, "Stationsgebied Erfurt," **de Architect** (1995) 11, pp. 72–73.
▸ S. Allen, "Railway Station, Erfurt (1995)," in J. Bosman (red.), **Wiel Arets. Strange Bodies/ Fremdkörper,** Basel, 1996, pp. 48–51.
▸ W. Arets, K. Frampton, R. v. Toorn, "Wiel Arets," **Context 3** (1999) 04, pp. 78–85.

058 (107)
project: Academy of Art (competition, first prize)
location: Steinfurterstrasse, old military barracks at the edge of the city of Münster, Germany
project team: Wiel Arets, Caroline Krogh Andersen, Dominic Papa, Sibylle Thomke, René Thijssen, Henrik Vuust, Richard Welten
date of design: 1995
models: Andrea Gustafson
client: city of Münster
program: academy of arts
area: building area 10,500 m^2
structural consultant: Ingenieurbureau A. Palte bv
building physics consultant: Cauberg-Huygen Raadgevende Ingenieurs bv

bibliography
▸ An., "Kunstacademie Münster," **de Architect** (1995) 11, pp. 74–75.
▸ L. Diller, "Academy of Art, Münster (1995)," in J. Bosman (red.), **Wiel Arets. Strange Bodies/ Fremdkörper,** Basel, 1996, pp. 100–101.
▸ W. Arets, K. Frampton, R. v. Toorn, "Wiel Arets," **Context 3** (1999) 04, pp. 96–101.

....

059 (108)
project: Study for the Stubaital
location: Innsbruck, Austria
project team: Wiel Arets
collaborator: Dominic Papa
date of design: 1995
photographs: Kim Zwarts
client: city of Innsbruck
program: Stubaital redevelopment

....

060 (109)
project: Study for Remise Ottakring
location: Ottakring in Vienna, Austria
project team: Wiel Arets, Nynke Joustra, Critian Sabella Rossa
collaborators: Silvia Braun, Joseph Bula, Ursula Eckelmann, Paulus Egers, Jan Endemann, Susanne Farwer, Jens Fehlig, Mathias Frey, Valentin Gorencic, Manfred Gräber, Michaela Heilmann, Olaf Hoffmann, Astrid Lipka, Dominic Neidlinger, Dominic Papa, Domenico Antonio Potenza, Marialessandra Secchi, Guido Vonester, Rene Holten
date of design: 1994
models: Paulus Egers and all collaborators
photographs: Kim Zwarts
client: Stadtentwicklung, Stadtplanung und Verkehr, Wien
program: apartments, cinema, restaurants, nightclub and parking

bibliography
▸ B. v. Berkel and C. Bos, "Remise Ottakring, Vienna (1994)," in J. Bosman (red.), **Wiel Arets. Strange Bodies / Fremdkörper,** Basel, 1996, pp. 34–41.
▸ W. Arets, K. Frampton, R. v. Toorn, "Wiel Arets," **Context 3** (1999) 04, pp. 74–77.

....

061 (110)
project: Police Headquarters (competition)
location: Berlin, Germany
project team: Wiel Arets, Caroline Krogh Andersen, Pauline Bremmer, Andrea Gustavson, Rhea Haebers, Ralph van Marmeren, Michel Melenhorst, Dominic Papa, René Thijssen, Sybille Thomke, Henrik Vuust, Richard Welten
date of design: 1995
models: Paul Egers
client: Senatsverwaltung für Bau- und Wohnungwesen
program: offices, sports hall, outside sportsground car park, cafe,
structural consultant: Ingenieursbureau A. Palte bv
building physics consultant: Cauberg-Huygen Raadgevende Ingenieurs bv

bibliography
▸ D. v/d Heuvel, "Stedelijke sculptuur in Berlijn," **de Architect** (1995) 12, pp. 16–17.

....

062 (111)
project: Body House
location: Münster, Germany
project team: Wiel Arets, Kim Egholm, Andrea Gustafson, Dominic Papa, Sibylle Thomke, Henrik Vuust, Richard Welten
date of design: 1995
models: Kim Egholm
photographs: Kim Zwarts
client: Mr. H. Lohmann
program: single-family house

bibliography
▸ W. Arets, "Das Körper Haus / Body House," in Galerie Sophia Ungers, **Houses for Sale,** Cologne, 1997 [catalogue].
▸ R. C. Levene, F. Márquez Cecilia (red.), "Wiel Arets 1993–1997," **El Croquis** (1997) 85, pp. 176–183.
▸ W. Arets, "Body House," **GA Houses** (1997) 52 [Apr.], pp. 18–19.
▸ R. Barke, C. Wieacker, "Transluzente Körper," **Tain** (1998) 3, pp. 6–13.
▸ W. Arets, K. Frampton, R. v. Toorn, "Wiel Arets," **Context 3** (1999) 04, pp. 120–123.

....

063 (112)
project: Jacobplaats Housing
location: St Jacobstraat 9–267, uneven housing complex in the center of Rotterdam, the Netherlands
project team: Wiel Arets, Pauline Bremmer, Dorthe Keis, René Thijssen
collaborators: Lars Dreessen, Roel van der Linden, Dominic Papa, Sybille Thomke
date of design: 1996
models: Ralph Blättler, Kees Lemmens
photographs: Kim Zwarts
client: Patrimonium Woningbouw Stichting
program: 98 appartments
structural consultant: Ingenieursbureau A. Palte bv
mechanical, electrical consultant: Huygen bv Installatie Adviseurs
building physics consultant: Cauberg - Huygen Raadgevende Ingenieurs bv

bibliography
▸ R. C. Levene, F. Márquez Cecilia (red.), "Wiel Arets 1993–1997," **El Croquis** (1997) 85, pp. 156–163.
▸ An., "Una austeridad retórica / A Rhetorical Austerity," **AV Monografías** (1998) 73, pp. 44–53.
▸ W. Arets, K. Frampton, R. v. Toorn, "Wiel Arets," **Context 3** (1999) 04, pp. 124–129.

....

064 (113)
project: House Geurten
location: Pijnseweg in Heerlen, the Netherlands
project team: Wiel Arets, Richard Welten
collaborator: Harold Hermans
date of design: 1995
date of completion: 1998
models: Kim Egholm
photographs: Kim Zwarts
client: Mr. P. Geurten
program: single-family house
structural consultant: Ingenieursburo A. Palte bv
building contractor: Coppelmans bouwbedrijven bv

bibliography
▸ R. C. Levene, F. Márquez Cecilia (red.), "Wiel Arets 1993–1997," **El Croquis** (1997) 85, pp. 184–189.
▸ W. Arets, K. Frampton, R. v. Toorn, "Wiel Arets," **Context 3** (1999) 04, pp. 114–119.

....

065 (114)

project: Academy for Sculptural Art
location: Vienna, Austria
project team: Wiel Arets, Dominic Papa
date of design: 1994
models: Thomas Alzinger, Karin Christof, Friedemann Derschmied, Anuska Frick, Julia Gruber,
Roland Kollnitz, Thomas Kosma, Andrea Passler, Stefan Pfeffer, Thomas Stepany,
Detlef Tautenhahn, Robert Temel, Constance Weiser
photographs: Kim Zwarts
client: Hochschule für Anewandte Kunst Vienna
program: Academy for Sculptural Art

....

066 (115)

project: Binnenrotte Rotterdam
location: Binnenrotte in Rotterdam, the Netherlands
project team: Wiel Arets,
collaborators: Dominic Papa, Sibylle Thomke
date of design: 1996
models: Sibylle Thomke
client: LOC Laurens Quartier Ontwikkelings Combinati

....

067 (116)

project: Restoration "Ulo-School"
location: Heerlen, the Netherlands
project team: Wiel Arets, Richard Welten, Roel van der Linden, Paul van Dongen
site supervisors: Hein Urlings
garden architect: Pieter Kromwijk
date of design: 1996
date of completion: 1998
photographs: Kim Zwarts
client: AZL Beheer bv
program: offices
management consultant: PRC Bouwcentrum bv
mechanical consultant: Huygen Installatieadviseurs
structural consultant: Palthe Ingenieursbureau

bibliography
▸ W.P.A.R.S. Graatsma, **Van 1931 tot 1998 van ULO tot AZL Beheer,** Heerlen, 1998.

....

068 (117)

p. 34   **project:** Cathedral for Ghana
location: gently sloping hill near the sea at Cape Coast, Ghana
project team: Wiel Arets, Bettina Kraus, Dominic Papa
collaborators: Pedro Anão, Saturo Umehara, Richard Welten, Victor Kwesi Quagraine
date of design: 1997–2001
models: Hayley Eber, Kees Lemmens
photographs: Kim Zwarts
client: Archbishop Peter Turkson, Alliance of Africa
program: Cathedral Complex-Weekday Chapel, Eucharistic Chapel, priest's residence
management consultant: Veldhoen Facility Consultants bv
structural consultant: ABT Rob Nijsse
mechanical consultant: Cauberg - Huygen Raadgevende Ingenieurs bv

bibliography
▸ An., "Catedral a Cape Coast, Ghana," in J. Cargol, **Màster intervencions arquitectòniques en el medi rural,** Girona, 1998.
▸ W. Arets, K. Frampton, R. v. Toorn, "Wiel Arets," **Context 3** (1999) 04, pp. 92–95.
▸ J. Rodermond, "Monumenten voor een nieuwe tijd. Recent werk van Wiel Arets," **de Architect** (2000) 4, pp. 48–59.

....

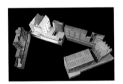

069 (118)

project: Extension Dutch Parliament (competition)
location: site in the historical center of The Hague, the Netherlands
project team: Wiel Arets, Paulien Bremmers, Ivo Daniëls, Paul van Dongen, Harold Hermans,
Dominic Papa, Michiel Vrehen, Henrik Vuust, Richard Welten
date of design: 1997
models: Kees Lemmens
client: Ministry of VROM
program: extension and renovation of an existing building for the Dutch parliament
area: building area 4,490 m^2; room area 7,970 m^2

bibliography
▸ W. Arets, K. Frampton, R. v. Toorn, "Wiel Arets," **Context 3** (1999) 04, pp. 86–91.

....

070 (119)

project: Urban Study
location: Venlo, the Netherlands
project team: Wiel Arets
collaborators: Dominic Papa, René Thijssen
date of design: 1996
program: housing

....

071 (120)
project: Proposal for "Schlossplatz"
location: Berlin, Germany
project team: Wiel Arets, Dominic Papa, Richard Welten
collaborators: René Thijssen, Henrik Vuust
date of design: 1996
client: Tagespiegel
program: housing, offices and public function

bibliography
▸ C. Käpplinger, "Drehbuch für einen Ort im Werden," in M. Zimmermann, **Der Berliner Schloßplatz; Visionen zur Gestaltung der Berliner Mitte**, Berlin, 1997, pp. 22–25.

....

072 (121)
project: Hazendans Social Housing
location: Maastricht, the Netherlands
project team: Wiel Arets, Richard Welten, Lars Dreessen, Frederik Vaes, Carl Augustijns
date of design: 1996
date of completion: 2000
client: Stienstra
program: housing
mechanical, electrical engineer: Huygen bv
building constructor: Smeets Bouw

....

073 (122)
project: Museum of Modern Art (competition)
location: part of the Downtown Manhattan Grid caught between 53 and 54 Street in the middle between 5th and 6th Avenue in New York, United States of America
project team: Wiel Arets, Dominic Papa, Henrik Vuust
collaborators: Bettina Kraus, Ivo Daniels, Martine Nederens
date of design: 1997
models: Ralph Blättler, Mette Rasmusen, Jeroen Storm, Janneke Wessels
photographs: Kim Zwarts
client: Museum of Modern Art
program: expansion of the museum

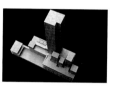

bibliography
▸ A. Lange, "MoMA's Boys," **New York** (1997) 12 [March 31], pp. 38–44.
▸ An., "Wiel Arets; from the architect's statement," in J. Elderfield (ed.**), Imagining the Future of The Museum of Modern Art; Studies in Modern Art 7,** New York, 1998, pp.160–169.
▸ C. Davidson, "Falsas esperanzas: Museo de Arte Moderno, Nueva York / False hopes: Museum of Modern Art, New York," **AV Monografías** (1998) 71, pp. 104–113.
▸ W. Arets, K. Frampton, R. v. Toorn, "Wiel Arets," **Context 3** (1999) 04, pp. 66–73.

....

074 (123)
p. 44 **project:** University Library
location: university campus "De Uithof" in Utrecht, the Netherlands
project team: Wiel Arets, Pauline Bremmer, René Thijssen, Richard Welten, Dominic Papa, Henrik Vuust
collaborators: Pedro Anão, Harold Aspers, Lars Dreessen, Eva Gjessing, Franziska Herb, Harold Hermans, Petra Jacquet, Peter Kaufmann, Guido Neijnens, Michael Pedersen, Frederik Vaes, Michiel Vrehen
garden architect: West 8
date of design: 1997–2001
date of completion: 2001–2004
models: Pedro Anão, Mai Henriksen, Kees Lemmens, Anniina Koivu
photographs; Hélène Binet, Kim Zwarts
client: University Utrecht (UU)
program: library, parking
structural consultant: ABT adviesbureau voor bouwtechniek bv
mechanical, electrical consultant: Huygen installatieadviseurs bv
building physics consultant: Cauberg - Huygen Raadgevende Ingenieurs bv
building acoustics consultant: Adviesbureau Peutz & Associates bv
building contractor: IBC-Heymans
installation contractor: GTI
facade contractor: Gerdner bv, Vogt bv

bibliography
▸ T. Notten, B. Lootsma, **Universiteitsbibliotheek Utrecht. Ontwerp Wiel Arets,** Utrecht, 1999.
▸ J. Rodermond, "Monumenten voor een nieuwe tijd. Recent werk van Wiel Arets," **de Architect** (2000) 4, pp. 48–59.
▸ F. Kaltenbach, "Über den Dächern von…- Wiel Arets über sein Konzept der Stadt / On the roofs of…- Wiel Arets on his Concept for the City," **Detail** (2000) 5, pp. 806–810.
▸ H. Ibelings (red.), **Het kunstmatig landschap: Hedendaagse architectuur, stedenbouw en landschapsarchitectuur in Nederland,** Rotterdam 2000, pp. 33–37.
▸ V + K Publishing, "Universiteitsbibliotheek" in **Architectuur Universiteit Utrecht,** Blaricum 2001, pp. 66–67 + 79.

....

075 (124)
p. 292 **project:** Villa van Zanten
location: Lisse, the Netherlands
project team: Wiel Arets, Richard Welten
collaborator: Lars Dreessen
site supervisors: Richard Welten
garden architect: West 8
date of design: 1997–1999
date of completion: 2000
models: Kees Lemmens, Ulrike Papperitz
photographs: Hélène Binet
client: family Van Zanten
program: single-family house
building physics: Van Zanten Raadgevende Ingenieurs
structural advisor: Corsmit Raadgevend Ingenieursbureau
mechanical advisor: Van Zanten Raadgevende Ingenieurs
building contractor: Bouwbedrijf G.J. van der Hulst bv

....

076 (128)
project: Apartment tower cinema annex
location: Poelestraat, Groningen, the Netherlands
project team: Wiel Arets, Michiel Vrehen
date of design: 1998
models: Ulrike Papperitz
client: Groningse Filmonderneming
program: cinema and apartments

077 (129)
project: Theater (competition)
location: Urban Place in Basel, Switzerland
project team: Wiel Arets, Bettina Kraus
collaborators: Paul van Dongen, Lars Dreessen, Harold Hermans, Rolf Jenny, Michiel Vrehen,
Richard Welten
date of design: 1997
models: Andreas Rubin
client: city of Basel
program: theater and shops
theater consultant: The Karten Materne / Theater Technik

bibliography
▸ W. Arets, K. Frampton, R. v. Toorn, "Wiel Arets," **Context 3** (1999) 04, pp. 202–203.

078 (130)
project: Leidsche Rijn Campus
location: Leidsche Rijn / Utrecht, the Netherlands
project team: Wiel Arets, Peter Kaufmann
collaborators: Massimo Adario, Pedro Anão, Harold Hermans, Bettina Kraus, Silke Oetsch,
Michiel Vrehen
date of design: 1998–2001
date of completion: 2002–2004
models: Franka Böhm, Nikolaj Froelund Thomsen
client: Leidsche Rijn College / Gemeente Utrecht
program: school, sport center, fitness center
structural consultant: Ingenieursbureau Palte bv
mechanical, electrical consultant: Huygen installatieadviseurs bv
building contractor: Aannemersbedrijf Xhonneux bv
building physics consultant: Cauberg-Huygen Raadgevende Ingenieurs bv

079 (131)
p. 54   project: Hedge House
location: pleasure garden of Castle Wijlre, the Netherlands
project team: Wiel Arets, Bettina Kraus, Lars Dreessen, Frederic Vaes, Richard Welten
site supervisors: Hein Urlings
date of design: 1999–2000
date of completion: 2001
models: Jeremy Bryan, Frederik Vaes
photographs: Hélène Binet
client: Mr. & Mrs. Eyck
program: art gallery, lounge, orchid room, greenhouses, seven poultry-houses, room for garden-tools
structural consultant: Ingenieursbureau Palte bv
mechanical, electrical consultant: Huygen installatieadviseurs bv
building contractor: Aannemersbedrijf Xhonneux bv
building physics consutlant: Cauberg-Huygen Raadgevende Ingenieurs bv

bibliography
▸ J. Rodermond, "Monumenten voor een nieuwe tijd. Recent werk van Wiel Arets," **de Architect** (2000) 4, pp. 48–59.

080 (132)
p. 62   project: Theater (competition, first prize)
location: gently sloping site at the waterfront of Almere, the Netherlands
project team: Wiel Arets, Bettina Kraus
collaborators: Pedro Anão, Lars Dreessen, Harold Hermans, Johannes Kappler, Michel Vrehen
date of design: 1998
models: Daniel Cranach, Kees Lemmens, Paul Tesser
photographs: Hélène Binet
client: city of Almere
program: theater, music school
structural consultant: ABT Rob Nijsse
building physics consultants: Cauberg–Huygen Raadgevende Ingenieurs bv

bibliography
▸ An., "Theater met Centrum voor Kunstzinnige Vorming," in M. Provoost, B. Colenbrander, F. Alkemade, **Dutchtown / O.M.A.'s meesterproef in Almere,**
Rotterdam, 1999, p. 104.
▸ W. Arets, K. Frampton, R. v. Toorn, "Wiel Arets," **Context 3** (1999) 04, pp. 102–107.

081 (134)
p. 68   project: Urban Plan Europapark
location: post-industrial terrain in the south-eastern part of Groningen, the Netherlands
project team: Wiel Arets, Johannes Kappler
collaborators: Pedro Anão, William Fung, Bettina Kraus, Fabiola Magan, Frank Menzel, Satoru Umehara
Jette Lindquist, Bert Pogehen, Chris Möller, Chris Ema
date of design: 1998–2001
date of completion: 2006
models: Vicky Anders, Jeremy Bryan, Vanessa Keith, Joost Körver, Kees Lemmens, Lutz Mürau,
Paul Tesser, Joost Vanderhoydonck
photographs: Hélène Binet, Arjen Schmitz, Kim Zwarts
client: city of Groningen
program: Euroborg Stadium, railway station Kempkensberg, 800 apartment units, 240,000 m^2 office units, 4,500 parking places
area: 55 hectares

bibliography
▸ K. Frenay, "Wonen, werken, uitgaan én voetballen in het Europapark," **Stadsmagazine Groningen** (1999) 3, pp. 24–25.
▸ W. Arets, **Europapark Groningen**, Groningen, 1999 [i.s.m. Gemeente Groningen].
▸ W. Arets, K. Frampton, R. v. Toorn, "Wiel Arets," **Context 3** (1999) 04, pp. 62–65.
▸ R. Koopman, **Euroborg / Europapark,** Moordrecht, 1999.
▸ J. Rodermond, "Monumenten voor een nieuwe tijd. Recent werk van Wiel Arets," **de Architect** (2000) 4, pp. 48–59.
▸ L. Fischer, "Lucca in Groningen: Das Euroborg-Projekt," **Bauwelt** 91 (2000) 30/31, pp. 24–25.
▸ An., "Het Europapark is een uniek project," **de Selectie** 1 (2000) 1, pp. 72–75.
▸ An., "Interview met Wiel Arets: Het stadion moet onderdeel van de stad zijn," in M. Provoost (red.), **Het stadion: de architectuur van massasport,** Rotterdam, 2000, pp. 175–177.
▸ H. Wapperom, "Sport en handel 'hand in hand'," **Cement** (2000) 4, pp. 11–15.
▸ F. Kaltenbach, "Über den Dächern von…- Wiel Arets über sein Konzept der Stadt / On the roofs of…- Wiel Arets on his Concept for the City," **Detail** (2000) 5, pp. 806–810.
▸ H. Ibelings (red.), **Het kunstmatig landschap: Hedendaagse architectuur, stedenbouw en landschapsarchitectuur in Nederland,** Rotterdam, 2000, pp. 33–37.
▸ Dienst RO/EZ, **Europapark Groningen: Station Kempkensberg Groningen,** Groningen, 2000.

....

082 (135)

p. 68 **project:** Euroborg Stadium
location: Groningen, the Netherlands
project team: Wiel Arets, Johannes Kappler, Bettina Kraus, Barend Christmas
collaborators: Pedro Anão, William Fung, Satoru Umehara
date of design: 1998–2001
date of completion: 2002–2006
models: Vanessa Keith, Jaap Kraayenhof, Kees Lemmens
photographs: Hélène Binet, Arjen Schmitz, Kim Zwarts
client: Euroborg NV
program: FC Groningen soccer stadium, offices, sport store, cinema, hotel, entertainment/leisure facilities, apartments, parking garage

bibliography
▸ K. Frenay, "Wonen, werken, uitgaan én voetballen in het Europapark," **Stadsmagazine Groningen** (1999) 3, pp. 24–25.
▸ W. Arets, **Europapark Groningen,** Groningen, 1999 [i.s.m. Gemeente Groningen].
▸ W. Arets, K. Frampton, R. v. Toorn, "Wiel Arets," **Context 3** (1999) 04, pp. 62–65.
▸ R. Koopman, **Euroborg / Europapark,** Moordrecht, 1999.
▸ J. Rodermond, "Monumenten voor een nieuwe tijd. Recent werk van Wiel Arets," **de Architect** (2000) 4, pp. 48–59.
▸ L. Fischer, "Lucca in Groningen: Das Euroborg-Projekt," **Bauwelt** 91 (2000) 30/31, pp. 24–25.
▸ An., "Het Europapark is een uniek project," **de Selectie** 1 (2000) 1, pp. 72–75.
▸ An., "Interview met Wiel Arets: Het stadion moet onderdeel van de stad zijn," in M. Provoost (red.), **Het stadion: de architectuur van massasport,** Rotterdam, 2000, pp. 175–177.
▸ H. Wapperom, "Sport en handel 'hand in hand'," **Cement** (2000) 4, pp. 11–15.
▸ F. Kaltenbach, "Über den Dächern von…- Wiel Arets über sein Konzept der Stadt / On the roofs of…- Wiel Arets on his Concept for the City," **Detail** (2000) 5, pp. 806–810.
▸ H. Ibelings (red.), **Het kunstmatig landschap: Hedendaagse architectuur, stedenbouw en landschapsarchitectuur in Nederland,** Rotterdam, 2000, pp. 33–37.

....

083 (136)

project: Takeo Kikuchi Store, Restaurant & Office
location: Tokyo, Japan
project team: Wiel Arets, Leekyung Han, Satoru Umehara, Richard Welten
site supervisors: Mr. Haijme Yatsuka, UPM Co. LTD
furniture design: Wiel Arets architect & associates bv
date of design: 1998
models: Leekyung Han, Fabiola Magan
client: World CD.ltd
program: fashion shop, restaurant, offices
mechanical and electric engineering: Huygen bv

....

084 (137)

p. 78 **project:** Jelly-Fish House
location: gently sloping site close to the sea of Marbella (Malaga), Spain
architect: Wiel Arets, Bettina Kraus
project team: Wiel Arets, Bettina Kraus, Lars Dreesen
collaborators: Paul Draaijer, William Fung, Johannes Kappler
site supervisors: Iñaki Pérez de la Fuente
date of design: 1999–2001
date of completion: 2001–2002
models: Franka Böhm, Kees Lemmens, Nikolaj Froelund Thomson
photographs: Hélène Binet
client: Mr. & Mrs. Wielheesen
program: vacation villa including guest unit and swimming pool
structural consultant: ABT adviesbureau voor bouwtechniek bv
building physics consultant: Cauberg-Huygen Raadgevende Ingenieurs bv

....

085 (138)

project: Housing Vroendael
location: Maastricht, the Netherlands
project team: Wiel Arets, Bettina Kraus, Satoru Umehara
collaborators: Philippe Dirix, Mai Henriksen
date of design: 1999–2001
date of completion: 2003
models: Satoru Umehara
client: Grouwels-Daelmans bv
program: 14 apartments and parking garage

....

086 (139)

p. 84 **project:** Apartment tower Amsterdam Zuid-Oost
location: next to the Ajax Arena, Amsterdam, the Netherlands
project team: Wiel Arets, Bettina Kraus, Satoru Umehara
collaborators: Pedro Anão, William Fung
date of design: 1999–2000
date of completion: 2005
models: Lutz Mürau, Joost Vanderhoydonck
photographs: Hélène Binet
clients: Delta Roa, SBB, BAM
program: 300 apartments, shops, leisure facilities
structural consultant: Van Rossum
mechanical, electrical consultant: Hiensch Engineering bv
building physics consultant: Cauberg-Huygen Raadgevende Ingenieurs bv
building acoustics consultant: Adviesbureau Peutz & Associes bv
building contractor: Smit's Bouwbedrijf bv, BAM Wooningbouw bv

....

087 (140)

p. 94 **project:** Bijenkorf Apartment Tower
location: next to the existing Bijenkorf shopping center in Rotterdam, the Netherlands
project team: Wiel Arets, Mai Henriksen, Bettina Kraus, Satoru Umehara
collaborators: Paul Tesser, Frederik Vaes
date of design: 1999–2000
models: Pioter Brzoza, Paul Tesser, Frederik Vaes
photographs: Hélène Binet
clients: M.A.B and K.B.B.
program: extension of the existing Bijenkorf and parking garage, apartments, offices
structural consultant: Ingenieursbureau Zonneveld bv
building physics consultant: Cauberg–Huygen Raadgevende Ingenieurs bv
mechanical, electrical consultant: Huygen bv Installatie adviseurs

....

088 (141)

project: Medical Center
location: Leidschendam, the Netherlands
project team: Wiel Arets, Jette Lindquist
collaborators: Harold Aspers, Bettina Kraus
date of design: 1999–2001
models: Jette Lindquist
client: J. Blijdendijk
program: doctors practise, physiotherapy, pharmacy

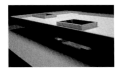

....

089 (142)

project: Kwakkel Showroom & Offices
location: Apeldoorn, the Netherlands
project team: Wiel Arets, William Fung, Harold Hermans
collaborators: Harold Aspers, Elsa Caetano, Jacques van Eyck, Frank Menzel, Mai Heneiksen, Markus Elminger
date of design: 1999–2001
date of completion: 2001–2002
models: William Fung, Sebastian Nau
client: Mr. W. Kwakkel
program: showroom, offices, storage accommodation
mechanical, electrical consultant: Huygen installatieadviseurs bv
building physics consultant: Cauberg-Huygen Raadgevende Ingenieurs bv
structural consultant: ABT adviesbureau voor bouwtechniek bv Bremen
building contractor: Draisma bv

....

090 (143)

project: Urban Plan Molenberg
location: Heerlen, the Netherlands
project team: Wiel Arets, Philippe Dirix
collaborators: Elsa Caetano, Jos Eliens, Johannes Kappler, Frank Menzel
date of design: 1999
date of completion: 2009
models: Elsa Caetano
client: Wonen Zuid, Municipality of Heerlen, Grouwels Dadman
program: reconstruction and extention of housing program for 1650 units

....

091 (146)

project: "Schunck" Glaspalace Music Center
location: Bongerd/Pancratiusplein in Heerlen, the Netherlands
architect: ABBC, a cooperation of Ir. Wiel Arets Architect & Associates, Bureau Bouwadvies, Jo Coenen & Co Architekten
project team: Daniel Meier, Bettina Sättele, W.M. Ummels
collaborators: Bettina Sättele, W.M. Ummels, Joost Vanderhoydonck, Massimo Adario, Chris Smith
site supervisors: Theo Goebbels
date of design: 1999–2001
date of completion: 2002–2003
models: Massimo Adario, Chris Smith
client: city of Heerlen
program: music school, academy of art, urban gallery, urban archive, cinema, cafe/restaurant
area: 9,150 m^2
structural engineer: ABT Adviesbureau voor bouwtechniek bv
mechanical, electrical consultant: Huygen bv Installatie Adviseurs
building physics consultant: Cauberg-Huygen Raadgevende Ingenieurs bv
building acoustics consultant: Adviesbureau Peutz & Associates bv
building contractor: Laudy Bouw & Planontwikkeling bv

bibliography
▸ An., "Glaspaleis wordt weer een lichtend baken," **Bouwen aan Limburg** 2 (2000) 2, pp. 12–17.

....

092 (147)

project: Hoofddorp Center Urban Plan
location: center of Hoofddorp, the Netherlands
project team: Wiel Arets, Johannes Kappler, Bettina Kraus
collaborators: Elsa Caetano, Frank Menzel, Massimo Adario, Vicky Anders
date of design: 1999–2000
models: Massimo Adario, Vicki Anders
client: municipality of Haarlemmermeer
program: offices, shopping center, apartments, parking, library, leisure center, museum, city hall, cinema, cultural center, city park
management consultant: Twynstra Gudde bv
traffic consultant: Goudappel Coffeng bv

....

093 (148)

project: Beukenhorst Urban Plan
location: Hoofddorp Haarlemmermeer, the Netherlands
project team: Wiel Arets, Johannes Kappler, Frank Menzel, Jette Lindquist, Mai Hendriksen
date of design: 1999–2001
date of completion: 2001–2005
models: William Fung, Frank Menzel, Vicky Anders
client: municipality of Haarlemmermeer
program: service facilities (hotel and retail), office units, parking places

....

094 (150)

p. 102 **project:** Kwakkel House
location: Oude Zwolseweg 203, Wenum, Wiesel, on the outskirts of Apeldoorn, the Netherlands
project team: Wiel Arets, William Fung, Mai Henriksen
collaborators: Elsa Caetano, Lars Dreesen, Frank Menzel, Erik Moederscheim
date of design: 2000–2001
date of completion: 2001
models: Elsa Caetano, William Fung, Frank Menzel, Nikolaj Froelund Thomson
photographs: Hélène Binet
client: Mr. and Mrs. Kwakkel
program: single-family house, stables, garage/workshop, greenhouse
mechanical, electrical consultant: Weterig bv
structural engineer: ABT adviesbureau voor bouwtechniek bv
building contractor: Dijkhof

bibliography
▸ M. Koivisto, "Arkkithti Wiel Arets," **Betoni** (2001) 1, pp. 22–29.

....

095 (153)

project: Brusselsestraat Urban Plan
location: Brusselsestraat in Maastricht, the Netherlands
project team: Wiel Arets, Johannes Kappler, Frank Menzel, Jette Lindquist
date of design: 2000
models: Franka Böhm
client: city of Maastricht
program: study center (University of Maastricht), leisure center, apartment units, hotel

....

096 (154)

project: Pergamon Museum (competition)
location: Museumsinsel in Berlin, Germany
project team: Wiel Arets, Elsa Caetano, Mai Henriksen, Johannes Kappler, Bettina Kraus, Satoru Umehara, Nicolaj Froelund Thomson
date of design: 2000
models: Nicolaj Froelund Thomson
client: Pergamon Museum
program: extension of the existing Pergamon Museum

....

097 (155)

project: Apeldoorn Housing (competition, first prize)
location: Apeldoorn, the Netherlands
project team: Wiel Arets, Carl Augustijns, Elsa Caetano, Mai Henriksen, Bettina Kraus, Nikolaj Froelund Thomsen, Satoru Umehara
date of design: 2000
date of completion: 2003
models: Nikolaj Froelund Thomsen
client: Mr. & Mrs. Kwakkel
program: 60 family houses
mechanical, electrical consultant: Weterig bv
structural engineer: Nickels bv
building contractor: Le Clercq bv

....

098 (158)
project: Hotel Promenade
location: Van Stolkweg 1, Den Haag, the Netherlands
project team: Wiel Arets, Satoru Umehara
collaborators: Bettina Kraus, Sadamu Shirafuji
date of design: 2000
date of completion: 2004
models: Michael Olsen, Carl Augustijns
photographs: Satoru Umehara
client: Crowne Plaza Den Haag
program: extension of the hotel

....

099 (159)
project: Beukenhorst Office
location: Tauruslaan, Beukenhorst-South, the Netherlands
project team: Wiel Arets, Mai Henriksen, Johannes Kappler, Bettina Kraus, Jette Lindquist
date of design: 2000–2001
models: Jette Lindquist, Mai Henriksen
client: Bouwfonds Vastgoedontwikkeling
program: 50,000 m^2 office building

....

100 (160)
project: Villa Veranda
location: Gerlingshof 17, Valkenburg, the Netherlands
project team: Wiel Arets, Bettina Kraus, Lars Dreesen
collaborator: Satoru Umehara
date of design: 2000–2001
date of completion: 2002
models: Jacques van Eijck, Erik Moederscheim, Frederik Vaes
client: Mr. & Mrs. Buijs
program: single family house
structural engineer: Palte bv
installation consultant: Cauberg-Huygen Raadgevende Ingenieurs bv

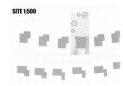

SITE 1:500

....

101 (161)
project: Dordrecht Medical Center
location: Blaauwweg, Dordrecht
project team: Wiel Arets, Jette Lindquist
collaborators: Mai Hendriksen, Bettina Kraus, Harold Aspers, Rasmus Rodam
date of design: 2000–2001
client: Mr. J. Bijdendijk
program: medical center
structural engineer: Palte bv
installation consultant: Wetering bv

....

102 (162)
project: Oostpoort Haarlem
location: Amsterdamse Vaart, Haarlem, the Netherlands
project team: Wiel Arets, Johannes Kappler, Bettina Kraus
collaborators: Carl Augustijns, Mai Henriksen, Jette Lindquist, Sadamu Shirafuji
date of design: 2001–2002
models: Sebastian Nau
client: IMCA
program: multi functional stadium, offices, entertainment / leisure facilities, hotel, apartments
structural engineer: Van Rossum
installation consultant: Wetering bv

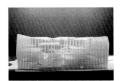

....

103 (163)
project: BMW (competition)
location: Olympiapark, Munich, Germany
project team: Wiel Arets, Bettina Kraus, Jette Lindquist, Satoru Umehara, Sadamu Shirafuji
date of design: 2001
models: Sadamu Shirafuji, Satoru Umehara, Tim Wenzel
client: BMW Group
program: BMW delivery and event center
area: 70,000 m^2

Monographs

1989	Wiel Arets and Anthony Vidler, Wiel Arets, architect, 010 Publishers, Rotterdam.
1992	Geert Bekaert, Macchina Arte Jan van Eijk Academy, i.c.w. Wim v.d. Bergh, "Rosbeek," 32, Nuth.
1992	Wiel Arets, An Alabaster Skin, 010 Publishers, Rotterdam.
1994	Wiel Arets and Greg Lynn, Maastricht Academy for the Arts and Architecture, 010 Publishers, Rotterdam.
1994	Wiel Arets, A Virological Architecture, "A+U" 2, Tokyo.
	Bart Lootsma, Wiel Arets. Strange Bodies / Fremdkörper, Birkhäuser Verlag, Basel.
1996	Bart Lootsma and Moritz Küng, Wiel Arets, architect, De Singel, Antwerp.
1997	Dominic Papa and others, Wiel Arets 1993-1997, "El Croquis" 85, Madrid.
1998	Manfred Bock, Wiel Arets, architect, 010 Publishers, Rotterdam.
	Kenneth Frampton and Roemer van Toorn, Wiel Arets, Context 3 Group, Seoul.
1999	Tanja Notten and Bart Lootsma, University Library Utrecht, Architectuurcentrum Aorta, Utrecht.
1999	Stan Allen, Wiel Arets, AZL Heerlen, 010 Publishers, Rotterdam.

Biography

1955	Born in Heerlen, the Netherlands
1983	Graduates from Technical University Eindhoven
1984	Establishes architectural office "ir Wiel Arets architect & associates" in Heerlen
1984–1985	Travels in Russia, Japan, America, Europe
1986–1989	Teaches at Academy of Architecture, Amsterdam and Rotterdam
1986	Founding-member of Wiederhall
1987	Victor de Stuers Award for Fashion shop Beltgens, Maastricht
1988	Charlotte Köhler Award
1988–1992	Diploma Unit Master at Architectural Association, London
1989	Rotterdam Maaskant Award
1991–1992	Visiting Professor at Columbia University, New York
1991	Edmund Hustinx Award
1992–1994	Visiting Professor at Berlage Institute, Postgraduate School of Architecture, Amsterdam
1992	Visiting Professor at Cooper Union, New York
1994	Visiting Professor at the Hochschule für Angewandte Kunst, Vienna
1994	Visiting Professor at the Royal Danish Academy of Fine Arts, Copenhagen
1994	Victor de Stuers Award for Academy for the Arts and Architecture, Maastricht
1994	Mies van der Rohe Pavilion Award for European Architecture, special mention for Academy for the Arts and Architecture, Maastricht
1995	Concrete Award for Academy for the Arts and Architecture, Maastricht
1995–2001	Dean Berlage Institute, Postgraduate Laboratory of Architecture, Amsterdam
1997	Establishes architectural office "ir Wiel Arets architect & associates" in Maastricht
1998	UIA nomination of the Academy for the Arts and Architecture as one of world's thousand best buildings of the twentieth century
1999	Member of the jury for the EEC European Price in Architecture by the Mies van der Rohe Foundation in Barcelona
2000	Visiting Professor at Mies van der Rohe Chair, Barcelona
2000	Professor Berlage Leerstoel at the Faculty Bouwkunde, Delft University
2001	Member of the Jury for the EEC

Exhibitions

1985	"La Biennale di Venezia. III Mostra Internazionale di Architettura," Venice, Italy
1987	"Biënnale jonge Nederlandse architecten," Beurs van Berlage, Amsterdam, Netherlands
1987	"Luce," Wiederhall Galerie, Amsterdam, Netherlands (solo exhibition)
1987	"L'Architettura Macchina," Van Rooy Gallerie, Amsterdam, Netherlands (solo exhibition)
1988	"Autobiographical Architecture," Stadsgalerij, Heerlen, Netherlands, (solo exhibition)
1988	"De Eindhovense School," De Singel, Antwerp, Belgium
1989	"Macchina Arte," Bonnefantenmuseum, Maastricht Wiel Arets i.c.w. Wim v.d Bergh, Netherlands
1989–1990	"Architectonische denkbeelden Wiel Arets & Wim v.d. Bergh," Stichting Architectuurmuseum – Museum voor Sierkunst, Ghent, Belgium
1990	"Wiel Arets Architect," phai, Diepenbeek, Belgium (solo exhibition)
1991	"Energeia – Recent work Wiel Arets," Thermenmuseum, Heerlen, Netherlands (solo exhibition)
1991	"La Biennale di Venezia. v Mostra Internazionale di Architettura," Venice, Italy
1992	"Urban Eco," Galerie Artikel, Tilburg, Netherlands (solo exhibition)
1992	"Modernisme zonder dogma: een jonge generatie architecten in Nederland," NAI Rotterdam, Netherlands
1993	"Hoog voor Amsterdam," Arcam Galerie, Amsterdam, Netherlands (solo exhibition)
1993	"Archi-Arché; A White Tower for Atuatuca, Tungrorum," Tongeren, Belgium
1993	"Fifth International Biennale for Architecture," Buenos Aires, Argentina
1994	"Housing for the Elderly," De Pont Museum, Tilburg, Netherlands
1995–1996	"Fundació Mies van der Rohe Barcelona," Frankfurt, Rotterdam, Madrid, Barcelona, Copenhagen
1995	Rotterdam 2045, Laurenskwartier, NAI Rotterdam, Netherlands
1996	"Virological Architecture," Architekturmuseum, Basel, Switzerland (solo exhibition)
1996	"La Biennale di Venezia, Headquarters AZL Pension Fund, Heerlen
1996	"Virologische Architectuur," De Singel Antwerp, Belgium (solo exhibition)
1996	"Houses for Sale," Galerie Sophia Ungers, Cologne, Germany
1997	"Police Station Vaals," Bonnefantenmuseum Maastricht, Netherlands
1998	"Police Station Vaals," Fundació Mies van der Rohe Barcelona," Milan, Berlin, Madrid and Barcelona
1998	Headquarters AZL Pensionfund Heerlen, Work & Culture, Vienna, Austria
1999	University Library Utrecht, Architectuurcentrum Aorta, Utrecht, Netherlands
1999	"Bienale Internacional de Arquitetura," São Paulo, Brazil
2000	"The Stadium" NAI Rotterdam, Netherlands
2000	"La Biennale," Venice, Italy

Colophon

General editor for the architectural series: Francisco Rei

Concept: Wiel Arets
Editor: Xavier Costa
Co-editing: Johannes Kappler, Andrea Tontsch
Photography: Hélène Binet with Mila Hecke
Bibliography: Marcelle van Bokhoven
Text: Xavier Costa, Stan Allen, Greg Lynn, Anthony Vidler, Bart Lootsma, Wiel Arets
Translation Dutch-English: Victor Josep
Translation Spanish-English: Graham Thomson
Design: Simon Davies, Rotterdam
Design Production: Studio LSD (Simon Davies, Lauran Schijvens), Rotterdam
Coordination: Montse Holgado, Carolina Moreno
Copy editing: Rafael Galisteo, Susan Brown Bridge
Production Manager: Rafael Aranda
Colour Separation: Format Digital, Barcelona
Printing: Filabo, Barcelona
Binding: Bardenas, Barcelona

Wiel Arets would like to thank all the people who contributed to this book, all collaborators who worked over the years in the office, all the clients who put their trust in our work and all firms who helped us to complete the buildings.

Wiel Arets
Bettina Kraus (associate)

Massimo Adario
Vicky Anders
Thomas Alzinger
Pedro Anão
Doris Annen
Anca Arenz
Harold Aspers
Carl Augustijns
Wendy Bakker
Max van Beers
Ralph Blätter
Franka Böhm
Marcelle van Bokhoven
Eric Bolle
Reina Bos
Tina Brandt
Pauline Bremmer
Mathieu Bruls
Jeremy Bryan
Pioter Brzoza
Elsa Caetano
Ramun Capaul
Barend Christmas
Karin Christof
Delphine Clavien
John Cleater
Daniel Cranach
Ivo Daniëls
William H. Deegan
Freidemann Derschmied
Scott Devere
Philippe Dirix
Paul van Dongen
Paul Draaijer
Lars Dreesen
Sven Dyckhoff
Hayley Eber
Paul Egers
Kim Egholm
Jos Eliens
Markus Elminger
Lars van Es
Kevin Estrada
Jacques van Eyck
Anuska Frick
Nikolaj Froelund Thomsen
William Fung

Marianne Geers
Eva Gjessing
Charlotte Greub
Piet Grouls
Julia Gruber
Andrea Gustafson
Leekyung Han
Rhea Harbers
Mai Henriksen
Franziska Herb
Harold Hermans
René Holten
Petra Jacquet
Jo Janssen
Rolf Jenny
Dorte Jensen
Malin Johanson
Nynke Joustra
Johannes Kappler
Peter Kaufmann
Dorthe Keis
Vanessa Keith
Nadim Khattar
Elmar Kleuters
Anniina Koivu
Lonnie Koken
Roland Kolinitz
Joost Körver
Thompke Kosma
Jaap Kraayenhof
Caroline Krogh Andersen
Paul Kuitenbrouwer
Victor Kwesi Quagraine
Kees Lemmens
Jette Lindquist
Frank van der Linden
Roel van der Linden
Katharina Lundeberg
Fabiola Magan
Ralph van Mameren
Annette Marx
Rick Maund
Daniel Meier
Michel Melenhorst
Frank Menzel
Erik Moederscheim
Anita Morandini

Lutz Mürau
Sebastian Nau
Martine Nederens
Guido Neijnens
Silke Oetsch
Michael Olsen
Dominic Papa
Ulrike Papperitz
Maurice Paulussen
Michael Pedersen
Stefan Pfeffer
Mette Rasmussen
Andreas Rubin
Henri Rueda-Coronel
Rasmus Rodam
Cristan Sabella Rossa
Bettina Sättele
Harold Schout
Sadamu Shirafuji
Chris Smith
Thomas Stepany
Jan Stoeldraaier
Isabel Martinez Stolche
Jeroen Storm
Harald Straatveit
John Swagten
Joanna Tang
Detief Tautenhahn
Robert Temel
Paul Tesser
René Thijssen
Sibylle Thomke
Neda Todorovic
Andrea Tontsch
Satoru Umehara
Hein Urlings
Frederik Vaes
Joost Vanderhoydonck
Ani Velez
Jeroen van der Ven
Gonrad Vleugels
Michel Vrehen
Henrik Vuust
Andrea Wallrath
Constance Weiser
Richard Welten
Janneke Wessels